IMAGINATIVE LITERATURE II

from Cervantes to Dostoevsky

Imaginative Literature II

from Cervantes to Dostoevsky

By

Mortimer J. Adler

and

Seymour Cain

Preface by

Joseph Wood Krutch

Formerly Professor of English Literature,

Columbia University

ENCYCLOPÆDIA BRITANNICA, INC.

Chicago • London • Toronto • Geneva

PREFACE

This second volume of the Reading Plan *Imaginative Literature* covers the subject from the beginning of the seventeenth century to the present day. The reader will probably notice at once that what we call "the novel" appears here for the first time, and that, indeed, five of the seven works to be treated belong in that category.

Most readers who have never thought much about such matters have probably tended to feel that the novel is the most natural, the almost inevitable, form of imaginative literature. Yet the fact remains that it was the latest to be evolved, and there would be some justification for saying that *Don Quixote* is the first modern novel.

This does not mean that narratives in prose have not existed since late classical times, but they were of secondary importance and none of them would be recognized as having the characteristics that we assume without definition distinguish this form of writing. We have also come to think of it as less formal, less "artificial," than any other imaginative writing, and in a sense it is. But in all the arts the earlier are, paradoxical though it may be, the most formal, the most closely tied to established conventions and (in a good sense) the most artificial.

Why should this new kind of writing have become so popular as to have all but monopolized the attention of the common reader; as well as, for that matter, the creative energies of the vast majority of writers of imaginative literature? One answer would be that it is thought of by many as the easiest to read—and the easiest to write. It has been said that every man's life would provide him with what is necessary for one good novel. And though this is not really true, no one would ever have thought of saying that every man should be able to write one epic or one tragedy.

Actually, the sense of ease of this kind of writing and this kind of reading are illusory at best except in the case of very inferior novels. As the reader of those treated in this guide will soon perceive, they must be read with attention if their real merits are to be appreciated. If he considers them carefully, he will also come to realize that, far from being loose or casual in construction, each has a style and form of its own—sometimes one which seems to have been invented by the author—and that the architecture is planned with masterly skill. They did not grow casually. They are not natural but extremely artful.

He will also observe that this new kind of writing, which seems to have replaced former kinds, has actually absorbed into its complex structure many of the characteristics of the more easily defined genres. None of them is actually an epic, or a comedy, or a tragedy by the old formal definitions. Yet we inevitably find ourselves calling at least certain passages comic, or tragic, or epic in their tone and effect. The question repeated often in the Guide, "Is this an epic, is it a tragedy, etc.," is never answerable with a simple "yes" or "no." But it is always a necessary question which leads to a fruitful discussion.

The modern novel—at least the great novel—treats in its own way the same great themes which the older poets and playwrights have treated. It may give them a modern setting and state them in modern terms, but the world of ideas to which the reader is introduced will not be new or strange to him if he is familiar with earlier literature. All five of the novels as well as *Paradise Lost* and *Faust* are concerned in one way or another—as perhaps all great literature is—with the nature of good and evil and with the meaning of the fact that both exist.

In many ways no two works could be more different than *Paradise Lost* and *Tom Jones*. One is exalted; the other down to earth. One is austere; the other relaxed and sometimes seemingly (though never actually) cynical. Milton seems to expect the most of man; Fielding to be saying that you must not expect too much. Yet the theme of both is good and evil—Milton tracing evil as sin which begins with "man's first disobedience"; Fielding drawing the contrast between the false-good man who lives, or pretends to live, by rules, and the truly good man whose heart is sound. He says in his own way the same thing which Milton had said elsewhere: "I admire not a cloistered virtue."

Another characteristic which all seven works have in common is this: none gives a formal, unambiguous solution to "the problem of evil," and hence all leave the universe, to a large extent, mysterious. In *Moby Dick*, Captain Ahab pursues the embodiment of evil in the white whale, but is not quite certain that it is not he rather than the whale who most truly embodies that evil. Adams' sin destroyed innocence forever, but is it not perhaps true that virtue, which consciously chooses in the full knowledge of what good and evil are, is more admirable than innocence which has no need to choose? And it is Dostoevsky who, more powerfully than any other modern writer, has represented the unfathomable mystery of the dark side of man's universe.

After what has been said, it is perhaps unnecessary to warn the reader against the once common assumption that a novel cannot be "serious" reading. For a long time after novels became extremely popular, the prejudice of the learned was strong against them. The opposition of the pious was even more vehement. To men of puritanical temper "fiction" meant merely "lies." But a good novel is not something which is false. It may or may not be superficially realistic, but the author is not escaping into a dream or a fantasy. He is in pursuit of truth by his own method. Imaginative literature can be, and often is, a way of knowing.

How, then, distinguish "imaginative literature" from philosophy? One criterion is given elsewhere in the guide: De Quincey's contrast between "the literature of knowledge" and "the literature of power." Perhaps much the same thing could be said in a different way. Philosophy, like science and all the quasi-sciences such as psychology and sociology, undertakes to prove and to demonstrate. Since the imaginative writer invents his characters and situations and has also the power to make them what he wills, he cannot in this sense demonstrate or prove anything. What he can and must do is simply to carry conviction. If we find ourselves believing his story, and the implications he draws from it, then to that extent he has succeeded.

JOSEPH WOOD KRUTCH

FOREWORD

I

This Reading Plan is an aid to the appreciation and understanding of great works of imaginative literature from Cervantes to Dostoevsky. It is preceded by another Reading Plan, *Imaginative Literature I*, covering works from Homer to Shakespeare. You may pursue the readings in this Reading Plan without having read any of the other Reading Plans. However, you will find in it references to the discussion of parts of *Paradise Lost* and *The Brothers Karamazov* in the Reading Plan on *Religion and Theology*. And there are frequent references in *Imaginative Literature II* to material and discussions contained in *Imaginative Literature I*, since similar problems are involved. These references are suggestions for further study.

How to Use the Reading Plan. The Reading Plan contains three parts: (1) a list of readings, (2) guides to each of the readings, and (3) suggestions for additional readings.

1. *The Reading List.* This Reading Plan consists of seven readings, each of them a whole work, varying considerably in length. Proper enjoyment and understanding of these works require that each reader proceed at his own pace. Hence, there are no specific time limits set for these readings. Reading time may vary from a week to a month or two, depending on the particular selection and the reader.

2. *The Guides*. These are intended to help the reader who is on his own, without a teacher or other study aids. They provide relevant background material and stimulate appreciation and understanding of the readings. Background material may include information about the particular historical setting in which the work was written—tradition, culture, contemporary conditions, and literary movements. It may also tell something about the author—his life, character, other writings, and his place in literature—and about the composition of the particular book. Each guide also includes a comprehensive summary of the work, together with salient citations from the text. This summary refreshes your memory of the work, sets forth the substance in a methodical manner, and provides the basis for our discussion in the final section of the guide.

The discussion raises thoughtful questions about the form, content, and style of the work—for instance, whether it is an epic and what an epic is, or whether the work is a unified whole, or why the author handled a situation in one way rather than another. These questions are intended to arouse your awareness and appreciation of literary values and meanings. They do not have any simple "yes" or "no" answers, but call for a sensitive and thoughtful response to the reading. A brief discussion follows each question, in order to indicate its significance and suggest some possible answers. The discussions do not provide any final or "right" answers—indeed, they sometimes provide contradictory answers. They are simply suggestions intended to stimulate your own awareness and understanding, and to get you started on answering the questions yourself.

The guide concludes with a set of "Self-Testing Questions," which are quite distinct from the discussion questions. These questions, dealing with particular details of the text, call for definite answers. They are intended to help you test the thoroughness and retentiveness of your reading. You can keep score on yourself by checking the list of answers on page 248.

3. *Additional Readings*. We have added a list of books that will help you in the reading and appreciation of imaginative literature. These range from philosophical works on literary

criticism to practical aids to reading poetry and prose. We have also included works on other aspects of imaginative literature—moral, religious, and social.

II

The term "literature" refers generally to any written matter. The works of Locke, Berkeley, and Hume are just as much part of English literature as those by Shakespeare, Milton, and Keats. But the term is also applied in a special sense to lyric poetry, drama, the epic, the novel, the short story, and other forms of imaginative writing. This is the type of literature with which we are concerned in this Reading Plan—imaginative literature.

It is sometimes difficult to draw the line between imaginative literature and other literature by merely formal criteria. Plato uses dramatic dialogue and myths to express philosophical principles and problems. The works of Plutarch, Tacitus, and other historians are models of literary structure and style. Portraits of actual men and events often have the same literary qualities as portraits of fictional characters and events.

Despite the borderline cases and the common literary excellence of the two types of literature, however, it is obvious that they are different types with different functions. Imaginative literature presents a fictional world, not the factual world of historians and biographers. It appeals to our imagination, our emotions, our sense of delight, our intimate personal experience, not to the powers of disinterested thought required by the scientists and philosophers. De Quincey's distinction between "the literature of power"—the emotionally moving—and "the literature of knowledge"—the intellectually instructive—is to the point in most cases.

It may be illuminating to note that imaginative literature is often more akin to the oral sagas, legends, folk tales, and romances of an earlier period of culture than to "the literature of knowledge." Homer's epics are closely related to the chants of the ancient bards at banquets or around the campfire. Chaucer and Cervantes openly mimic the form of oral storytelling in their works and reflect the avid audience listening to the tell-

ing of a good yarn. The oral bard was a man talking or singing to men, using his face, body, gestures, and especially the
sound of his voice. Something of these elemental qualities is
expressed in written works in other ways. Rhetorical power,
the "gift of gab," the love of word sounds and combinations,
the powerful or tender organ tones of the human voice—these
are to be found in great imaginative writers all through the ages
—in Aristophanes, Rabelais, Shakespeare, Milton, Fielding,
Melville, Joyce, and Dylan Thomas, our twentieth-century
embodiment of the ancient bard.

Reading imaginative literature, therefore, is not just a visual
process of discerning symbolic signs on a piece of paper; it is
also a process of hearing sounds, either in the mind's ear or
through oral recitation. It is a response to the human voice, to
the human breath and pulse, to the throbbing life, which no
electronic reading machine can detect or interpret. Through
the "physical" sound and rhythm of words, as well as through
their logical sense, imaginative writers engage our imagination
and feeling and afford us enjoyment.

While sharing these characteristics with oral works—and the
elements of narrative interest, verbal power, and sheer delight
are always there—imaginative literature in the West has
achieved complex and refined forms, technical sophistication,
and a range of subject matter appropriate to a late stage of
culture. Some of the greatest minds in the Western world have
devoted themselves to the creation of imaginative literature,
and they have usually been conscious inheritors of the culture
of the past and active participants in the culture of their own
day. Their works raise questions of form and substance, of
manner and matter, of the intent and result of literary expression.

III

Unfortunately, or perhaps fortunately, there is only one
formal work of literary criticism in the *Great Books of the
Western World*, Aristotle's *Poetics*. In the guides, we have
often cited Aristotle's distinctions in order to illuminate our
reading and to suggest other distinctions, where Aristotle's

seemed inadequate or irrelevant. We have also cited biographical, historical, and critical works where they shed light on the
author and his work. But, on the whole, we have proceeded
from the actual texts to the general questions they call forth
on the function, forms, and nature of imaginative literature.
Among the questions which have recurred persistently are
these:

1. *Questions about formal kinds or genres.* Philosophers and
literary critics have distinguished various kinds of imaginative
writing, that is, definite forms or species, as in animal life. For
example, Aristotle in the *Poetics* distinguishes tragedy, epic, and
comedy. As we read the specific works in the Reading Plan, we
may find it interesting and illuminating to discern the particular
forms of literature that they represent. We may find that
certain works make previous definitions of a form questionable,
possibly calling for a redefinition or even for the naming and
definition of a new form. For instance, the works of Cervantes,
Fielding, Melville, Tolstoy, and Dostoevsky in this Reading
Plan raise the question, "What is a novel?" They also raise
the question whether the prose novel may be the modern expression of the ancient forms of tragedy, epic, and comedy.
What kind of epic is *Paradise Lost,* if it is an epic? And what
kind of tragedy is *Faust,* if it is a tragedy?

2. *Questions about the effectiveness of literary devices.*
Writers down through the ages have used various devices to
obtain their effects. The further away we get from an era
and its literary conventions, the more we tend to question the
effectiveness of these devices. We can, however, try to discern
what the author was trying to do and to see whether or not
the particular devices detract from the work's plausibility
and our enjoyment of it. One such device is the use of the
narrator in the modern novel. Is it plausible for the narrator
to intrude and give his analysis and opinion of the action and
characters, as in *Tom Jones?* May he pop in and out of the
narration, as he does in *Moby Dick* and *The Brothers Karamazov,* so that the narrative changes from the first to the
third person? Should the point of view remain fixed or may it
change? Is character revealed best through direct analysis or

dramatic presentation? These are some of the technical questions raised by these readings.

3. *Questions about prosody and prose style.* The adept use of language is one of the essential marks of literary excellence, both in prose and in poetry. Because of the importance of John Milton in the development of English poetry, we deal in the Second Reading with blank verse in general and with the particular use that Milton made of it in *Paradise Lost.* The whole question of Milton's unique style, and its possible merits or demerits, is pursued. We also note the way Goethe swings from poetry to prose and from Greek to modern verse rhythms in *Faust,* to convey transitions in thought and action. Achievements in prose style of writers such as Cervantes and Melville are also discussed.

4. *Questions about the relation of imagination and truth.* Many of the works in this Reading Plan center on theological and philosophical themes and raise the problem of the relation between poetic fiction and ideas or facts. The question arises as to whether it is legitimate or possible to present such themes in imaginative literature, and if so, as to the best artistic way to present them. Such questions come up near the very start of this Reading Plan, with Milton's *Paradise Lost,* and they recur constantly down to the end. Tolstoy's *War and Peace* raises again the whole question of the relation of poetry and history, first discussed in Aristotle's *Poetics.*

CONTENTS

A NOTE ON
REFERENCE STYLE

In referring to *Great Books of the Western World,* the same style is used as in the *Syntopicon.* Pages are cited by number and section. In books that are printed in single column, "a" and "b" refer to the upper and lower halves of the page. In books that are printed in double column, "a" and "b" refer to the upper and lower halves of the left column, "c" and "d" to the upper and lower halves of the right column. For example, "Vol. 53, p. 210b" refers to the lower half of page 210, since Vol. 53, James's *Principles of Psychology,* is printed in single column. But "Vol. 7, p. 202b" refers to the lower left quarter of page 202, since Vol. 7, Plato's *Dialogues,* is printed in double column.

THE READING LIST

CERVANTES

The History of Don Quixote de la Mancha

Vol. 29

Don *Quixote* is a masterpiece that was a great popular success in its own day as well as a work for the ages. It has been one of the most widely read and best beloved books ever since the day it was published. It is both the great book of Spanish literature and a book for all mankind. Works of a somewhat similar form appeared before Cervantes' time, but *Don Quixote* is a unique creation towering above all rival works.

The reasons why this book appeals to a wide public are not hard to determine. First of all, it is a humorous book, varying from the subtlest wit to the coarsest slapstick. Secondly, it depicts everyday reality and, like Chaucer's *Canterbury Tales*, gives us a good picture of the society of the author's time. Thirdly, it is a wonderful story or series of stories, for Cervantes is a master of fictional invention and the smooth and easy unrolling of a tale. And, above all, it is a tale of human characters, two of whom have achieved literary immortality.

Don Quixote, the mad visionary who seeks to be a knight-errant in days when chivalry is long past, and Sancho Panza, the grossly practical and common-sense peasant who cannot see beyond the end of his nose— these two characters have become universal human types in whom we may see ourselves and others more lucidly. The mad Knight of the Rueful Countenance, who always seeks to transcend and transform everyday reality in order to see it in an ideal light, and his pragmatic squire, who always seeks for immediate, tangible gain, are two typical aspects of human character. The tale of the exploits of this odd pair has left traces in our common speech, as in the term "quixotic" and the expression "tilting at windmills."

This tale is also one of the great examples of antiliterary literature. It is a satire directed not so much against chivalry as against the literature about chivalry —"the extravagant and silly tales of chivalry." This enjoyable entertainment is also a purposeful protest, in the form of a burlesque, against what had become a degenerate, stereotyped, and ridiculous literary form. The greatness of the work, however, lies in its transcending its announced negative purpose of "an attack upon the books of chivalry" to become itself one of the great tales of life and adventure, as we follow enthralled the strange and droll episodes of the lanky would-be knight and his fat squire-in-spite-of-himself.

First Reading

I

Cervantes' *History of Don Quixote de la Mancha* was written during the golden age of Spanish literature, which occurred from about 1550 to 1650. It was a period of national unity, centralized monarchical government, and military conquests, including the great naval victory at Lepanto in which Cervantes was badly wounded. In this age of the great Armada, which Cervantes helped to provision, sailed against England. The literature of Spain, which had previously looked abroad for its models, principally to Italy and France, became more original and authentically Spanish.

The "picaresque" novel (so called because it told the tale of the adventures of a *picaro*, or rogue), one of the peculiarly Spanish forms of literature, was originated and developed in this period. It revealed the various modes of life and social conditions, and hence is called a "novel of manners." This story form was later combined with the adventure romance, based on Italian models, of the type written by Cervantes in his *Exemplary Novels*. A good English example of the picaresque adventure novel is Defoe's *Moll Flanders*. The term "picaresque" has been broadened to refer to any story of the adventures of an itinerant hero, such as Fielding's *Tom Jones* and Saul Bellow's *The Adventures of Augie March*.

Don Quixote is in form akin to the picaresque novel, social romance, or adventure story. But it is something unique and unrepeatable. This tale of itinerant adventures through the the attitudes and values of the ancient chivalric tales have bemances set in the time when knighthood was in flower. The literature which *Don Quixote* parodies is of the type familiar to us in the stories of King Arthur and the Knights of the

3

Round Table, revolving around such characters as Lancelot, Galahad, Merlin, Tristam, and Queen Guinevere. The French originals of these stories were translated into Spanish and Portuguese, and a whole literature of chivalric romances developed in Spain. The prototype and best known of these is the *Amadis of Gaul*, often referred to admiringly by Cervantes in *Don Quixote*. It is an old legend of a perfect knight who, after various adventures and ordeals, wins the hand of his fair lady. This story, in a new Spanish version, won popular success in Spain early in the sixteenth century and became the subject of a vast number of inferior imitations which were widely read in Cervantes' time.

Don Quixote is directed against these imitations, in which the attitudes and values of the ancient chivalric tales have become clichés, ridiculous and unbelievable extravagances. Most critics agree that the butt of Cervantes' humor is not chivalric ideals, but the trashy imitations of chivalric romance and their effect on the minds of contemporary readers. Some critics also see an underlying criticism of the narrow, provincial, unrealistic temper of the Spanish *hidalgo*, or country gentleman, marked by an intense pride in lineage and locality and a disregard of practical needs.

The fictitious friend of the author in the Preface to Part I says, "this piece of yours aims at nothing more than to destroy the authority and influence which books of chivalry have in the world and with the public." The author then proceeds to give us the story of "the famous Don Quixote of La Mancha . . . the chastest lover and the bravest knight that has for many years been seen in that neighborhood," and also of "the famous Sancho Panza, his squire, in whom . . . I have given thee condensed all the squirely drolleries that are scattered through the swarm of the vain books of chivalry" (p. xiiid). However, he and we become so involved with these two characters and their adventures and misadventures that we find not a mere burlesque, a ribbing of the tales of chivalry, but a most appealing and enriching story in its own right.

II

The History of Don Quixote de la Mancha consists of two parts. Part I was published in 1605 and Part II in 1615. Some publishers have printed editions of *Don Quixote* that include only Part I, and many readers have been unaware that they were missing the second half of Cervantes' masterpiece. Some critics think that, as far as style and literary form go, the book gets better and better as it goes on, and that the second part is superior to the first and should not be neglected. You will note other "parts" referred to in Part I. These are actually subparts, called "books" in some translations, and are not to be confused with the main parts. (See the references at the end of Chapters 8, 14, and 27 in Part I.)

The book begins with a charming Preface, which apologizes to the reader for "the story of a dry, shrivelled, whimsical off-spring, full of thoughts of all sorts and such as never came into any other imagination—just what might be begotten in a prison . . ." (p. xia). This may mean that *Don Quixote* was first conceived while Cervantes was in jail. (See the Biographical Note, pp. v-vi, for an account of Cervantes' life.) In a satirical thrust at the literary mode of his day, he calls his work "a book as dry as a rush, devoid of invention, meagre in style, poor in thoughts, wholly wanting in learning and wisdom, without quotations in the margin or annotations at the end, after the fashion of other books I see . . . I am by nature shy and careless about hunting for authors to say what I myself can say without them" (pp. xic-xiia). At the suggestion of a friend, however, he has made up some pieces himself and used famous names as pretended authors. These we find in the "Commendatory Verses" following the Preface, signed by such famous characters of chivalric romance as Urganda the Unknown, Amadis of Gaul, and Don Belianis of Greece. Of the ten poems, the first eight are straight parodies of the manner and sentiments of chivalric romance, as if meant to be taken seriously. The last two, however, are in the modern style and poke fun gently at Don Quixote and Sancho Panza, as in this sonnet which offers a capsule preview of the book:

Your fantasies, Sir Quixote, it is true,
   That crazy brain of yours have quite upset,
   But aught of base or mean hath never yet
Been charged by any in reproach to you.
Your deeds are open proof in all men's view;
   For you went forth injustice to abate,
   And for your pains sore drubbings did you get
From many a rascally and ruffian crew.
If the fair Dulcinea, your heart's queen,
   Be unrelenting in her cruelty,
     If still your woe be powerless to move her,
   In such hard case your comfort let it be
That Sancho was a sorry go-between:
   A booby he, hard-hearted she, and you no lover. (p. xvib-c)

We meet the hero at the start of the first chapter. He is described as a country gentleman of about fifty, "of a hardy habit, spare, gaunt-featured, a very early riser, and a great sportsman . . . one of those gentlemen that keep a lance in the lance-rack, an old buckler, a lean hack, and a greyhound for coursing." This typical Spanish country gentleman, who is at leisure almost all the time, has become so infatuated with chivalric romances that he has neglected his sports and the management of his estate, even to the extent of selling acres of good land to buy books on chivalry. He is so obsessed by these romances that he reads them all day and all night, until "his brains got so dry that he lost his wits." It is this imaginary world of "wounds, wooings, loves, agonies, and all sorts of impossible nonsense" that becomes more real to him than any historical reality, and he takes these chivalric ideals so seriously that he decides to act them out.

In short, his wits being quite gone, he hit upon the strangest notion that ever madman in this world hit upon, and that was that he fancied it was right and requisite, as well for the support of his own honor as for the service of his country, that he should make a knight-errant of himself, roaming the world over in full armor and on horseback in quest of adventures, and putting in practice himself all that he had read of as being the usual practices of knights-errant; righting every kind of wrong, and exposing himself to peril and danger from which, in the issue, he was to reap eternal renown and fame. (p. 2b)

Whereupon he cleans up some old armor of his great-grand-father's, patches up a helmet with pasteboard and iron bars, and bestows on his lean, old horse the name of Rocinante as properly befitting the steed of a famous knight-errant. For himself, previously known as Quixada or Quesada or Quixana ("Lantern-Jaws"?), he takes the name of Don Quixote of La Mancha (his home district) on the model of Amadis of Gaul. One thing is still lacking for a proper knight-errant—"a lady to be in love with." For, after all, when one conquers a giant or other fearsome foe, one must have a ladylove to whom the conquered foe will be dispatched as a trophy and narrator of knightly deeds. The new knight chooses a local country girl, Aldonza Lorenzo, whom he had once been in love with, though without her knowing it, and bestows on her the name of Dulcinea del Toboso, as a name like her own and yet "a name, to his mind, musical, uncommon, and significant, like all those he had already bestowed upon himself and the things belonging to him."

So, with everything in order, the Don sets out in full regalia before dawn and rides out of his back yard on the road to adventure. He is troubled for a moment by the realization that he has not yet been dubbed a knight, as the law of chivalry requires, but he resolves to have it done at the first opportunity. He follows the course his horse takes, "for in this he believed lay the essence of adventures." As he rides along he muses on the way in which some future chronicler will tell of the first sally of the great Don Quixote, and imagines it in the extravagant, windy, florid style of the chivalric romances he has read. At the end of his first day, which is disappointingly bare of adventures, he comes to an inn, which he takes to be a castle, just as he takes the innkeeper to be its castellan, or governor, and two common prostitutes to be pure young maidens of high degree. Since he refuses to take off his helmet, it is almost impossible for him to eat; the two girls have to put the food into his mouth and the landlord pours wine into him through a reed. He gets the "castellan" to agree to dub him a knight, and keeps a vigil over his armor, which is in a water trough out in the yard. When some teamsters remove the armor, in order to water their horses, he bashes them so seriously with his lance that the innkeeper decides to cut the vigil short and dub him a knight forthwith. Now a fully legitimate knight, Don Quixote takes off again at dawn to do knightly deeds.

Almost immediately he encounters his first adventure, an opportunity to right wrong and aid those in need. He comes upon a farmer whipping his shepherd boy, and forces him to stop and promise to pay the boy his back wages. Despite Quixote's fearsome threats, after he leaves the master flogs the boy cruelly and sends him off without his wages. (The boy complains later in the story,

". . . for all which your worship is to blame; for if you had gone your own way and not come where there was no call for you, nor meddled in other people's affairs, my master would have been content with giving me one or two dozen lashes, and would have then loosed me and paid me what he owed me . . ." (p. 116c)

And he begs Don Quixote never to help him again even if he sees him being cut to pieces, for no misfortune could be greater than what would result from the great knight's aid.) But at the time Don Quixote innocently believes he has made a great beginning in his career of righting wrongs and succoring those in need. Thus encouraged, he attacks a company of traders whom he takes to be knights-errant, but Rocinante stumbles and Quixote is laid out on the ground; then a muleteer breaks the Don's lance to pieces and beats him so vigorously that he is unable to rise on his own power.

Nothing daunted by his beating, Don Quixote takes this to be a normal occupational hazard of knight-errantry. By the time a neighbor peasant finds him and helps him home he has thoroughly confused himself with various figures in chivalric ballads. When the peasant objects that Don Quixote is not Baldwin the Knight but Señor Quixada, the Don replies,

"I know who I am . . . and I know that I may be not only those I have named, but all the Twelve Peers of France and even all the Nine Worthies, since my achievements surpass all that they have done all together and each of them on his own account." (p. 12b)

At home, his housekeeper, his niece, and his friends the curate and the barber are relieved to have him back. They proceed to burn almost all his library of chivalry, as the root and source of his obsession. We get a brief survey of chivalric literature and even a critical comment on Cervantes' pastoral novel *Galatea*. (See p. 16a-b.)

The redoubtable Don Quixote is undeterred by the loss of his books and even of the room that contained them, which his friends have had walled up—a disappearance which he accepts as the work of magical enchantment. He is convinced more than ever that the world needs the return of knight-errantry and that he is the man to bring it back. In view of this mission, he inveigles a dull-witted neighbor, a farm laborer by the name of Sancho Panza, to accompany him as his squire. He holds out the lure of an island kingdom which he will bestow on Sancho as a reward for his services. So, in the dead of night, Don Quixote sets out on his second sally, he on his old nag and Sancho following behind on an ass. "Don't forget about the island," the squire reminds his master.

III

There follows now a series of adventures which reveals the essential attitudes of Don Quixote and Sancho Panza toward the world and also reveals a good deal of contemporary Spanish life. Don Quixote's second sally begins with the famous tilt with the windmills, which he takes to be giants. When Sancho Panza points out his error, the Don says his squire does not know anything about "this business of adventures," charges a windmill, and is thrown to the ground when his lance gets caught in the sails. Coming upon a coach, preceded by two Benedictine monks, he takes the monks to be enchanters kidnaping some princess and vanquishes them with his lance. He also beats a Biscayan squire in a sword fight, but spares his life at the request of the ladies in the coach, on condition that the squire go to the lady Dulcinea del Toboso, and be at her disposal.

Impressed by this victory, Sancho asks for his island, but the Don informs him that this is not an adventure of islands but of crossroads, "in which nothing is got except a broken head or an ear the less." Sure enough, in their next adventure the two of them are beaten to a pulp by a group of teamsters. When Sancho, dismayed by this turn of events, proclaims a policy of peace at any price and nonresistance to evil, Don Quixote points out that "the life of knights-errant is subject to a thousand dangers and reverses," which should be accepted and not lead to dismay. They stop at an inn (which the Don, of course, takes to be a castle) to recuperate from their battering. Another beating results for the pair as a servant girl (whom the Don takes to be the princess of the castle) wanders into the beds of the Don and his squire by mistake and arouses the ire of her intended lover. A scene out of Keystone comedy ensues as the lover beats up Sancho, he the girl, she him, and the innkeeper her, "cat to rat, rat to rope, rope to stick." These events leave the Don with the firm conviction that "this castle is enchanted."

Don Quixote's next misadventure occurs when he takes two flocks of sheep to be armies out of chivalric legend. "Seeing in his imagination what he did not see and what did not exist," he is not disturbed by Sancho's insistence upon empirical reality, but "brimful and saturated with what he had read in his lying books," he charges and begins to spear the sheep. The angry shepherds stone him until he falls off his horse, minus a good many teeth. "We who profess the austere order of chivalry," he tells Sancho, "are liable to all this" (p. 54a). The undiscouraged Don triumphs in his next encounter—with a funeral procession in the dead of night. Sancho and Don Quixote react typically to "this strange spectacle at such an hour and in such a solitary place." Sancho is paralyzed with fear and dread. But the Don

. . . took it into his head that the litter was a bier on which was borne some sorely wounded or slain knight, to avenge whom was a task reserved for him alone; and without any further reasoning he laid his lance in rest, fixed himself firmly in his saddle, and with gallant spirit and bearing took up his position in the middle of the road . . . (p. 55a-b)

When the mourners ("knights" to him) do not heed his order to stop, he charges them, wounding one badly and sending the rest scurrying off into the night, "for they all thought it was no man, but a devil from hell come to carry away the dead body they had in the litter." Sancho is quite impressed by his master's victory over a score of foes. "Clearly this master of mine is as bold and valiant as he says he is" (p. 55c). The wounded man turns out to be one of a dozen priests who have been accompanying the corpse to its burial place. When Don Quixote informs him that he is a knight-errant whose mission is to right wrongs, the poor fellow retorts

"I do not know how that about righting wrongs can be . . . for from straight you have made me crooked, leaving me with a broken leg that will never see itself straight again all the days of its life; and the injury you have redressed in my case has been to leave me injured in such a way that I shall remain injured forever; and the height of misadventure it was to fall in with you who go in search of adventures." (p. 56a)

The knight and his squire emerge from the encounter with a store of tasty provisions looted from the priests' sumpter mule. Also Don Quixote gets a distinctive name, as is proper for a knight-errant in all the tales of chivalry. Sancho tells the Don that he has "the most ill-favored countenance I ever saw." Thereupon Quixote decides he will be called the "Knight of the Rueful Countenance" and have a sad face painted on his shield. No need for that, Sancho assures him. People will just have to look at his face to know he is the one with the rueful countenance.

The contrast in the attitudes toward danger between knight and squire is again emphasized in the encounter with the fulling hammers, the clanking of which in the dark night terrorizes Sancho, "who was by nature timid and faint-hearted," but not Don Quixote, who is "supported by his intrepid heart." This encounter is just one more opportunity to fulfill his mission of reviving the golden age in the present base age of iron. (See his pronouncement on pp. 57d-58a.) The more awesome the sights and sounds, says the Don, the more the "incentive and stimulant to my spirit, making my heart burst in my bosom through eagerness to engage in this adventure, arduous as it promises to be" (p. 58a). When the fearsome giants that the Don is courageously set to charge turn out to be six fulling hammers, Sancho Panza's fear gives way to laughter and he pokes fun at the Don and his mission. The Don rebukes him thus:

"Look here, my lively gentleman, if these, instead of being fulling hammers, had been some perilous adventure, have I not, think you, shown the courage required for the attempt and achievement? Am I, perchance, being, as I am, a gentleman, bound to know and distinguish sounds and tell whether they come from fulling mills or not; and that, when perhaps, as is the case, I have never in my life seen any as you have, low boor as you are, that have been born and bred among them? But turn me these six hammers into six giants, and bring them to beard me, one by one or all together, and if I do not knock them head over heels, then make what mockery you like of me." (p. 62b)

He also instructs Sancho in the niceties of chivalry when the latter complains that the Don's deeds will not elicit the rewards they deserve without publicity, and hence he should enter the service of some great emperor or prince.

"Thou speakest not amiss, Sancho . . . but before that point is reached it is requisite to roam the world, as it were on probation, seeking adventures, in order that, by achieving some, name and fame may be acquired, such that when he betakes himself to the court of some great monarch the knight may be already known by his deeds and that the boys, the instant they see him enter the gate of the city, may all follow him and surround him, crying, 'This is the Knight of the Sun'—or the Serpent, or any other title under which he may have achieved great deeds . . ." (p. 65d)

Then the king will welcome him and the princess will fall in love with him, and he will accomplish world-famous deeds and wed the princess and succeed the king—and reward his squire, with a title, estate, and highborn damsel. At this point the Don makes an interesting point on social status, noting

". . . that there are two kinds of lineages in the world; some there be tracing and deriving their descent from kings and princes, whom time has reduced little by little until they end in a point like a pyramid upside down; and others who spring from the common herd and go on rising step by step until they come to be great lords; so that the difference is that the one were what they no longer are, and the others are what they formerly were not . . ." (p. 67b)

One of the high lights of Part I is the encounter with the chain gang of convicts being led to service as galley slaves. The Don considers this another golden opportunity to fulfill his mission, "to put down force and to succor and help the wretched" (p. 68c). He finds excuses for the crimes these men have been convicted of and uses his lance and sword to gain their release. The convicts, anxious to make good their escape, refuse to proceed to Dulcinea del Toboso to narrate Don Quixote's exploits as he requests, and they bombard the knight and his squire with a shower of stones, strip them of their coats, and take off for the hills, leaving "Don Quixote fuming to find himself so served by the very persons for whom he had done so much" (p. 73a).

The adventures we have sketched above are narrated in the first twenty-two chapters of Part I. The remaining thirty chapters of Part I deal with the Don's adventures in the Sierra Morena mountains and with the attempt of his friends, the curate and the barber, to bring him back home. New characters are introduced, side stories, and stories within stories. The main subplot deals with the tangled affairs of a young man, Cardenio, who is betrayed in winning the girl he loves by his false friend, Don Fernando, a grandee's son. This cad has also seduced the peasant girl Dorothea with a false promise of marriage. Dorothea, a sprightly, intelligent, and comely young woman, is the most interesting and well-drawn of the new characters. In the end things come out all right for the lovers, and each girl ends up with the right man.

There are many stories told by characters in Part I that have nothing to do with the main story, such as "The Novel of the Ill-advised Curiosity" in Chapters 33-35, and "The Captive's Story" in Chapters 39-42. The goatherd's tale of Marcela and Chrysostom is another such insert, although it is worked into the main story. (See Chapters 12-14.) Such tales may be skipped in the first reading, if the reader is anxious to get on with the main story. J. M. Cohen, a recent translator of *Don Quixote*, advocates this procedure and even advises skipping the inserts of the Cardenio-Fernando story that intersperse Chapters 24-28. Whatever the reader chooses to do, he should not get so sidetracked or bogged down in the incidental material that he gets too weary or bored to follow the adventures of the Don and his squire. For there is much interesting and enjoyable material about this pair in the last half of Part I.

One of the most wonderful of the concluding episodes is the tale of Don Quixote's imitation of the penance of Amadis of Gaul, who withdrew from the world and went mad with despair over his rejection by the Lady Oriana. When Sancho Panza objects from his common-sense standpoint that Don Quixote has no such provocation or cause, the knight points out

"There is the point . . . and that is the beauty of this business of mine; no thanks to a knight-errant for going mad when he has a cause; the thing is to turn crazy without any provocation, and to let my lady know, if I do this in the dry, what I would do in the moist . . ." (p. 83b)

Sancho protests that all of the Don's chivalric notions "must be made up of wind and lies, and all pigments or figments, or whatever we may call them," for he considers what everyone knows is a barber's basin to be Mambrino's golden helmet (out of the chivalric romance *Orlando Furioso*). Don Quixote is scornful of his squire's limited understanding.

". . . Is it possible that all this time thou hast been going about with me thou hast never found out that all things belonging to knights-errant seem to be illusions and nonsense and ravings, and to go always by contraries? And not because it really is so, but because there is always a swarm of enchanters in attendance upon us that change and alter everything with us, and turn things as they please, and according as they are disposed to aid or destroy us; thus what seems to thee a barber's basin seems to me Mambrino's helmet, and to another it will seem something else; and rare foresight it was in the sage who is on my side to make what is really and truly Mambrino's helmet seem a basin to everybody, for, being held in such estimation as it is, all the world would pursue me to rob me of it; but when they see it is only a barber's basin they do not take the trouble to obtain it; as was plainly shown by him who tried to break it, and left it on the ground without taking it, for, by my faith, had he known it he would never have left it behind . . ." (p. 83d)

Don Quixote goes through the ritual of tearing his garments, banging his head on the rocks, and other actions, so that Sancho Panza may be able to give a truthful report of his sufferings and madness to the Lady Dulcinea del Toboso. When Sancho finds out that this exalted lady is actually the hefty farm wench Aldonza Lorenzo, he objects that it is silly to send captives to kneel before her, when she will most likely be baling flax or threshing wheat. Again the Don points out to his thickheaded squire that

". . . for all I want with Dulcinea del Toboso she is just as good as the most exalted princess on earth. It is not to be supposed that all those poets who sang the praises of ladies under the fancy names they give them, had any such mistresses. Thinkest thou that the Amaryllises, the Phyllises, the Sylvias, the Dianas, the Galateas, the Filidas, and all the rest of them that the books, the ballads, the barbers' shops, the theatres are full of were really and truly ladies of flesh and blood, and mistresses of those that glorify and have glorified them? Nothing of the kind; they only invent them for the most part to furnish a subject for their verses, and that they may pass for lovers or for men who have some pretensions to be so; and so it is enough for me to think and believe that the good Aldonza Lorenzo is fair and virtuous; and as to her pedigree it is very little matter, for no one will examine into it for the purpose of conferring any order upon her, and I, for my part, reckon her the most exalted princess in the world. For thou shouldst know, Sancho, if thou dost not know, that two things alone beyond all others are incentives to love, and these are great beauty and a good name, and these two things are to be found in Dulcinea in the highest degree, for in beauty no one equals her and in good name few approach her; and to put the whole thing in a nutshell, I persuade myself that all I say is as I say, neither more nor less, and I picture her in my imagination as I would have her to be, as well in beauty as in condition; Helen approaches her not, nor does Lucretia come up to her, nor any other of the famous women of times past, Greek, Barbarian, or Latin; and let each say what he will, for if in this I am taken to task by the ignorant, I shall not be censured by the critical." (p. 86c-d)

Don Quixote asserts his capacity to see things as they really are, undeceived by the appearances which mislead common sense and experience. Nothing that happens to him or that he witnesses can disturb his absolute certainty in the truth of his vision. The dispute about Mambrino's golden helmet (the barber's basin) in Chapter 45 is an uproarious example of this. See also the dispute between the Don and his squire about whether Don Quixote is enchanted (pp. 187d-189a), and the argument between Don Quixote and the canon in Chapters 49-50 about whether chivalric romances are truth or fiction. Cervantes puts in Don Quixote's mouth an eloquent and lovely appreciation of the enjoyment afforded by reading the tales of chivalry. (See pp. 191d-193a.) The canon is astonished both at Quixote's "methodical nonsense" and Sancho's simplicity.

We, too, begin to wonder about just how rooted in empirical actuality Sancho is. Don Quixote has already observed earlier, "to all appearance thou art not sounder in thy wits than I am" (p. 87d). Sancho is interested in proving to Quixote that he is not enchanted, because Sancho understands that it is a trick of Quixote's friends to get the Don home, an event which would deprive Sancho of the island and title that his master will bestow on him if they continue their adventures. The irate barber remarks,

. . . "so you are of the same fraternity as your master, too, Sancho? By God, I begin to see that you will have to keep him company in the cage, and be enchanted like him for having caught some of his humor and chivalry. It was an evil hour when you let yourself be got with child by his promises, and that island you long so much for found its way into your head." (p. 183d)

But a country of his own, to have and to rule, doing as he pleases, is Sancho's heart's desire, and he refuses to give it up. (See p. 193a-b.)

In the end, after one last mad defeated charge, Don Quixote is brought safely home in a cage on an oxcart by his friends, the barber and the curate. Sancho tells his wife, anxious to find out how much money he has made,

". . . that there is nothing in the world more delightful than to be a person of consideration, squire to a knight-errant, and a seeker of adventures. To be sure most of those one finds do not end as pleasantly as one could wish, for out of a hundred that one meets with, ninety-nine will turn out cross and contrary. I know it by experience, for out of some I came blanketed, and out of others belabored. Still, for all that, it is a fine thing to be on the lookout for what may happen, crossing mountains, searching woods, climbing rocks, visiting castles, putting up at inns, all at free quarters, and devil take the maravedi to pay." (p. 199c-d)

The book ends with the author's hint of a Second Part, which will narrate Don Quixote's third sally and with it some epitaphs and eulogies discovered in some old archives. These verses are dedicated to "the scatterbrain" and "ill-errant" Don Quixote, Dulcinea del Toboso, Rocinante, and Sancho Panza, of whom it is said:

Within an ace of being Count was he . . .
Delusive hopes that lure the common herd
With promises of ease, the heart's desire,
In shadows, dreams, and smoke ye always end. (pp. 200d-201a)

IV

Part II continues and concludes the story of the remarkable Don Quixote and his adventures. In his Preface to the new work Cervantes indicates that one reason why he wrote a sequel to Part I was that a spurious Second Part had been published in the previous year by a writer who called himself Alonso Fernandez de Avellaneda of Tordesillas. Cervantes was not only offended as an artist by the low, vulgar, dull imitation of his work, but also deeply hurt by a malicious preface which showered abuse on Cervantes as a man and a writer. The plagiarist ridiculed Cervantes as being old and poor and maimed—"with more tongue than hands." To this Cervantes replies that he bears his battle wounds as a badge of honor, that age improves the understanding which creates literature (Part I was published in his 58th year, Part II in his 69th year), and that honor and nobility may be retained intact in poverty.

The allusion to an author of genius who is behind "Avellaneda" (see p. 203b-c) may be intended for Lope de Vega, the most prolific and popular playwright of Cervantes' time. Possibly De Vega was hurt by the opinion of the popular Spanish theatre expressed by the canon in Part I (see Section V below), or he may have been jealous of the great popularity suddenly achieved by the comparatively obscure Cervantes. Anyway, the true author of *Don Quixote*, disturbed by the false Part II, assures us that this is the genuine article, that

. . . this Second Part of *Don Quixote* which I offer thee is cut by the same craftsman and from the same cloth as the First, and that in it I present thee Don Quixote continued, and at length dead and buried . . . (p. 204c)

As the book opens we find the Don still imbued with the spirit of knight-errantry. He is interested in the reactions of his neighbors to his exploits and particularly in the book about his exploits, just published, called *The Ingenious Gentleman Don*

Quixote of La Mancha. He discusses with the bachelor Samson Carrasco the various criticisms of the book and the prospects of a Second Part coming out. Sancho Panza says that if they go out on another sally, they will furnish the author material for a hundred parts. So the two of them decide to go to the city of Saragossa where Don Quixote may joust with the best knights in the kingdom of Aragon.

As they start on the journey to Saragossa there occurs one of the most remarkable incidents in the story of Don Quixote, as Sancho Panza invents a fake Dulcinea to placate his master, who wants to bid farewell to the fair lady he knows only by hearsay. Since his master is always taking one thing for another, as windmills for giants and barbers' basins for golden helmets, why not pass off the first country girl he comes across as the Lady Dulcinea? So when he sees three peasant girls mounted on asses, he rides back to tell his master that the Lady Dulcinea del Toboso and her damsels, attired in rich jewels and fabrics and magnificently mounted, are nearby. But this time it is Don Quixote who believes the evidence of his senses. He says, "I see nothing . . . but three country girls on three jackasses" (p. 232d). And this time it is Sancho Panza who reprimands Don Quixote for his blindness and who goes down on his knees before the startled girls, addressing them in the high chivalric style. The girls think the gentry are making fun of peasant girls and are eager to get away. Don Quixote is convinced that the enchanter that is always persecuting him has transformed his beautiful highborn lady to appear as a plain peasant girl in his eyes. In the confusion the supposed Dulcinea is thrown from her mount, and

. . . as Don Quixote was about to lift up his enchanted mistress in his arms and put her upon her beast, the lady, getting up from the ground, saved him the trouble, for, going back a little, she took a short run, and putting both hands on the croup of the ass she dropped into the saddle more lightly than a falcon, and sat astride like a man . . . (p. 233c)

As she speeds away Quixote laments the malicious enchantment which has even taken away the sweet fragrance of highborn ladies and substituted raw garlic, the unmistakable whiff of which he inhaled as he bent down to aid his fallen "lady."

Also near the beginning of the new sally occurs the queer adventure of the Knight of the Mirrors (also called the Knight of the Grove), whom Don Quixote vanquishes and forces to confess the superiority of Dulcinea del Toboso to the strange knight's own lady fair. That the knight turns out to be the bachelor Samson Carrasco does not faze Don Quixote a bit— he understands immediately that the knight's face has been transformed into Carrasco's through enchantment. One of the intriguing things about this odd, dreamlike, mirrorlike passage is that Sancho Panza, too, has an opposite number, the squire of the strange knight, with whom he discusses the ups and downs of the squire business. When the squire's disguise (consisting mainly of a tremendous nose, "so big that it almost overshadowed his whole body") is also pierced and he turns out to be a friend and neighbor of Sancho, the latter is convinced that this, too, is the work of enchantment and literally does not believe his eyes.

A host of new adventures and new characters is presented in Part II. Sancho Panza finally gains—and loses—his island. Don Quixote is finally defeated—by the Knight of the White Moon, who turns out again to be Samson Carrasco—and he is forced to renounce knight-errantry for a year. The vanquished knight returns home, falls into a fatal illness in which he recovers his senses, and foreswears all belief in the vulgar tales of knight-errantry. He announces,

". . . I am no longer Don Quixote of La Mancha, but Alonso Quixano, whose way of life won for him the name of Good. Now am I the enemy of Amadis of Gaul and of the whole countless troop of his descendants; odious to me now are all the profane stories of knight-errantry; now I perceive my folly, and the peril into which reading them brought me; now, by God's mercy schooled into my right senses, I loathe them." (p. 427c-d)

He makes a will bequeathing his estate to his niece, on condition that she shall not marry any man who knows "what books of chivalry are." He asks his executors to find the author of the forthcoming *Second Part of the Achievements of Don*

Quixote of La Mancha to tender his apologies for being the cause of the "monstrous absurdities" he has been forced to detail. So Don Quixote dies in bed after properly receiving the sacraments. Samson Carrasco's new epitaph for Don Quixote closes with this apt summing up:

> *He for the world but little cared;*
> *And at his feats the world was scared;*
> *A crazy man his life he passed,*
> *But in his senses died at last.* (p. 429b-c)

Cervantes ends his great work with these words, put in the mouth of Cid Hamet, the fictitious author of *Don Quixote*, and aimed at the vulgar plagiarist from Tordesillas.

". . . For me alone was Don Quixote born, and I for him; it was his to act; mine to write; we two together make but one, notwithstanding and in spite of that pretended Tordesillesque writer who has ventured or would venture with his great, coarse, ill-trimmed ostrich quill to write the achievements of my valiant knight;—no burden for his shoulders, nor subject for his frozen wit: whom, if perchance thou shouldst come to know him, thou shalt warn to leave at rest where they lie the weary mouldering bones of Don Quixote, and not to attempt to carry him off, in opposition to all the privileges of death, to Old Castile, making him rise from the grave where in reality and truth he lies stretched at full length, powerless to make any third expedition or new sally; for the two that he has already made, so much to the enjoyment and approval of everybody to whom they have become known, in this as well as in foreign countries, are quite sufficient for the purpose of turning into ridicule the whole of those made by the whole set of the knights-errant; and so doing shalt thou discharge thy Christian calling, giving good counsel to one that bears ill-will to thee. And I shall remain satisfied, and proud to have been the first who has ever enjoined the fruit of his writings as fully as he could desire; for my desire has been no other than to deliver over to the detestation of mankind the false and foolish tales of the books of chivalry, which, thanks to that of my true Don Quixote, are even now tottering, and doubtless doomed to fall forever. Farewell." (p. 429c-d)

V

Besides the pure enjoyment of its story, *Don Quixote* provides the reader with instruction in literary history and criticism. We should note that the very aim and form of the work—the parody of chivalric romance—is in itself a form of literary criticism. Besides this implicit criticism, there are many passages of explicit literary analysis and interpretation that may be of interest to readers of this study plan. Right at the start, in the Preface to Part I, there is wry comment on the practice of filling books with citations from various sources, and advice to keep style and diction both musical and plain, "with clear, proper, and well-placed words." And Chapter 6 of Part I furnishes a critical history of chivalric romances. There is also a genial discussion of this literature in Chapter 32, Part I, between the curate and the people who run the inn. The curate condemns such books as lies, leading to unfortunate consequences when naïve persons believe they are true stories. But the landlord and his household find enjoyment, recreation, and elevation in listening to these tales, identifying with the characters and participating in their adventures. We get a picture of the reapers listening spellbound to the reading of these tales in the respite from their labors. The landlord is absolutely sure that these are true stories, since it is unbelievable that the Lords of the Royal Council would license what the curate calls "the fabrication and invention of idle wits."

The most ambitious discussion of literature occurs in Part I, Chapters 47-50, where the canon holds forth on chivalric romances and other types of literature. He objects to chivalric romances, first, because they aim only at amusement, and secondly, because they fail to amuse. His first objection stems from the ethical principle that literature must both instruct and amuse. His second objection is aesthetic, based on the principle that enjoyment derives from the mind's contact with beauty and harmony. Chivalric romance, he insists, is full of ugliness, disproportion, and implausibility. He believes that fiction should imitate reality, and that plots should be smooth, unified, and lead harmoniously from the beginning to the end. He also complains that chivalric romances are all alike—if you've read one, you've read them all—and that he has never been able to read one all the way through. The canon, however, is alive to the possibilities of such a spacious medium, which, like the ancient epic, permits the author to present so many incidents and characters and to depict concretely the cardinal human virtues, and thus to give both instruction and pleasure—"if this be done with charm of style and ingenious invention, aiming at the truth as much as possible" (p. 185b).

The canon points to debased popular taste, or what the author thinks the public wants, as the cause for the low level of both chivalric romance and contemporary drama. He insists that plays written according to the laws of art would be even more entertaining than the nonsensical drivel then in vogue. The curate joins in to point out the various barbarities perpetrated in the contemporary drama and its violation of the classical unities of place and time, "as plays have become a salable commodity" (p. 187a). He suggests that a state official, "some intelligent and sensible person," examine all plays before they are produced, so that only plays written in accord with artistic rules and other decencies may be put on. Thus good plays could be produced that would at the same time entertain the audiences. And the same might be done for chivalric romances.

The canon, however, fails to convince Don Quixote that the chivalric tales are fiction. Like the landlord, Quixote finds it utterly incredible that books licensed by the king, read with delight, and carrying such an appearance of truth—to the tiniest details—should be fiction. He constructs a wonderful, moving image of the content and effect of chivalric tales, which raise man's spirit out of melancholy and depression and lead to moral edification, the kind that is embodied in action.

". . . For myself I can say that since I have been a knight-errant I have become valiant, polite, generous, well-bred, magnanimous, courteous, dauntless, gentle, patient, and have learned to bear hardships, imprisonments, and enchantments; and though it be such a short time since I have seen myself shut up in a cage like a madman, I hope by the might of my arm, if Heaven aid me and fortune thwart me not, to see myself king of some kingdom where I may be able to show the gratitude and generosity that dwell in my heart; for by my faith, señor, the poor man is incapacitated from showing the virtue of generosity to any one, though he may possess it in the highest degree; and gratitude that consists of disposition only is a dead thing, just as faith without works is dead . . ." (pp. 192d-193a)

Besides these general criticisms of chivalric romance and popular drama, Cervantes provides us with a specific criticism of Part I, which probably conveys the reactions of various critics of his day. (See Part II, Ch. 3-4.) The criticism includes the objections that far too many beatings of Don Quixote are narrated; that Sancho Panza, though delightful, is too credulous about the island; that the insertion of pieces like "The Ill-advised Curiosity" is out of place in the story of Don Quixote; that there are lapses of memory and incongruity of details, as with Sancho's ass, Dapple, which he both has and has not at the same time. Don Quixote and Sancho Panza discuss these criticisms with Samson Carrasco, and Don Quixote makes this wise observation on the writing of books and especially of humorous ones:

". . . to write histories, or books of any kind, there is need of great judgment and a ripe understanding. To give expression to humor, and write in a strain of graceful pleasantry, is the gift of great geniuses. The cleverest character in comedy is the clown, for he who would make people take him for a fool, must not be one . . ." (p. 214c-d)

See also Quixote's praise of poetry, his demand that it be both edifying and elegant, his defense of poetry written in the common modern tongues, and the relation of art to nature in poetry (pp. 251b-252b).

VI

Is Don Quixote mad?

Many characters in the book (notably the canon in Part I) remark that Don Quixote shows good sense, critical learning, and even solid wisdom when he is not gripped by his obsession about knight-errantry. Is this plausible and acceptable *in the context of the story*, leaving aside any question of psychological plausibility? Is the hero split into two Quixotes, or are the good sense and the madness different expressions of one and the same man *in Cervantes' portrayal*? What would Don Quixote and his story be without his madness? Without his sanity?

Some literary critics maintain that degenerate or pathological characters or situations are unfitting subjects for fictional development and interest. Yet generations of readers all over the Western world have enjoyed the story of Don Quixote ever since it appeared. Where does their enjoyment lie? In the Don's being a ridiculous character whose mad ideas and mishaps they laugh at, as in slapstick comedy? The citations in this guide indicate the comic flavor of *Don Quixote,* and few readers can avoid laughing at the Don and his deeds. But is this all? Do we just *laugh at* him or do we also *feel with* him? Is Don Quixote a lovable character? Is he admirable or noble in his madness? If so, in what respect?

Practically all the other characters in the book look on Don Quixote as a strange, unique person. Is he just an abnormal oddity to you as you read the story, or is there anything in him, in his mad state, that you sympathize with, that expresses anything in your mind? Are you for him or against him in his struggle to assert his ideal vision against the solid reality of actual existence? Or do you just enjoy his antics as a mere spectator?

Is Sancho Panza the representative of solid common sense?

A common reaction to the lanky knight and his squat squire is that they represent two polar types of human thought and character, Don Quixote embodying an utterly visionary though noble idealism—pure imagination—and Sancho Panza representing a practical though unimaginative common sense—pure earthiness. They may both be seen as deviations from the normal human type, the one too rarefied, the other too gross for fully human existence. But, as we have noted, Don Quixote's expressions and actions do not always conform to the visionary type, and there are many things about Sancho Panza that do not conform to the stereotype of the gross lout.

For one thing, his credulity in believing Quixote's promises to give him an island and other rewards hardly seems concordant with common sense. Or is this just an indication that the material desires of gross souls lead to just as great a departure from reality as the idealistic aspirations of noble minds? More than one of the characters remark that the credulous squire is as mad as his master—"of the same fraternity," says the barber.

For another thing, as the book goes on, this man who starts out as an utterly stupid and unimaginative fellow develops surprising qualities of mind. In Part I, he invents a whole story about carrying a message to Don Quixote's Lady Dulcinea, down to the tiniest and most plausible details. In Part II, he invents a fantastic tale to account for a lapse of detail by Cervantes in Part I. (See p. 215c-d.) And in Part II, Chapter 10, occurs the most remarkable turnabout of all, where *Sancho Panza* insists that three homely peasant girls are three beautiful princesses, and it is only *Don Quixote* who is able to see the manifest empirical reality.

What has happened to Sancho Panza? Has some of Don Quixote's imaginative capacity rubbed off on him? (See Sancho's own opinion about this, p. 237d.) Does he still remain Sancho Panza? What is the difference between his imaginative inventions and Quixote's idealized vision? Is the one just a crafty contriver and the other a sincere madman or visionary? Does Sancho have any effect on Quixote, or is it essential to Quixote's character that he have no development, be responsive to no influence?

What is Sancho's role in the novel? Is he a "straight man" or vaudeville partner to the burlesque knight? Does he help to convey Don Quixote's essential character and intention? Is Don Quixote conceivable without Sancho Panza? Couldn't we have a novel with the same basic theme and background without this remarkable character? Would we find Quixote's idealism more acceptable if we did not have Sancho's constant heckling? Or do we get a richness of content and tone from the two voices that we would not get from a solo performance.

Is Don Quixote *a criticism of contemporary society?*

We have noted that Cervantes' announced aim is to satirize third-rate imitations of chivalric romance. Is *Don Quixote* also a satire or criticism of contemporary society? This is a "novel of manners," a picaresque social novel. Characters from various social classes are portrayed, and the problem of romance and marriage between persons of different classes is handled in the love stories. The clergy are as omnipresent in this novel as in Chaucer's *Canterbury Tales*, and some of them are shown in an unflattering or ridiculous light. Quixote even claims a higher status of holiness for the knights. There is a surprising amount of talk about equality, about one man being as good as another. And there is the remarkable incident where Quixote frees the galley slaves.

But is this a novel of social protest, written in a reforming spirit? Does Quixote, like Dante, shake his finger at contemporary abuses and call for their abolition? Or does he, like Chaucer, merely describe the social types and conditions of his time for our enjoyment? Is Don Quixote imbued with a reforming spirit when he sees his time as a base one which has to be elevated by the renaissance of knight-errantry? Is this novel actually a satire against *hidalgism,* the spirit and code of the decayed Spanish country gentry? Does Cervantes ever take sides for or against anything? Or is this novel intended for one purpose alone—aesthetic enjoyment?

How is love between the sexes portrayed in this novel?

Don Quixote's prevailing attitude toward women is the one of lady worship (or "domnei") which he found expressed in chivalric romance. The knight dedicates his heart to his lady and offers his deeds and prowess as a sacrifice of love. She stands on the highest level, rivaling or even superseding that of the divine personages of religious faith, as more than one character warns the Don. Dante's Beatrice comes of this tradition of courtly love.

Is Cervantes making fun of this kind of love, this idealization of woman, this setting of the object of desire in the heavens? Or does he accept it seriously and portray it understandingly, ridiculing only the vulgarization that it takes in the cheap imitations of chivalric romance? What are we to make of the fact that Quixote's "queen" is a common country girl?

And what is the meaning of that wonderful scene in Part II where Quixote kneels down before one whom he admits his senses show to be only a plain peasant wench? Does Quixote see in the ugly reality before him an inner beauty and spirit? Or is this merely the triumph of obsessions over experience, having nothing to do with actual reality? Note what Quixote himself says on mistaking the country wench for a princess. (See p. 15 above.)

How is the carnal side of sexual love handled in this novel? As the canon points out, there is a good deal about adultery and other illicit loves in the romantic tales themselves—together with their transcendental lady-worship. How about Quixote? Does he reflect this interest? What are his expectations and intentions when the maid stumbles into his bed by accident? When the Duenna enters his chamber? (See Part II, Ch. 48.) Are they concordant with his knightly mission and character? See Quixote's bawdy analogy between his choice of the peasant girl and the widow's choice of a rather dull divinity student for her lover (p. 86b-c).

How are we to take the story of Don Fernando, the gay seducer and the betrayer of his friend's trust? Are we to accept it as the normal behavior of a grandee's son, finally made right by his marrying Dorothea? And what of "The Novel of the Ill-advised Curiosity," where the husband prevails on his best friend to try to seduce his wife in order to test her virtue? Is this plausible or edifying? Is it amusing and enjoyable as one of Chaucer's smoking-car stories or something out of Rabelais? Does Cervantes want us to take this story seriously?

What was Cervantes' intention in writing this novel, and did he succeed?

Cervantes announces his intention as the parody of the stereotyped, third-rate imitation of chivalric romance that was popular in his day. But we have noted that besides parodying the third-rate he achieves beautiful imitations of what must be the genuine article, masterful renditions of the chivalric style of writing. Obviously we are meant to laugh at the ridiculing parodies, and we do. But what about the beautiful imitations and the critical appreciation of genuine chivalric romance? Are we to take this seriously or laugh at this too? Is *Don Quixote* a bad mixture of the serious and the comical? And what of the way the story develops on its own, with its own interest and elaboration, aside from any parody of chivalry? And what of the two leading characters, who start out by being comic types, the butt of laughter and ridicule, and develop into something far wider, deeper, and more compelling? Did Cervantes let his story and his characters run away with him? And if so, is this a good or a bad thing, from the artistic point of view? Or does the genius of the novel and the great novelist lie in just this open, sprawling development, unprescribed by critical canons or the author's original intentions?

The modern Italian philosopher Benedetto Croce proposed as a rule of criticism that an author's artistry should be judged by how closely he fulfills his basic intention. What do you think of this as a criterion of good writing? Could a work fulfill the intention of its author perfectly and yet be trivial, shallow, and dull? Is it permissible for the author or artist to change his idea as he goes along? As to basic form? As to essential content? As to methods? Or only as to incidental details?

Does it matter for us readers what the author's intention may or may not have been? Is the book as it appears on the printed page before us the sole object of our attentions? Would it help our understanding and appreciation of *Don Quixote* to know what Cervantes' contemporaries found enjoyable in the book—features that we possibly miss the point of? Would we find the parody of stereotyped romance more hilarious if we were familiar with the original, as in a Bob Hope or Tony Randall parody of Western movies? How important is this factor in our enjoyment and understanding of *Don Quixote* as a whole? Do we see anything in the work that Cervantes' contemporaries may have missed? Can a work take on additional or different meanings for each era? What social type today would be the closest equivalent for Quixote's decayed country gentleman? What anachronistic ideal would be most impelling for such a type?

Is the ending proper to the story?

Does the ending contradict the whole tone and interest of the story, or is it the only way the story can definitely end? Does it make the world all right and Don Quixote all wrong, a crazy man who dies in his senses? Or is this the way all adventures of the imagination must finally end? Or was it just the most convenient way for Cervantes to end the story?

How would the canon have rated Don Quixote?

Is *Don Quixote* both amusing and instructive? Is it perfectly formed, proportionate, and smooth? Are these proper criteria for novels? What do you think of the curate's suggestion of a censor who would permit only plays written according to the classical rules to be performed? Do you think it would increase the number of good plays written? Do you think plays must observe the classical unities of time and place to be artistically proper?

The following questions are designed to help you test the thoroughness of your reading. Each question is to be answered by giving a page or pages of the reading assignment. Answers will be found on page 248 of this Reading Plan.

1 Who has *the best hand of any woman in all La Mancha for salting pigs*?

2 What is Marcela's defense against the charge that she caused Chrysostom's suicide?

3 What is Don Quixote's criticism of the way Sancho Panza tells a story?

4 What is the story of "Princess Micomicona"?

5 Who is warned that seeking for the impossible may result in the withholding of what is possible?

6 What is the curate's criticism of "The Novel of the Ill-advised Curiosity"?

7 What is the plot of "The Captive's Story"?

8 What is there about Sancho's talk in Chapter 5 of Book II that makes the translator consider it apocryphal?

9 What art form is "a mirror in which we may see vividly displayed what goes on in human life"?

10 What exploit earns Don Quixote the self-bestowed title of "The Knight of the Lions"?

30

MILTON

Paradise Lost

Vol. 32, pp. 93-333

Milton's *Paradise Lost* has long been regarded as the great epic poem of the English language. It has had an immense influence on the writing of English poetry. The stature and influence of this work are no accident. Its author set out to write a poem that would rival the ancient epics of Homer and Virgil, adorn his native tongue, and be a work for future ages. This poem is not the product of youthful ardor, of a momentary burst of creative power, or of sudden "inspiration." *Paradise Lost* is the work of decades—"long choosing, and beginning late"—and its author gave to it all that he had and was.

John Milton was no ordinary man or writer. He was a man of great learning, intimate with ancient and modern literatures, versed in secular and sacred writings, erudite both in the new sciences and in traditional religious learning. He was also an active participant in the religious and political struggles of his time, writing vigorous pamphlets in favor of popular rule and liberty in church and state. At the time he wrote this poem he was living in danger and disgrace, for the monarchical rule and the ecclesiastical government he had long fought had been restored to power.

It was in this dark period—literally dark, too, because of his total loss of vision—that John Milton wrote the great English epic. But this was not the usual epic, with its stories of battles and heroes of history and legend, glorifying and commemorating a people's past. This new blind Homer attempted nothing less than the story of the Fall of Man—the original sin that brought sin and death into the world. It covers the whole biblical story of creation and redemption. Into the telling of this tale John Milton put all his learning, secular and sacred, all his experience of love and agony.

Milton contributed one unforgettable character to world literature, that of Satan, the Hinderer, the intransigent opponent of God and man. The scenes in which he acts and reacts will remain in your mind long after you lay down this book. Just as unforgettable are the scenes of Adam and Eve in the Garden, their simple happy life, their busy work, their joyous lovemaking, their corruption, their fall, and finally of their departure from Eden and their entering upon a new life in the imperfect world we know.

Second Reading

I

The epic poem has a long and distinguished history in Western literature. (See the remarks on the epic in *Imaginative Literature I*, page 17.) Homer, the first and probably the greatest of the epic poets, launches our set of *Great Books of the Western World*. Two of the ancient epics, Homer's *Odyssey* and Virgil's *Aeneid*, have already been considered in *Imaginative Literature I*. The foremost writers of the new European literatures strove to emulate Homer and Virgil and to write epics in their own tongues for their own peoples. Italian writers achieved great narrative poems in the grand style—Dante (1265-1321) in his *Divine Comedy*, Ariosto (1474-1533) in *Orlando Furioso*, and Torquato Tasso (1544-1595) in *Jerusalem Liberated*. The English and French writers of the Renaissance were eager to match the Italian achievement and to write a great epic, or "heroic," poem—just as modern American writers have long striven to write "the great American novel" in emulation of the great European writers.

In England, Edmund Spenser's allegorical romance *The Faerie Queene* (published 1590-1609) was the first notable attempt in the epic form. Spenser used the old tales of King Arthur and his knights, and made allegorical references to Queen Elizabeth I and other national topics, but he failed to achieve the great English epic. *The Faerie Queene* lacks unity of structure, and—despite its undeniable loveliness and technical perfection—Spenser's verse lacks the power and character necessary for the epic style. Moreover, it is an unfinished work, with only six of its planned twelve books completed.

Milton owed much to Spenser and admired him as the

greatest of poets, but he knew that the great English epic remained to be written; and he wanted to be the poet who would write it. In an autobiographical passage in his essay "The Reason of Church-Government," he tells us that he had "an inward prompting . . . that by labour and intent study . . . joyn'd with the strong propensity of nature, I might perhaps leave something so written to aftertimes, as they should not willingly let it die. . . . That what the greatest and choycest wits of *Athens, Rome,* or modern *Italy,* and those Hebrews of old did for their country, I in my proportion with this over and above of being a Christian, might doe for mine own Citizens throughout this Iland in the mother dialect." He muses on whether he will write epic, tragedy, or odes.

Milton goes on to extol the edifying power of the poetic art for individuals and nations: lyric powers are the gift of God and suited to convey the divine teachings. With superb confidence, he asks the reader to share his faith that someday he will complete "a work not to be rays'd from the heat of youth, or the vapours of wine, like that which flows at wast from the pen of some vulgar Amorist, or the trencher fury of a riming parasite, nor to be obtain'd by the invocation of Dame Memory and her Siren daughters, but by devout prayer to that eternall Spirit who can enrich with all utterance and knowledge, and sends out his Seraphim with the hallow'd fire of his Altar to touch and purify the lips of whom he pleases: to this must be added industrious and select reading, steddy observation, insight into all seemly and generous arts and affaires." He admits, twenty years before the completion of *Paradise Lost,* that it is difficult to ask anyone to believe that he will accomplish all this.

It soon became clear to Milton that it was an epic that he must write, but at first he decided to write a national rather than a religious epic. In a passage from one of his Latin poems, *Epitaphium Damonis,* he tells of his plan to write a British *Aeneid* ("I have a theme of Trojans cruising our southern headlands"), using the Arthurian legend as his material, and singing of British rivers and valleys in the English tongue ("your Latian music/Changed for the British war-screech"). This seems a natural subject matter for an English epic, and we do not know why Milton changed his mind. We do know that the political and religious situation in England had changed considerably between the time he wrote that Latin poem as a young man of thirty and the time he started *Paradise Lost*. Perhaps that un-reconstructed Puritan was disinclined to write a poem celebrating the glories of England in a time when the Stuart monarchy and the Established Church—to him symbols of corruption—dominated the scene.

Be that as it may, we know from the essay mentioned above that he had long had an interest in biblical writings both as models and as themes for poetic art. He refers there to the Book of Job as a "brief model" of the epic form, to the Song of Solomon as a "divine pastoral Drama," and to the Revelation of St. John as "the majestick image of a high and stately Tragedy." (See also Milton's biblical tragedy *Samson Agonistes*, pp. 337-378.)

There is considerable daring, but also a certain logic, in Milton's choosing a biblical theme—given his understanding of what an epic should be. First, an epic had to have a *grand theme*, and what grander theme could Milton choose than the Fall of Man, with the Creation and the Redemption thrown in? Secondly, an epic had to be *true*, based on actual events rather than on fables and fictions. Tasso, Milton's great forerunner, taught that the subject of an epic must be *historical*, to give it the necessary semblance of truth; and that it must deal with a *true* religion, that is, Christianity. For Milton, the Bible was pre-eminently true above all other sources; beside it, the pagan stories were mere fripperies of the imagination. He justifies his choice of subject thus, at the beginning of Book IX of *Paradise Lost:*

> . . . Sad task, yet argument
> Not less but more Heroic then the wrauth
> Of stern *Achilles* on his Foe pursu'd
> Thrice Fugitive about *Troy* Wall; or rage
> Of *Turnus* for *Lavinia* disespous'd,
> Or *Neptun's* ire or *Juno's*, that so long
> Perplex'd the *Greek* and *Cytherea's* Son;
> If answerable style I can obtaine
> Of my Celestial Patroness, who deignes
> Her nightly visitation unimplor'd,

And dictates to me slumbring, or inspires
Easie my unpremeditated Verse:
Since first this Subject for Heroic Song
Pleas'd me long choosing, and beginning late
Not sedulous by Nature to indite
Warrs, hitherto the onely Argument
Heroic deem'd, chief maistrie to dissect
With long and tedious havoc fabl'd Knights
In Battels feign'd; the better fortitude
Of Patience and Heroic Martyrdom
Unsung; or to describe Races and Games,
Or tilting Furniture, emblazon'd Shields,
Impreses quaint, Caparisons and Steeds;
Bases and tinsel Trappings, gorgious Knights
At Joust and Torneament; then marshal'd Feast
Serv'd up in Hall with Sewers, and Seneshals;
The skill of Artifice or Office mean,
Not that which justly gives Heroic name
To Person or to Poem. Mee of these
Nor skilld nor studious, higher Argument
Remaines, sufficient of it self to raise
That name, unless an age too late, or cold
Climat, or Years damp may intended wing
Deprest, and much they may, if all be mine,
Not Hers who brings it nightly to my Ear.
(pp. 247b-248a)

Milton had chosen a tremendous task: to tell the story of the Creation, Fall, and Redemption of man and the world; to deal with abstract ideas and immaterial beings in poetic language. This was a far different and more difficult task than that of Tasso in writing an epic about the First Crusade. Satan appears occasionally in *Jerusalem Liberated*, but the other characters are the Crusaders and their enemies, human beings on the earthly plane. When Milton speculated about writing something like this in the essay mentioned above, his problems were on this historical level of verisimilitude: "And lastly what K. [King] or Knight before the conquest might be chosen in whom to lay the pattern of a Christian *Heroe*." Even his biblical tragedy deals with human figures and events: Samson is human—all too human.

In *Paradise Lost*, Milton had to create a convincing picture of the infinite and invisible Being who exists beyond the sphere of time and space, and of His Son, His ministering angels, and the rebellious spirits. He had to kindle and maintain interest in a contest between lesser beings and the omnipotent Ruler of the universe, where the result is a forgone conclusion. He had to observe Aristotle's precept that the epic poet must make even the most marvelous and impossible event seem probable and at the same time break Tasso's rule that the epic poet should not deal with articles of faith, since dogmas are fixed and leave no scope for poetic fancy. Eminent critics, from his contemporary John Dryden to our contemporary Mark Van Doren, have asserted that he chose an impossible task and failed. Other critics have regarded Milton's poem as a magnificent achievement, the only work in the English language that deserves the name "epic." Milton himself was aware of the magnitude of his task and exactly what his problem was, as this speech he put into Raphael's mouth bears witness:

> High matter thou injoinst me, O prime of men,
> Sad task and hard, for how shall I relate
> To human sense th' invisible exploits
> Of warring Spirits; how without remorse
> The ruin of so many glorious once
> And perfet while they stood; how last unfould
> The secrets of another world, perhaps
> Not lawful to reveal? yet for thy good
> This is dispenc't, and what surmounts the reach
> Of human sense, I shall delineate so,
> By lik'ning spiritual to corporal forms,
> As may express them best, though what if Earth
> Be but the shaddow of Heav'n, and things therein
> Each to other like, more then on earth is thought?
> (p. 187b)

The poet must make the invisible visible through sensuous imagery, the things of heaven apparent through the things of earth. Milton held in his theological writings that the biblical writers, too, had recourse to allegorical imagery as well as to literal statements about God, and that the literal descriptions did not really describe God as He is, but only insofar as the human mind can grasp the divine reality.

Milton devoted to the rendition of this tremendous theme everything he had learned as a practicing poet and as a discerning and erudite reader of ancient and modern literature. Much of the poem is a literary rendering of biblical narrative, but he did not confine himself to Christian Scriptures for his literary "machinery." The pagan gods and goddesses are invoked and welded into the orthodox Christian framework. To read *Paradise Lost* with a grasp of all its allusions and references requires the use of a good biblical dictionary and a handy manual on classical literature (such as *The Oxford Companion to Classical Literature* or *Everyman's Smaller Classical Dictionary*).

The main event of *Paradise Lost* is Adam's sin in eating the forbidden fruit of the Tree of the Knowledge of Good and Evil. The Bible tells the story tersely and emphatically in a single chapter of twenty-four verses. (See Genesis 3.) Milton tells the tale in twelve "books" with thousands of lines. In telling it, he fuses it with other biblical material, with pagan allusions, and with his own inventions. Perhaps the most important and vivid of the added material is that dealing with Satan and his cohorts, the rebellious angels or demons. None of this is in the original story. Identification of the snake with Satan is a much later interpretation, appearing in apocryphal and New Testament writings. Chapter 12 of the Book of Revelation is the only obvious biblical source for the additional material, which contributes so much to the color and drama of *Paradise Lost*. This final book of the Christian Bible tells of a war in heaven and the fall of the rebellious angels, with their leader, "that old serpent, called the Devil, and Satan, which deceiveth the whole world" (Rev. 12:9; see also 20:2). There are other references to the fall of Satan, or Lucifer, from Heaven in Isa. 14:12-15 and in Luke 10:17-19. The Bible contains many allusions and references to angels and demons, especially in later Old Testament books like Daniel, in the "apocalyptic" books, and in the books of the New Testament. And Satan appears as man's tempter and accuser in Job 1:6-12. (See also Zech. 3:1-2, and I Chron. 21:1.)

But all these were for Milton just germinal ideas, suggestions, sources. He did not feel limited by the biblical passages or bound to mimic them unaltered. Despite his Protestant Puritan awe of the Bible as the written Word of God, he felt no compunction about using and molding these materials to his own purposes, as the poet, the "maker," of *Paradise Lost*. He identifies the devils with the pagan gods, according to an ancient Christian tradition, and thereby obtains sanction for the various poetic allusions to pagan figures. Biblical synonyms for Satan or evil, such as Beelzebub and Belial, become separate devils, newly created characters. Moloch, the horrible pagan god of the Old Testament, and Mammon, the personification of covetousness in the New, are also added to his dramatic gallery of devils.

Others had written imaginative works on similar biblical themes before Milton. He undoubtedly knew these works, and he may have borrowed from them or learned from them before he wrote his own. Among the works frequently cited as possible influences on the writing of *Paradise Lost* are *La Divine Sepmaine* ("The Divine Week") by Guillaume du Bartas (1578), an epic poem on the creation story in Genesis; the play *L'Adamo* ("Adam") by Giambattista Andreini (1613); Phineas Fletcher's poem *The Locusts or Apollyonists,* 1627 (for the portrait of Lucifer); and Joost van den Vondel's play *Lucifer,* 1654 (for the portrayal of the revolt of the angels and the Fall of Man). An ancient Latin work by the sixth-century churchman St. Avitus, on *The Creation, the Fall, and the Expulsion from Paradise,* may have been Milton's model for his portrayal of Paradise and Satan.

II

Paradise Lost consists of twelve "books," written in blank verse (discussed in Section V below). Preceding the first line of verse in each book there appears an "argument," in prose, summarizing the theme and events of the book. Thus in Book I we read first:

THE ARGUMENT

This first Book proposes first in brief the whole Subject, *Mans disobedience, and the loss thereupon of Paradise wherein he was plac't:* Then touches *the prime cause of his fall, the Serpent, or rather* Satan *in the Serpent; who revolting from God, and drawing to his side many Legions of Angels, was by the command of God driven out of Heaven with all his Crew into the great Deep.* Which action past over, the Poem hasts into the midst of things, presenting *Satan with his Angels now fallen into Hell* . . . (p. 93a)

At the end of the Argument begins the first line of verse, "Of Mans First Disobedience, and the Fruit," and the poet states his theme, invokes the Spirit of God that hovered over the waters, and presents his purpose:

> That to the highth of this great Argument
> I may assert Eternal Providence,
> And justifie the wayes of God to men. (p. 94a)

With this preamble to the book and the poem out of the way, the poet sets out to tell his story, starting in "the midst of things," at the point where Satan and his fellow rebels have been driven out of Heaven into *"a place of utter darknesse, fitliest call'd Chaos,"* and are *"lying on the burning Lake, thunder-struck and astonisht."*

Let us pause here for a brief survey of the work as a whole, to see how Milton has distributed the action in the twelve books. Books I-IV deal with Satan's rallying of his forces and his journey to the earth to attempt the Fall of Man. Books V-VIII deal with the revolt of the angels, their defeat and fall, and the creation of the universe and of Adam and Eve. Books IX-XII deal with the Fall of Man, his punishment, and the prophecy of his ultimate redemption. Thus, chronologically speaking, we start the story in the middle; only when we get to Book V do we get the beginning of the story; and it takes the middle four books to fill us in on the background of the events that began in Book I. The climax occurs in Book IX (by far the longest) with the Fall of Man, the basic theme of the poem, and the last three books give us an understanding of its permanent meaning and consequences.

Now let us see how this scheme works out concretely in the actual reading of the poem. Undoubtedly, *Paradise Lost* starts out with immediate interest, color, and force. Even the greatest detractors of Milton's effort admire the portrait of Satan in the first few books. This archspirit of perverseness and rebellion is magnificent as he stands indomitable and intransigent, hurling defiance at his omnipotent conqueror out of the depths of darkness and despair. He cries,

> ... What though the field be lost?
> All is not lost; the unconquerable Will,
> And study of revenge, immortal hate,
> And courage never to submit or yield:
> And what is else not to be overcome?
> That Glory never shall his wrath or might
> Extort from me. (pp. 95b-96a)

He rallies his stunned and battle-weary followers, proclaiming that the war against God and the good must go on. They must strive to bring evil out of good, in perfect opposition to God's purpose to bring good out of evil. Satan is, in the original meaning of his name, the Adversary, the Hinderer, the perfect expression of the perverted will. "Evil be thou my good," he cries in a later passage of the poem (p. 154b).

Satan is proud as well as perverse—as our common simile "as proud as Lucifer" reminds us. "Better to reign in Hell, than serve in Heav'n," says he. He does not want to be second to anyone, not even to God. In Hell, as he thinks, the rebel angels are free from the dominion of the Almighty. Moreover he insists

> The mind is its own place, and in it self
> Can make a Heav'n of Hell, a Hell of Heav'n. (p. 99a)

Nevertheless, he cannot remain content with this limited security and freedom. He must carry on the struggle for power against God and His Providence.

He calls a council of his leaders—"The great Seraphic Lords and Cherubim"—to decide whether they shall wage a hot or a cold war—"Whether of open Warr or covert guile." Satan's own choice is the way of fraud and guile and the exploration of the new world rumored to have been created by God. (See p. 107b.) But he sits on his throne like a good constitutional monarch and lets his associates—"A thousand Demy-Gods on golden seat's"—debate the issues. We hear the chiefs speak out: Moloch, Belial, Mammon, and Beelzebub. The proposal of the latter, to seek out new opportunities on earth, wins in the ensuing vote. Satan himself assumes the dreadful task of journeying through infinite darkness and chaos to discover the new creation and subvert it.

The crafty "Adversary of God and Man" induces the monsters Sin (his daughter) and Death (his recently begotten son) to open up the Gates of Hell, and he flies into the infinite realm of chaos and night that extends between Heaven and Hell. Chaos, the ruling spirit, gives Satan directions on how to get to the earth, in the hope that the newly created order will be reduced to its original formlessness and darkness. After a hard and dangerous journey, Satan reaches the border where nature—the physical order—begins and "the sacred influence/of light appears." Above him is his native homeland Heaven, from which he is permanently exiled; below him is the earth.

> Thither full fraught with mischievous revenge,
> Accurst, and in a cursed hour he hies. (p. 134a)

But first he passes through the Limbo of Vanity, or Paradise of Fools, skirts the stairway to Heaven, and comes down to the sphere of the sun. He changes himself into the shape of a lesser angel, and gets directions from the archangel Uriel, the guardian angel of the sphere, on how to find earth and its new creature Man. Satan finally alights on Mount Niphates (in Assyria) and sees the earthly Paradise, the Garden of Eden ("delight").

Satan has reached his destination, but instead of feeling elated, he is overwhelmed with remorse and despair at his fall. The pleasant prospect of Eden awakens his conscience and the memory "Of what he was, what is, and what must be." He knows that he has come to his present state through his own free will, and there is no way out save by repentance and submission, which his obdurate pride forbids. He is imprisoned in his self-made state.

> Me miserable! which way shall I flie
> Infinite wrauth, and infinite despaire?
> Which way I flie is Hell; my self am Hell; (p. 154a)

To his utter despair is joined the lacerating envy of the new creature Man, God's "new delight," living in joy and innocence. With all hope gone and all good lost, all that remains for him now is to do evil.

He makes his way into the Garden and perches "like a Cormorant" on the Tree of Life, the highest tree there, from which he views this "Heaven on Earth." He sees the lovely landscape, the flowers, trees, and waters,

> ... all kind
> Of living Creatures new to sight and strange:
> Two of far nobler shape erect and tall,
> Godlike erect, with native Honour clad
> In naked Majestie seemd Lords of all,
> And worthie seemd, for in thir looks Divine
> The image of thir glorious Maker shon,
> Truth, Wisdome, Sanctitude severe and pure,
> Severe, but in true filial freedom plac't;
> Whence true autoritie in men ... (p. 158b)

He sees these first humans, living in joyful innocence, loving without shame, going about naked, doing their gardening work, resting, and supping from the fruit of the trees. Around them play the beasts, the lion with the kid, bears, tigers, and elephants, in mutual enjoyment, not destruction. Satan cries out with anguish at this pleasant sight, at the happy pair who are only slightly below the angels and who shine with the divine image. He is touched with wonder and confesses he could love them and could pity them for the disaster he is to bring on them. He has nothing against *them*, he protests; he seeks only mutual friendship and alliance, their company with him in Hell. They are the mere means to his revenge against God, and he pleads "The Tyrants plea"—necessity.

> And should I at your harmless innocence
> Melt, as I doe, yet public reason just,
> Honour and Empire with revenge enlarg'd,
> By conquering this new World, compels me now
> To do what else though damnd I should abhorre. (p. 161a)

Satan comes down closer, changing into the shapes of various animals, to spy on Adam and Eve. Listening to their conversation, he discovers the vulnerable point through which he may work their fall. Adam remarks to Eve that their life is one of ease and freedom, with only one restriction,

> ... not to taste that onely Tree
> Of knowledge, planted by the Tree of Life, (p. 161b)

God has pronounced the penalty of death if they disobey that "One easie prohibition." Despite his previous expression of friendly feeling, Satan is full of hateful envy at the sight of the caresses they exchange, and eager to make use of the information he has just learned.

> Sight hateful, sight tormenting! thus these two
> Imparadis't in one anothers arms
> The happier *Eden*, shall enjoy thir fill
> Of bliss on bliss, while I to Hell am thrust,
> Where neither joy nor love, but fierce desire,
> Among our other torments not the least,
> Still unfulfill'd with pain of longing pines;
> Yet let me not forget what I have gain'd
> From thir own mouths; all is not theirs it seems:
> One fatal Tree there stands of Knowledge call'd,
> Forbidden them to taste: Knowledge forbidd'n?
> Suspicious, reasonless. Why should thir Lord
> Envie them that? can it be sin to know,
> Can it be death? and do they onely stand
> By Ignorance, is that thir happie state,
> The proof of thir obedience and thir faith?
> O fair foundation laid whereon to build
> Thir ruine! Hence I will excite thir minds
> With more desire to know, and to reject
> Envious commands, invented with designe
> To keep them low whom knowledge might exalt
> Equal with Gods; aspiring to be such,
> They taste and die: what likelier can ensue? (pp. 163b-164a)

Satan goes on about his spying, but his presence has been detected by the guardian angels. When night falls, Gabriel, the watchman of the Gate of Paradise, dispatches his guards, who discover Satan, in the form of a toad, perched at Eve's ear attempting to influence her through dreams. Brought before Gabriel, Satan replies scornfully and proudly, ready to offer resistance to the angelic squadron that would thrust him from Eden back into the infernal pit. But a sign from God in the heavens warns him that he is too weak to fight God's angels, and he flees from the Garden.

This is the end of Book IV and of the introductory section of the poem. The first four books have centered on Satan, his character and motives, and his encounter with the situation

and persons that will be the scene and characters of the ensuing action. One notable exception to this continuous flow and
concentration occurs in the first half of Book III (lines 1-415),
which is set in Heaven and centered on God.

This complete change in scene and tone is signaled by the
beautiful hymn to light which opens Book III: "Hail holy light,
ofspring of Heav'n first-born." In it Milton expresses the contrast between the dark regions traversed by Satan in his flight
and the "Bright effluence of bright essence increate" which is
the God who is light. Milton also expresses the pain and yet
the opportunity of his blindness, which shuts out forever the
physical light, the sight of dawn and evening, and all the
things and creatures, making nature for him "a Universal
blanc." But though the outer sensible light is shut off, he hopes
and prays that he may all the more be granted the inner light
which irradiates the mind so that he may accomplish his poetic
task,

> ... that I may see and tell
> Of things invisible to mortal sight. (p. 136b)

He proceeds to the scene in Heaven, where God, seated on
His throne, witnesses Adam and Eve in their innocent bliss and
Satan speeding through the darkness on his way to the earthly
Paradise. God turns to His Son, "The radiant image of his
Glory," seated at His right hand, and tells Him that Satan will
succeed in his dreadful errand. God foresees all, for the future
is present to Him. But He refuses to intervene, for He has
given man free will, the power to choose good or evil, and man
must stand or fall by his own choice. Man alone is responsible
for what is to happen; it is his will, not the Creator's, not pre-
destination nor the force of fate or natural necessity, that will
decide what is to be. Man is an ingrate, a faithless, disloyal
traitor, who, with his progeny, must suffer dire punishment.
But because man shall fall through the temptation of another
rather than through his own depravity, God promises him
mercy and grace.

The Son begs God not to destroy His own creation, the human race ("thy youngest Son"), and satisfy the malice of the
Adversary. God assures the Son that man will be saved,

through God's free grace, but insists that satisfaction must be offered for man's treasonable disobedience, by man himself or by a substitute.

> He with his whole posteritie must die,
> Die hee or Justice must; unless for him
> Som other able, and as willing, pay
> The rigid satisfaction, death for death.
> Say Heav'nly Powers, where shall we find such love,
> Which of ye will be mortal to redeem
> Mans mortal crime, and just th' unjust to save,
> Dwels in all Heaven charitie so deare? (p. 140a)

An awful silence follows as man's fate hangs in the balance. It seems that no substitute will appear to bear his punishment, and that his destiny must be death, and Hell his ultimate abode. Then the Son, the voice of infinite compassion, speaks up for the unhappy creature who through his sin is incapable of seeking grace and offering atonement.

> Behold mee then, mee for him, life for life
> I offer, on mee let thine anger fall;
> Account mee man; I for his sake will leave
> Thy bosom, and this glorie next to thee
> Freely put off, and for him lastly die
> Well pleas'd, on me let Death wreck all his rage; (p. 140b)

He proclaims that He will not really die, but will be resurrected and victorious over Death and Hell and all His foes; He will return to Heaven to the Father whose wrath will have been appeased, and with Him He will bring the redeemed human race.

God hails the Son as the new Adam, who through taking on human form shall save mankind. The Son through His merit shall erase the consequences of Adam's sin, and "Heav'nly love shal outdoo Hellish hate." God praises the virtue which is evident in the Son's unselfish offer, making Him "By Merit more than Birthright Son of God," through His goodness and humiliation rather than through His greatness and glory. For this He shall reign over the universe until the Day of Judgment, when "God shall be All in All." And He calls on the heavenly beings to "Adore the Son, and honour him as mee." The heavenly choir of angels sings "loud Hosannas" and praises God the Father and His Son, the "Divine Similitude." Here the scene ends, and we cut again to Satan alighting on the outermost sphere of the universe.

What Milton has done in this passage is to dramatize the New Testament view, found especially in Paul's Epistles, that the Passion of Christ is the propitiation for Adam's sin. He stages a dialogue between God the Father and the Son (whom, for poetic purposes, and perhaps also for theological reasons, he makes a distinct and secondary being). In this way he tries to fulfill his announced fundamental purpose: to justify the ways of God to man. And he tells us in advance, through the voice of an omniscient and all-foreseeing being, what is to happen. This whole passage is an anticipation—what the rhetoricians call a "prolepsis"—of the things that are to come. Milton foregoes the advantage of suspense, in what already is a well-known story, with a foregone conclusion, and trusts confidently in his poetic powers to maintain the reader's interest in his rendering of that story.

Milton is necessarily limited in his description of God and the Son. God is not described at all. He is all voice and tone. He is expressed in His speech. The Son is described to some extent, but not graphically. It is stated that "Divine compassion visibly appeerd" in His face, or that He had a "meek aspect"; or superlatives are used, such as "Beyond compare," "most glorious," "Love without end, and without measure Grace." No concrete imagery is used. Tact, if not reverence, lays a restraining hand on the poet here.

III

Books I-IV tell us how Satan set off to work man's fall, and leave him temporarily frustrated by the alert guardian angels. Books V-VIII give us the background that provides the basis and reason for Satan's attempt, including the revolt and fall of the angels, and the Creation of the world. The angelic fall is filled in to provide a parallel with the human fall that is narrated in Books IX-XII.

This middle section of Milton's work, filled with many lovely songs and verses, begins with a tender and touching dialogue between Adam and Eve. Eve has been disturbed by a dream (inspired by Satan the night before) in which she was tempted to eat of the Tree of Knowledge and become like the gods. Adam comforts her with his explanation that such dreams are the result of pure imagination, uncontrolled by reason, and that even when they are inspired by external evil forces, they come and go without staining the virtue of the dreamer. The original couple then proceed to offer worship to their Creator, with simple, unrehearsed, informal rites, singing a magnificent hymn of praise of the glorious works of God. Here is the ending of the hymn:

> Joyn voices all ye living Souls, ye Birds,
> That singing up to Heaven Gate ascend,
> Bear on your wings and in your notes his praise;
> Yee that in Waters glide, and yee that walk
> The Earth, and stately tread, or lowly creep;
> Witness if I be silent, Morn or Eeven,
> To Hill, or Valley, Fountain, or fresh shade
> Made vocal by my Song, and taught his praise.
> Hail universal Lord, be bounteous still
> To give us onely good; and if the night
> Have gathered aught of evil or conceald,
> Disperse it, as now light dispels the dark. (p. 179b)

After this worship service they proceed to their labor, which for Milton is a distinguishing characteristic of man even in Eden, and sets him apart from the idle animals. (See pp. 165b-166a.)

At this point God sends Raphael, "the sociable Spirit," to warn Adam of Satan's plot against him. Thus, God emphasizes, man will not be able to say he was not warned. Raphael is received hospitably by Adam and Eve. The angel explains that man, like the angels in Heaven, has freedom of will, and that he too may fall and be justly punished as the fallen angels were. He proceeds to the story of the revolt of the angels. (See line 577 of Book V to the end of Book VI.) It begins before the Creation of the world, with God's appointment of His only begotten Son to be His vicegerent, ruling over the heavenly powers.

Satan, one of the highest of the angels, is filled with envy
and rancor at the new appointment. He plots rebellion and
takes a third of the heavenly host off with him into the northern regions of Heaven. High on his throne, he summons the
angels. Satan scoffs at this strange new doctrine, transferring
God's work to "secondarie hands." Moreover, he insists that the
angels are self-made beings, that they were not created at all.

> We know no time when we were not as now;
> Know none before us, self-begot, self-rais'd
> By our own quick'ning power, when fatal course
> Had circl'd his full Orbe, the birth mature
> Of this our native Heav'n, Ethereal Sons.
> Our puissance is our own, our own right hand
> Shall teach us highest deeds, by proof to try
> Who is our equal: then thou shalt behold
> Whether by supplication we intend
> Address, and to begirt th' Almighty Throne
> Beseeching or besieging . . . (p. 194a)

The faithful Abdiel, alone among the faithless angels, shouts
his imprecations at the rebel chieftain, and speeds to God's
throne to inform Him of what has transpired.

The omniscient Deity of course knows what is going on and
orders that force be used against those who will not obey the
law of right reason. He calls on his generals, the archangels
Michael and Gabriel, to lead the attack.

> Goe *Michael* of Celestial Armies Prince,
> And thou in Military prowess next
> *Gabriel*, lead forth to Battel these my Sons
> Invincible, lead forth my armed Saints
> By Thousands and by Millions rang'd for fight;
> Equal in number to that Godless crew
> Rebellious, them with Fire and hostile Arms
> Fearless assault, and to the brow of Heav'n
> Pursuing drive them out from God and bliss,
> Into thir place of punishment, the Gulf
> Of *Tartarus*, which ready opens wide
> His fiery *Chaos* to receave thir fall. (p. 197a-b)

The "Powers Militant" go forth with the heavenly bands
playing martial airs and meet the rebel forces headed by "Th'
Apostat in his Sun-bright Chariot." Abdiel again disputes with

Satan on the true nature of freedom and slavery (Abdiel holds
that to serve the law of God or Nature is freedom), and then
nearly fells the apostate angel with a mighty blow. Thereupon
the two armies meet in furious conflict and the heavens shake
under the movement of "Millions of fierce encountring Angels."
Satan is again beaten, this time by a sword stroke of Michael's,
which gives him his first experience of pain and causes him to be
carried from the battlefield, "Gnashing for anguish and despite
and shame." But since he is a spirit, his wound is soon healed.
He rallies the disheartened and panicky rebel angels, who have
been driven from the battlefield by the loyal onslaught. He
rolls back the loyal forces with his new weapon, cannon fire.
The loyalists retaliate with mountains which they uproot and
cast at the rebel forces.

With an endless stalemate in prospect between two such
evenly matched forces—equal in creaturely status—God sends
the Son to defeat the rebel forces decisively. God says to the
Son:

> For thee I have ordain'd it, and thus farr
> Have sufferd, that the Glorie may be thine
> Of ending this great Warr, since none but Thou
> Can end it. Into thee such Vertue and Grace
> Immense I have transfus'd, that all may know
> In Heav'n and Hell thy Power above compare,
> And this perverse Commotion governd thus,
> To manifest thee worthiest to be Heir
> Of all things, to be Heir and to be King
> By Sacred Unction, thy deserved right.
> Go them thou Mightiest in the Fathers might,
> Ascend my Chariot, guide the rapid Wheeles
> That shake Heav'ns basis, bring forth all my Warr,
> My Bow and Thunder, my Almightie Arms
> Gird on, and Sword upon thy puissant Thigh;
> Pursue these sons of Darkness, drive them out
> From all Heav'ns bounds into the utter Deep:
> There let them learn, as likes them, to despise
> God and *Messiah* his anointed King. (pp. 211b-212a)

The Son promises to hate those whom the Father hates and to
crush His enemies. This He does with dispatch, hurling the
rebels into the deep, down to the bottomless pit of Hell.

> ... Hell at last
> Yawning receavd them whole, and on them clos'd,
> Hell thir fit habitation fraught with fire
> Unquenchable, the house of woe and paine. (p. 215a-b)

The Son is hailed as victor by the saints, who sing a song of triumph to the "Victorious King, Son, Heire, and Lord," and accompany Him to the divine throne, where He is received into glory and seated at the right hand of the Father.

Thus Raphael completes his account of the strange "Warr in Heav'n/Among th' Angelic Powers," and Milton succeeds in getting into his epic poem the martial deeds he had forsworn relating when he selected a biblical theme. Raphael continues his story with a description of the Creation of the world and man through the agency of the Son, and an account of the motions of the heavenly bodies. A large part of Book VIII (lines 250-520) deals with Adam's own account of his creation—his first awareness of existing, his first conversation with God, his naming of the animals (and thus understanding their nature), his sense of loneliness and his petition for a mate, which is fulfilled in the creation from his rib of the lovely creature called "woman."

> ... To the Nuptial Bowre
> I led her blushing like the Morn: all Heav'n,
> And happie Constellations on that houre
> Shed thir selectest influence; the Earth
> Gave sign of gratulation, and each Hill;
> Joyous the Birds; fresh Gates and gentle Aires
> Whisper'd it to the Woods, and from thir wings
> Flung Rose, flung Odours from the spicie Shrub,
> Disporting, till the amorous Bird of Night
> Sung Spousal, and bid haste the Evening Starr
> On his Hill top, to light the bridal Lamp. (p. 243a-b)
> (See also pp. 162a-163a.)

Adam confesses to Raphael that the passion he feels for this lovely creature softens him so much that he becomes willing to subordinate reason and wisdom and his own superior authority to her. It is not merely externals, the sense of touch, which Raphael scorns as mere animal delight, but

> ... those graceful acts,
> Those thousand decencies that daily flow
> From all her words and actions, mixt with Love
> And sweet compliance, which declare unfeign'd
> Union of Mind, or in us both one Soule: (p. 245a)

Raphael admits that the angels too love and embrace, for without love there can be no happiness. He leaves Adam with this admonition,

> Be strong, live happie, and love, but first of all
> Him whom to love is to obey, and keep
> His great command; take heed least Passion sway
> Thy Judgement to do aught, which else free Will
> Would not admit; thine and of all thy Sons
> The weal or woe in thee is plac't; beware.
> I in thy persevering shall rejoyce,
> And all the Blest: stand fast; to stand or fall
> Free in thine own Arbitrement it lies.
> Perfect within, no outward aid require;
> And all temptation to transgress repel. (p. 246a)

IV

Book IX presents the main event of the story, for which the previous eight books have been prelude and the last three books are consequence. Adam has been warned; Satan's intent has been made plain. The latter returns to Eden and enters into the body of "The Serpent suttlest Beast of all the Field." Before he sets off to undo man, he sings a magnificent song in praise of the new creation.

> O Earth, how like to Heav'n, if not preferr'd
> More justly, Seat worthier of Gods, as built
> With second thoughts, reforming what was old!
> For what God after better worse would build?
> Terrestrial Heav'n, danc't round by other Heav'ns
> That shine, yet bear thir bright officious Lamps,
> Light above Light, for thee alone, as seems,
> In thee concentring all thir precious beams
> Of sacred influence: As God in Heav'n
> Is Center, yet extends to all, so thou
> Centring receav'st from all those Orbs; in thee,
> Not in themselves, all thir known vertue appeers
> Productive in Herb, Plant, and nobler birth

> Of Creatures animate with gradual life
> Of Growth, Sense, Reason, all summ'd up in Man. (p. 249b)

But he hates the good and is possessed by the will to destruction and to make others companions in his misery. He wants to destroy in one day what God took six to create and to get his revenge through the fall of

> ... this new Favorite
> Of Heav'n, this Man of Clay, Son of despite,
> Whom us the more to spite his Maker rais'd
> From dust: spite then with spite is best repaid. (p. 251a)

It is Eve who gives Satan the opportunity he requires. She insists that she and Adam work apart, to get more work done and to allow her to demonstrate her virtue singlehanded against any temptation that their enemy may attempt. Adam's admonition not to seek out temptation, which will come readily enough unsought, is unavailing, and like many another husband thereafter, he lets Eve have her way. Satan, elated to find her alone, is touched for a moment by the sight of her feminine loveliness and grace, but hate and the will to destruction prevail over this momentary softness. He lulls Eve's wariness by flattery, and tells her that he has attained the gift of speech through eating of the Tree of Knowledge. He deprecates her feeling that she must obey the divine interdiction and her fear of punishment, pointing out that she can become like God, just as he has become like man, attaining reason and speech. Moreover, he has eaten the fruit, he says, and he is not dead.

This argument, and the sight and smell of the delicious fruit, is too much for the lone woman, vulnerable without her man.

> ... her rash hand in evil hour
> Forth reaching to the Fruit, she pluck'd, she eat:
> Earth felt the wound, and Nature from her seat
> Sighing through all her Works gave signs of woe,
> That all was lost ... (p. 264b)

She sits in greedy enjoyment, "eating Death," while Satan slinks off into the underbrush. She is gratified by the prospect of experience, knowledge, and wisdom that lies open before her, making her equal or even superior to Adam. However, she bethinks herself:

> . . . but what if God have seen
> And Death ensue? then I shall be no more,
> And *Adam* wedded to another *Eve,*
> Shall live with her enjoying, I extinct;
> A death to think. Confirm'd then I resolve,
> *Adam* shall share with me in bliss or woe:
> So dear I love him, that with him all deaths
> I could endure, without him live no life. (p. 265a-b)

So this weak and vulnerable creature rushes to her man to tell him of the wonderful forbidden fruit she has partaken of, and that she is "growing up to Godhead." But, she tells Adam, she is unwilling to enjoy bliss and partake of divinity without him. Adam is aghast at what she has done. He cries,

> How art thou lost, how on a sudden lost,
> Defac't, deflourd, and now to Death devote? (p. 267a)

But he is so attached and bound to her that he feels compelled to share her fate. Eve is touched and contrite at his devotion and attestation of their indissoluble unity—"one flesh"—but she feels that "not Death, but Life/Augmented, op'nd Eyes, new Hopes, new Joyes" will result from eating the forbidden fruit. And he, won over—"Against his better knowledge"—eats voraciously and with gusto, while the earth trembles and groans at the completion of the original sin, which brings a Fall to Nature as well as to man.

The first result is lust, and possessed by carnal desire and wantonness—in contrast with their previous innocent joy in conjugal love—they proceed to enjoy one another and fall into exhausted sleep. This enjoyment is "of thir mutual guilt the Seale,/The solace of thir sin." When they awake, they realize their guilt and loss of primitive righteousness; they feel naked both within and without—"destitute and bare/Of all thir vertue." Ashamed to see each other naked now, they sew fig leaves together to cover their private parts. But it does not cover their inner guilt and shame, and they are shaken by inner disturbance and ugly emotions.

> ... but high Winds worse within
> Began to rise, high Passions, Anger, Hate,
> Mistrust, Suspicion, Discord, and shook sore
> Thir inward State of Mind, calme Region once
> And full of Peace, now tost and turbulent:
> For Understanding rul'd not, and the Will
> Heard not her lore, both in subjection now
> To sensual Appetite, who from beneathe
> Usurping over sovran Reason claimd
> Superior sway ... (pp. 271b-272a)

Now they go at one another, hammer and tongs, like many a couple thereafter. "I told you so," says Adam in effect—she should have done as he advised, then all would have gone well. But she maintains that it is his fault, for giving in to her and not preventing her from going by absolute command—he is the superior and responsible one. Adam is indignant—"after all I've done for you" is his retort—having given up immortal bliss to share death with her. Then he takes the same position toward Eve as God does toward man, asserting that he could not force her, but had to allow her to exercise her freedom of will. But he admits that he was wrong to trust in her virtue, and this is a warning to all future husbands.

> ... but I rue
> That errour now, which is become my crime,
> And thou th' accuser. Thus it shall befall
> Him who to worth in Women overtrusting
> Lets her Will rule; restraint she will not brook,
> And left to her self, if evil thence ensue,
> Shee first his weak indulgence will accuse. (p. 273a)

Books X-XII deal with the consequences of the original sin. On the one hand, sin and death have been brought into the world, all nature is infected with evil and death, and man is exiled from his original perfection—Adam and all his descendents, the human race. On the other hand, the assurance of redemption is held out, for the Son will eventually make the full payment for Adam's sin, the Son who is "Eve's seed," the "Second Adam," who will conquer death and sin, and revenge the original couple's seduction by "the Serpent." And there will be elevating compensations in ordinary human existence, despite a new life where love between the sexes is beset with frustrations, where joyful labor has become painful toil, where perfect bliss and immortality have been replaced by disease, old age, and death, and man cannot enjoy full intimacy with God anymore. Despite these obvious ills and imperfections, man will have the God-given gifts of culture and productivity; through God's grace and instruction man will learn the arts and sciences and make a path for himself in the world. Work is good (this is a constant theme in *Paradise Lost*) and knowledge will give man a home in the world. Moreover, through the Fall and his active repentance, man will achieve virtue, reason, and the will to do right, fulfilling the law of God through love—such will and obedience are true freedom.

All this is unfolded by the archangel Michael, who is commissioned by God to reveal to Adam the shape of things to come, prior to ejecting him from Paradise. Just as Raphael in Books V-VIII revealed the past to Adam, up to and including the creation of man and the world, so Michael in Books XI-XII reveals to Adam the future of the human race and the natural world from the original sin to the Last Judgment. Milton paraphrases the biblical account, including the Flood, the Patriarchs, the Exodus, the Incarnation, the Passion, and the Resurrection, down to the Second Advent and the Last Judgment, when Christ will raise the faithful to eternal bliss,

> Whether in Heav'n or Earth, for then the Earth
> Shall all be Paradise, far happier place
> Then this of Eden, and far happier daies. (p. 329a)

Adam is impelled to cry out his *Felix culpa!* ("fortunate sin!") at this joyful picture.

> O goodness infinite, goodness immense!
> That all this good of evil shall produce,
> And evil turn to good; more wonderful
> Then that by which creation first brought forth
> Light out of darkness! full of doubt I stand,
> Whether I should repent me now of sin
> By mee done and occasiond, or rejoyce
> Much more, that much more good thereof shall spring,
> To God more glory, more good will to Men
> From God, and over wrauth grace shall abound. (p. 329b)

This too is the tone of Michael's final words. He promises that when Adam has attained perfect obedience to God, attested in deeds and in the virtues of faith, patience, temperance, and charity,

> . . . then wilt thou not be loath
> To leave this Paradise, but shalt possess
> A Paradise within thee, happier farr. (p. 332a)

This idea also appears in the Son's plea for man, at the beginning of Book XI, when he points to the contrite prayers of Adam and Eve and he says to God,

> See Father, what first fruits on Earth are sprung
> From thy implanted Grace in Man, these Sighs
> And Prayers, which in this Golden Censer, mixt
> With Incense, I thy Priest before thee bring,
> Fruits of more pleasing savour from thy seed
> Sow'n with contrition in his heart, then those
> Which his own hand manuring all the Trees
> Of Paradise could have produc't, ere fall'n
> From innocence . . . (p. 299b)

Cheered by the expectation Michael has raised of an ultimate "happie end," Adam, accompanied by Eve, leaves Paradise. Behind them a troop of Cherubim preceded by the bright and blazing Sword of God, mounts guard on the Garden. They glance back and shed some tears at the loss of innocence and bliss, but

> The World was all before them, where to choose
> Thir place of rest, and Providence thir guide:
> They hand in hand with wandring steps and slow,
> Through *Eden* took thir solitarie way. (p. 333a)

And with these words *Paradise Lost* comes to a close.

V

We have now completed our survey of the matter of Milton's poem. Let us now glance briefly at the manner in which this story is told. *Paradise Lost* is written in blank verse, called "blank" because of its lack of rhyme. The meter of blank verse in English poetry is iambic pentameter, which we discussed in *Imaginative Literature I*. (See pp. 140-142.) In this meter, each line has five main stresses or accents, with a rising rhythm, in which an unaccented syllable is usually followed by an accented syllable. Chaucer used this meter, but wrote in rhymed couplets, not blank verse.

Henry Howard, Earl of Surrey, composed the earliest extant English poetry in blank verse—a translation of Books II and IV of Virgil's *Aeneid,* published in 1557. Dramatic poets soon seized on Surrey's device and used it for their plays; most notable among them were Christopher Marlowe and William Shakespeare. After Shakespeare, blank verse declined into a prosaic and indefinite meter, lacking the sonority and solidity of the blank verse of the great masters. Then Milton came along and molded this form into poetry of great force, intricacy, and expressiveness, the great "organ tone" which has made his verse famous.

Where Surrey had restricted the line of blank verse to ten syllables, with five equal iambic feet and a single pause, Milton's verse has an extraordinary variety of stresses, pauses, and inversions. Milton goes far beyond Chaucer in his variation from a mechanical model of ten-syllable, five-accent lines. No line in *Paradise Lost* has fewer than ten syllables, but there are many lines of eleven and twelve syllables. Often these extra syllables are accounted for by the "elision" or cutting off of sounds, as the *e* in "the" before a word beginning with a vowel ("th' Aonian Mount"). Milton not only elides vowels at the end of words but also in the middle of words ("Heav'n," "know'st"), and he also elides the so-called semivowels *l, n,* and *r* at the end of words (such elisions are not indicated by apostrophes).

Milton varies the number of syllables as well as the number of accents. Do not feel disappointed if you do not find five full stresses in each line. Sometimes there are only four, and in some cases only three. Certain syllables are just not heavy enough to take a full stress, and this may occur not only at the beginning of the line, but in any one of the five "feet." Here are some examples from Robert Bridges' fine book on *Milton's Prosody* (Oxford, 1921), with the unaccented, "weak" feet underlined:

As from the Center thrice to th' utmost Pole (Book I, line 74)
Serv'd only to discover sights of woe (I, 64)
A Dungeon horrible, on all sides round (I, 61)
Sole reigning holds the Tyranny of Heav'n (I, 124)
No light, but rather darkness visible (I ,63)

Milton also inverts the rising rhythm of iambic pentameter to a falling rhythm, in order to stress the sense or freshen the rhythm. The sense naturally demands that we accent "not" in "A mind not to be chang'd by Place or Time" (Book I, line 253). The rhythm is freshened by the stress on "due" in "From Noon, and gentle Aires due at thir hour" (Book X, line 93). Bridges again points out that this may occur in any foot, even in the fifth, where we would normally expect an accent on the final syllable.

Similarly, Milton makes an adroit and flexible use of the pause or break, technically called "caesura." The early writers of blank verse were aware that a constant reiteration of syllables, accented or unaccented, would produce a monotonous singsong, so they inserted a pause or break somewhere in the line. Traditionally the pause came in the middle of the line, usually on the accented fourth syllable. Surrey, however, varied this quite a bit, as the rhythm and feeling of the particular line demanded. Milton again exceeds previous poets in his variations, and breaks anywhere in the line, as either the sense or the rhythm may demand. Bridges shows that a break may occur in any syllable of the line, from the first to the last. In the first line of the poem, the break occurs at the grammatical pause, at the comma after "Disobedience." There are also lines with two breaks, as Bridges demonstrates. In blank verse even the grammatical pauses, indicated by semicolons, periods, etc., may occur anywhere in the line; for sentences and other word groups do not usually end at the end of a line.

It was through these variations, this flexibility and change of pace, that Milton achieved what has been called the "free musical paragraph," a consummate welding of sense and sound, combining the utmost in order with the utmost in freedom. Working in English, he had the advantage of not being restricted by "laws" of prosody that ruled in Greek, Latin, and the Romance languages. He had, too, the poetic genius to create ordered unity from all the variations and to see beyond the syllables and the lines to the big units, to complete thoughts, "periods," and paragraphs. T. S. Eliot, once a harsh critic of Milton's style, has this to say of Milton's poetic mastery:

It is the period, the sentence and still more the paragraph, that is the unit of Milton's verse; and emphasis on the line structure is the minimum necessary to provide a counter-pattern to the period structure. It is only in the period that the wave-length of Milton's verse is to be found: it is his ability to give a perfect and unique pattern to every paragraph, such that the full beauty of the line is found in its context, and his ability to work in larger musical units than any other poet— that is to me the most conclusive evidence of Milton's supreme mastery. The peculiar feeling, almost a physical sensation of a breathless leap, communicated by Milton's long periods, and by his alone, is impossible to procure from rhymed verse. Indeed, this mastery is more conclusive evidence of his intellectual power, than is his grasp of any *ideas* that he borrowed or invented. To be able to control so many words at once is the token of a mind of most exceptional energy. (*T. S. Eliot—Selected Prose,* Penguin Books, 1953, p. 145 f.)

Those who may be interested in how one of Milton's "musical paragraphs" would sound if set to music may consult the article on "Rhythm" in Volumn 19 of the *Encyclopædia Britannica,* which includes two exercises in the musical notation of the first lines of *Paradise Lost.*

As for Milton's spelling, which may intrigue or baffle the reader, Bridges concludes that it is uniquely Milton's, and intended—save for a few mannered or antique forms—to reproduce as closely as possible the sounds denoted by the words. In other words this is a phonetic spelling, of the type many language reformers have advocated. Bridges explains the inconsistencies in spelling by the fact that Milton was blind and could not see to it himself that the text was perfectly accurate and in accord with his intentions. On the other hand, he may have felt no compulsion to be perfectly consistent.

Another peculiarity of Milton's style is its latinity—the extraordinary number of words of Latin derivation and his adherence to Latin syntax in his writing of this English poem. He has been accused by critics from Samuel Johnson to the present day of having written in a foreign language, "completely unlike anything used in common speech, producing a language peculiarly his own." T. S. Eliot said in his anti-Milton mood that "Milton writes English like a dead language." And Mark Van Doren says that Milton's diction "is starched with latinity, as if Milton did not trust his own language." But many such critics also admire the things Milton achieved with his peculiar language. Eliot later considered "the remoteness of Milton's verse from ordinary speech, his invention of his own phonetic language . . . one of the marks of his greatness." If you are interested in the effect of Latin terms and syntax on the English language, see the chapter on "Latin and Greek" in Otto Jespersen's *Growth and Structure of the English Language*. (One of Jespersen's prime examples of excessive latinity is a paragraph of prose by Samuel Johnson!)

VI

Who is the hero of Paradise Lost?

Some readers have suggested that Satan is the real hero of the poem, because of the good lines that Milton gives him and the indomitable character that is attributed to him. But even if there were some underlying truth in this suggestion, would that make Satan the hero of the story in its full unfolding? Who, then, is the hero *inside the poem?* Is it God, who triumphs now and will triumph ultimately? Or is it the Son, God's champion and agent, the actual doer of the deeds, the conqueror of Satan, and the ultimate redeemer and judge of the world? But does this jibe with our notion of the epic hero? Does he have to be a human being, like Odysseus or Aeneas? Is Adam, then, the hero?

Assuming that Adam is the hero, we may consider whether he fits the role and whether he possesses heroic qualities. Does Adam have enough room to act within the poem, to display the resourcefulness, courage, and other virtues of an Odysseus or an Aeneas? What does Adam do, before or after the Fall, to set him apart as a hero? Is it enough to make him the hero that he is the human figure around whom the whole story centers, whose fall from perfect happiness to earthly imperfection is the theme of the poem? What admirable characteristics that can be compared with the vivid qualities ascribed to Satan does he display? Is Adam a believable, individualized character? Would it be possible for Milton to create an individualized portrait of the first man, the generic prototype of the human race? Does Adam achieve only after the Fall the human characteristics and virtue we are familiar with?

Is Paradise Lost an epic poem?

An epic poem is a serious narrative poem dealing with a grand theme and extraordinary actions. The epics discussed in *Imaginative Literature I* narrated the exploits of Odysseus and Aeneas, legendary heroes of the Greek and Roman peoples. They come through dangers and trials to a triumphant conclusion. Is *Paradise Lost* comparable to epics of this type?

Assuming that Adam is the hero, would you say that this poem is the epic of the past and destiny of the human race, as the *Aeneid* was with respect to the Roman nation? Even if the story in Genesis is taken literally, does *Paradise Lost* have a historical basis and bearing? Does not all that takes place in the Garden of Eden, within the action of the poem, occur before history began? Or is it only necessary that the story be regarded as essentially true, as Milton believed, to fulfill the requirements of truth and relevance required for epic poems?

Are epic poems supposed to end triumphantly? Epics are not supposed to end like tragedies, with a fall from happiness to misery. Dryden, Addison, and other critics have stated that this theme—"the losing of our happiness," in Dryden's words— is not suitable to an epic poem. Is this the only possible view of the theme and ending of *Paradise Lost*? Does Adam (or the human race) triumph in the poem?

Is it a defect of poetic form that so much of the material of epic quality—the trials and ventures of the human race through history—is narrated indirectly and not presented directly, as the Fall of Man is? Is it necessary for Milton to narrate the stories of Creation (before the Fall) and of Salvation (after the Fall) indirectly through the archangels Raphael and Michael? Even if it is necessary, does the indirectness of such a vast portion of the story detract from the dramatic force and immediacy of material that is essential to the epic quality of the poem?

Do the war of the angels and the military role assigned to God and the Son add to the epic quality of the poem? Are they analogous to the battle scenes and intervention of the gods narrated by Homer and Virgil? Are they out of place or absurd in Heaven?

Is it impossible to express Milton's theme in poetic images?

Some critics have complained that Milton attempted an impossible task when he tried to write an epic poem describing eternal realms and dramatizing divine activity. Milton himself expresses an awareness of the difficulty in more than one place in the poem. How does he propose to accomplish his admittedly difficult objective? Does he succeed in describing Heaven and Hell, in dramatizing Creation and Redemption, and in presenting God, the Son, Satan, and Adam as believable characters in the poem? Which of the characters mentioned is presented the most vividly, believably, and unforgettably? Is the Son or Satan the more impressively rendered as a character in the story? Is Adam or Eve the more believable and recognizable of the human characters?

How does the Bible present the story or stories that Milton tells? Is the biblical story simpler or more complicated than *Paradise Lost*? Is the biblical style more or less elevated than Milton's? What does each of the two versions of these events contribute that the other does not? May we compare sacred and secular writings as to their literary value? If so, which account would you rate higher and why—the Bible's or Milton's?

In *Imaginative Literature I*, we have another poetic work that deals with religious subject matter: Dante's *Divine Comedy*. Does Dante handle the eternal realms, the character and action of divine personages any differently than Milton? If so, just what is the difference in the way each poet handles Hell and Heaven, God and the Son, the Devil, and other characters? Are the two poems at all comparable? May we consider Dante's "comedy" as an epic too? Why or why not?

Is Milton's language a help or a hindrance in expressing his subject matter?

A horde of critics from Milton's day to our own have criticized the style of this poem. Their essential point is that an involved rhetorical language, often more musical than sensible, stands between the reader and what the poet is trying to convey. They maintain that Milton often fails to make us see what he is trying to describe because of the cloud of fantastic images or abstractions that stands in the way. What do you think of this criticism?

In the first place, is Milton's style the same throughout the poem? Is the style of the early books the same as that of the later books? Is the language and beat of Satan's speeches the same as that of God's or the Son's or Adam's? Where do you think the criticism is most justified or least justified—in the descriptions of the fallen angels in Hell, Satan's flight to Eden, the Garden of Eden, the war of the angels, the story of the Creation, the Fall of Man, the story of the future and Redemption of man, the passages where Satan acts and speaks, or those in which God or the Son appears?

There has been a strong movement among poets and critics —notably Wordsworth in the past and T. S. Eliot in the present day—to bring the language of poetry as close as possible to common speech. Putting aside the question of whether this is generally desirable, can we say that a language close to ordinary English speech would have been more suitable for this poem? Is Milton guilty of poetic perversity, blindness, and deafness, or is there a method in his "madness" of concocting a language of his own—involved, full of extraordinary expressions, circumlocutions, paradoxes, Latinisms, a wild mixture of metaphors, and all the other things he is accused of? By using this oddly sublime style does he convey anything that he could not convey otherwise? Would *Paradise Lost* be as well or better expressed in prose, as is Butler's translation of the *Odyssey*, or in rhymed verse, say heroic couplets, as is Chaucer's *Canterbury Tales?*

Is Milton's sense conveyed by the sound of his verse, or does he forget the sense for the sound? William Hazlitt thought Milton had the finest ear of any English poet for the perfect relation of music and sense in poetry. T. S. Eliot, in his anti-Milton period, said that the sound and the rhetoric get in the way so much that you have to read a passage in *Paradise Lost* once for the sound, the musical magic and evocation, and once for the sense. Who are right, the admirers or the detractors of Milton's style?

Aristotle in the *Poetics* considers invention—of plot, character, etc.—the main element of poetry, and such things as versification—rhythm, "music," etc.—minor or dispensable. At the other extreme, critics have made style, diction, and meter the main elements of poetry; Hegel, for instance, says that "metre is the first and only condition absolutely demanded by poetry." Is the poetic substance of a work like the *Aeneid*, the *Divine Comedy*, or *Paradise Lost* conveyable in any other way than through poetic rhythm and verse? Are the particular material sounds and the arrangements of words indissolubly linked to the meaning in these poems and indispensable for conveying it? Is poetry translatable? Would it be possible to translate *Paradise Lost* adequately into any modern European language? Granted that *Paradise Lost* is a glory of the English tongue, is it or can it be a glory in any other Western language?

What kind of knowledge do Adam and Eve attain through eating the forbidden fruit?

The forbidden fruit supposedly bestows knowledge of good and evil. In the poem Satan puts the question of why such knowledge is forbidden. What is wrong with knowing good and evil? Is not such knowledge essential to human virtue? And how can knowledge be a sin? (See the speeches of Satan and Eve, pp. 262a-264a; also Satan's speech, pp. 163b-164a.) Milton comments that this knowledge is "Knowledge of Good bought dear by knowing ill" (p. 157a). Adam says to Eve that they have come to know "Both Good and Evil, Good lost, and Evil got" (p. 270b). And God too says that man has lost his knowledge of good and attained that of evil, adding

> Happier, had it suffic'd him to have known
> Good by it self, and Evil not at all. (p. 301a)

Is this Milton's conclusion too? How does this accord with his picture of man attaining a happier Eden after the Fall and the new knowledge obtained through sin? Does he hold out the prospect of a surer virtue through the experience of evil than the state of innocence could foster? What kind of knowledge is this, anyway? Is it theoretical, objective knowledge about good and evil, or actual experience of—intimate participation in—evil? What are the immediate emotional and psychological consequences of the new knowledge in Milton's portrayal?

Turn now to the famous passage in Milton's *Areopagitica*, which begins "Good and evil we know in the field of this world grow up together almost inseparably. . . . " (See pp. 390b-391a.) Do you conclude from this passage that Milton did or did not believe that man could know good without knowing evil? Did he consider Adam's virtue before the Fall "a fugitive and cloistered virtue, unexercised and unbreathed, that never sallies out and sees her adversary"? What kind of knowledge of evil does he advocate in this passage—knowledge through seeing or knowledge through doing? If Adam had been tempted but had abstained, would he have attained the full human virtue Milton points to? Or is the journey through a world where moral choices loom at every turn necessary to achieve real human virtue?

Does Milton really consider the Fall a horrible doom, as he frequently says in *Paradise Lost*, or does he consider it a glorious opportunity for the moral education of man, for the perfection of man's humanity? Is Adam in Eden really perfect, virtuous, rational, and free? Or must he attain these virtues through effort and experience in the everyday world?

The following questions are designed to help you test the thoroughness of your reading. Each question is to be answered by giving a page or pages of the reading assignment. Answers will be found on page 248 of this Reading Plan.

1 Who is "the least erected Spirit that fell/From heav'n"?

2 Which of the fallen angels advocates a policy of "open Warr" against God?

3 Which of the fallen angels counsels "ignoble ease, and peaceful sloath"?

4 Who is the mother of Death?

5 Who is "the Anarch old"?

6 Which is more constricted—Hell or Eden?

7 Whose image does the newly created Eve see in the lake?

8 What is the attitude toward conjugal love expressed in this poem?

9 What is the devilish invention that some day may plague the human race?

10 Who has fallen "On evil dayes . . . and evil tongues/In darkness"?

FIELDING

Tom Jones

Vol. 37

*T*om Jones is the masterwork of one of the great creators of the modern novel. Its plot has been praised as one of the most perfect in world literature. It is for reasons such as these that "a mere novel" has been selected for inclusion in the *Great Books of the Western World*.

Like Chaucer's *Canterbury Tales* and Cervantes' *Don Quixote*, this book is full of humor, rich in characters, and presents a graphic portrait of the life and society of the times. Fielding's novel keeps the itinerant character of the old picaresque chronicle. We follow Tom Jones along the roads of eighteenth-century England, stop with him in the wayside inns, accompany him to London, and share his encounter with various provincial and city characters and levels of life.

But Fielding has given us something far more than a picaresque tale of adventures along the road. The adventures carry forward and complicate the plot and theme of the story. The characters that are encountered are connected with the story and contribute to the incidents that take place.

And what wonderful characters they are! There is the crusty, earthy, bullheaded Squire Western, with language right out of Rabelais or Chaucer. There is his sister, Mrs. Western, ridiculously proud of her wisdom on how to be an "operator" in high society and politics, but utterly blind and stupid about the workings of the human heart—a wonderful caricature of a perennial human type. And there is the naïve, garrulous, irrepressible, timid Partridge, who gives Tom a companionship on his adventures that rivals that of Sancho Panza for Don Quixote.

Such people as these, very real as individuals or types or both, make the story go. They inhabit the world Fielding has created in this novel and which he makes live for us through narration, characterization, dialogue, and commentary. This imaginary world provides us with an enjoyable experience and also affords some insight into the real world it is intended to mirror.

Third Reading

I

When we come to the study of the novel, we feel something like Molière's bourgeois gentleman, who, in his attempt to acquire culture, finds to his delight that he has been speaking prose all his life. However sketchy and occasional our knowledge of other literary forms may be, nearly all of us have read many novels during our lifetime. Even those who claim to be too busy to read any works that do not serve their vocational pursuits usually permit themselves the relaxation of reading novels—at least mysteries and westerns. The novel has been the predominant form of imaginative literature in modern times, and it is much more familiar to us than dramatic tragedy or epic poetry.

Despite our intimacy with the novel, however, we find it harder to describe or define than the traditional literary forms. The terms and analytical distinctions which Aristotle applies to tragedy and epic in the *Poetics* (see Vol. 9, pp. 681-699), such as plot, character, and diction, are also applicable to the novel. "Recognition" scenes and "reversals" occur in novels as well as in tragedies. The ancient forerunner of the novel seems to be the epic poem—we have already noted T. E. Lawrence's proclamation of the *Odyssey* as the first novel of Europe. (See *Imaginative Literature I*, p. 1.)

Yet we seem to be faced with a new and different form of literature, and the analysis of the old forms does not tell us what a novel is, or rather what it is like and how it is put together. Like the epic, it is a long narrative, at least the length of an ordinary book (from 200 to 1,000 pages). But the epic is written in verse, while the novel, as commonly known, is written in prose. Also the epic deals with extraordinary or "heroic" events and characters, while the novel does not seem to be thus limited. Indeed, most often it deals with events and characters on the ordinary level of experience—the kind we can "identify" with. But there have also been "heroic" novels as well as novels about ridiculous persons and actions. The novel apparently includes characters and events below, above, and at the level of the ordinary. (See Aristotle's *Poetics*, Vol. 9, pp. 681d, 683d, 687c-688b.)

Another distinction between the epic and the novel might be that the epic deals with legendary or historical subjects, while the novel, though usually depicting problems of everyday life, is pure fiction, made-up, "new" (and hence "novel"). But we have seen in the previous readings how little restricted the epic poets were by their original materials and how "new" their creations were. We know that many novels are based on the author's personal experience—sometimes directly autobiographical—and that there are such things as historical novels. Obviously, the important thing is what the author, whether of tragedy, epic, or the novel, makes of his material; wherever it comes from, he must make it unique. We really do not care whether the author is being faithful to historical fact or received tradition; we are interested in the particular story he is telling us. (See Aristotle's remarks on the difference between history and poetry in the *Poetics*, Vol. 9, p. 686a-c. The poet, he says, deals not with what *has been*, but with what *might be*. Not with the actual, but with the possible, the probable, or the necessary.) We appreciate and judge novels as we do paintings, by what we experience and enjoy through them, not by their photographic fidelity to particular objects. Of course, it is possible that we may get something beyond aesthetic enjoyment and merely formal appreciation from novels; we may reach awareness and understanding of man's existence in the world, but this extra perception does not derive from the faithful recording of actual incidents and persons.

A good way to learn what a novel is and how a novel is put together is to read one of the recognized models of the novel, such as *Tom Jones*. (For a partial sketch of the background of the novel of romance and of the picaresque novel, see Section I of the First Reading.) Fielding's *Tom Jones* was written in the early formative period of the English novel, in those middle decades of the eighteenth century in which Samuel Richardson, Henry Fielding, Tobias Smollett, and Laurence Sterne created their memorable works. Literary historians regard Richardson's *Pamela; or Virtue Rewarded* (1740) as the first English novel. Fielding's *The History of Joseph Andrews* (1742) was intended as a burlesque of *Pamela,* but ended as an original comic novel. Fielding rejected Richardson's method of writing a novel in the form of a series of letters between the characters in the story. Instead he adopted a straight narrative form, interspersed with essay-type passages. His second novel, *The Life of Mr. Jonathan Wild the Great* (1743), was a modern satire in the old picaresque tradition, based on the life and deeds of a notorious criminal. His third novel, *The History of Tom Jones, a Foundling* (1749), is regarded as his greatest. Some critics rate it as the most perfect novel ever written. Fielding himself claims to be "the founder of a new province of writing" (p. 20a).

Tom Jones is so highly praised because of the masterly organization with which Fielding welds a host of events and characters, with their individual actions and "histories," into a unified whole, in which the characters, the actions, and the style mutually illuminate one another. Such continuity and harmony among all the elements that make up a novel had not appeared until this time. Fielding's achievement was a challenge and inspiration to his contemporaries as well as a model to the great nineteenth-century novelists. During our own century novelists have attempted other tasks and devised other methods than those of the eighteenth and nineteenth centuries, and hence contemporary critics often deprecate Fielding as the model novelist. However, it is safe to say that *Tom Jones* is a model of the old-fashioned novel, and that reading it may bring us enjoyment as well as instruction about at least one type of novel.

II

Tom Jones is called a "history" and is written as if it dealt with actual events. This fictional device is reminiscent of the romances written by men like Daniel Defoe in the previous generation, such works as *Robinson Crusoe* and *Moll Flanders* which pretend to be true accounts of real events. Hence, Fielding's story proper begins thus: "In that part of the western division of this kingdom which is commonly called Somersetshire, there lately lived, and perhaps lives still, a gentleman whose name was Allworthy" (p. 2b). A naïve British reader of the time might want to take a ride out there to see Allworthy after reading the book. But the fictional character of this "history" is a pervading atmosphere, transmitted through many devices. One important device is that of the author as the omniscient narrator outside the story, in sharp distinction from the "autobiographical" first-person-singular accounts in Defoe's works. The author claims knowledge that no individual character or mere observer could possibly have, and thus avoids the "realistic" eyewitness tone which characterizes first-person narratives.

This method of narration is obvious from the start, but the author pushes the point home himself, speaking in his own voice. In the introductory essays which make up the first chapter of each of the eighteen books of *Tom Jones*, he tells us what he is doing and how he is doing it. He proclaims his right to comment as he pleases (pp. 2d-3a, 6d-7a, 45b-d), to select and arrange events as seems best to him (Book II, Ch. 1), to be omniscient about the events of the story (pp. 6c, 42d-43d); and he talks at length about the qualities necessary for "historical writers who do not draw their materials from records," but rely instead on "the vast authentic doomsday-book of nature" (Book IX, Ch. 1). This truth to nature makes the novelist a "historian" rather than a mere "romancer," Fielding proclaims. (See also Book I, Ch. 1, which lists human nature as his subject.) Fielding has it both ways, though. Frequently, he does not tell all he knows, and appeals to the reader's imagination to fill in the details. And when he narrates an odd action or response that does not follow the general course of human nature, he claims he is just reporting the facts as an honest historian: "I am not writing a system, but a history, and I am not obliged to reconcile every matter to the received notions concerning truth and nature" (p. 260a).

These introductory essays, which he throws in free with the story, amount to a course in literary appreciation by the author. We will take up their doctrine in Section VI below, where we discuss Fielding's technique. At this point let us proceed to the story this genial "historian" tells.

Tom Jones is the story of a foundling, of a man who starts his life as an abandoned infant of uncertain parentage. From the beginning his life is shadowed by this stigma and uncertainty, despite the security and affection offered by his foster parent, the benevolent Squire Allworthy. He encounters enmity, jealousy, and malice in Allworthy's household from relatives, servants, and teachers. When Allworthy disowns Tom because of his escapades and the malicious tales of his enemies, he takes to the road to seek his own way in life.

An amazing and variegated series of adventures follows, in the old picaresque tradition, as Tom Jones goes from one incident to another, through low life and high, in the countryside and in the metropolis of London. A parallel series of adventures is experienced by Tom's sweetheart, Sophia, daughter of the neighboring Squire Western, who runs away from home in order to avoid marrying Allworthy's detestable nephew, young Blifil. The rest of the story is made up of the crisscrossing and separation of the paths of the two lovers, including Sophia's rejection of Tom because of his escapades and her misunderstanding of him.

The latter part of the novel introduces many complications of the difficulties, a deeper cleavage between the two lovers, and the final resolution of the impasse, as well as Tom's reconciliation with Allworthy. Despite the pitfalls and dangers that Tom constantly encounters—and he comes dangerously close to fulfilling the malicious prophecy that he was born to be hanged—we always feel sure that he will come out of it all right and that there will be a happy ending, as with the hero in a western movie. He is the author's hero and ours too, and we like him from the start, and his girl also. Despite the evil and unpleasantness evident in some characters and events, we just know that this will be a "comedy" in the classic sense, with a happy ending, the good guys getting their reward and the bad guys getting their just deserts.

The story is told through a rich variety of characters and events, all of them, with rare exceptions (such as the Man of the Hill digression), connected in one way or another with the two neighboring families—the Allworthys and the Westerns. We encounter a wide variety of types, classes, and dialects in a very full and convincing imitation of life. No bare summary can do justice to this richness of content and tone.

We may break the story into three parts: (1) the period before the flight of Tom and Sophia (Book I to Book VII, Ch. 9); (2) the period on the road (Book VII, Ch. 10 through Book XII); (3) the period in London and the conclusion (Books XIII-XVIII).

III

In the first section of the work, Fielding presents the major characters and the situation around which the novel revolves. The benevolent Squire Allworthy finds a baby in his bed and decides to take care of it and raise it as if it were his own. His inquiries as to its parentage result in the admission by a village girl named Jenny Jones that the child is hers, but she refuses to name the father. Allworthy, after a paternal lecture on the viciousness of vice and the virtuousness of virtue, sends her away to a distant town, where he provides for her. The townsfolk, of course, conclude that he is the father of the child. But responsibility for this role is soon settled on a schoolmaster named Partridge, in whose household Jenny Jones had worked as a maid. Despite Partridge's protestations of innocence, Allworthy, acting as magistrate, believes the contrary testimony of Partridge's jealous wife, declares him guilty, and deprives him of the annuity he has been receiving from Allworthy. Partridge is plunged into misery and ultimately leaves the locality. Thus both of the parents assigned to Tom leave the scene early in the story. But the mystery of Tom's parentage remains unsolved until the end of the book.

Tom's life is complicated from early boyhood by the marriage of Squire Allworthy's sister Bridget to a Captain Blifil and by her bearing the latter a son, who vies with Tom for the favor and fortune of Squire Allworthy. Tom not only has to contend with the elder Blifil, who resents his intrusion and sharing in the Allworthy lot, but also with the ill will of the boys' teachers, Parson Thwackum and Mr. Square. Thwackum is a bigoted and narrow-minded pedant, a pious old fraud, who believes in frequent and severe floggings in the rearing of children. Square is a hypocritical moral philosopher, always talking about the proper and the fit, but arguing in specific cases so that the proper and fit turns out to be whatever is to his advantage. The worthy divine and the moralist are interested in sharing in the Allworthy estate, and they consider it wisest to gain the favor of young Blifil, who will most likely be Allworthy's heir. So it is Tom who gets the beatings and the black reports to Allworthy, while young Blifil is presented constantly as a model of virtue and character.

Tom's own character gives occasion for much of the trouble he gets into. Tom has an open, generous, unsuspecting disposition. He is also impulsive, daring, full of vitality, and a bit "wild." This combination of generosity and wildness makes him vulnerable to the machinations of those who bear him ill will.

Young Blifil and Tom Jones present a complete contrast in character. Blifil is crafty, selfish, malicious, and always finds cunning ways to put Tom in the wrong, while Tom unsuspectingly admires and loves him. He appears to his elders as the good boy, who always does and says the right thing, even when he is up to his most vicious acts. With this combination of character traits, Blifil is in a position to triumph over a boy like Tom Jones.

When Tom gets older, his generous disposition and passionate temperament lead him into serious trouble. By the time he is nineteen he has become "one of the handsomest young fellows in the world" and is attracted to Molly Seagrim, the gamekeeper's beautiful, sensuous daughter. The restraint of his own moral inhibitions is overcome by Molly's purposeful seductiveness; they have an affair and Molly is soon pregnant. Tom considers himself responsible for Molly and when Squire Allworthy, acting as magistrate again, sentences Molly to the House of Correction for her conduct, Tom stops the proceedings and confesses that he is the man involved. Allworthy is shocked by this news, but he withdraws the sentence, still holding Tom in his esteem for his manliness and other good qualities.

About this time another love relation emerges between Tom and his neighbor Sophia Western. Already in childhood the discerning Sophia has recognized "that Tom, though an idle, thoughtless, rattling rascal, was nobody's enemy but his own; and that Master Blifil, though a prudent, discreet, sober young gentleman, was at the same time strongly attached to the interest only of one single person . . ."—himself (p. 54d). Sophia, now a very beautiful, accomplished, and charming young lady, is strongly attracted to handsome Tom. But though he shows her the "natural gallantry and good-nature" that he shows to all women, he has no designs on her. Tom is a young man with an acute conscience and, being a foundling, he is incapable of scheming to make a good match with the daughter of the rich squire who has trusted him to come and go in his house. Nor does he feel free to fall in love with her, for he is already involved rather seriously with another girl.

All of this is changed by a sudden accident, when Tom in saving Sophia from a bad fall from her horse fractures his arm. He is cared for in the Westerns' house, and the very nature of the incident and the propinquity it throws them into soon reveals to the two young people that they are in love with one another. Mrs. Honour, the Westerns' housekeeper, a plain-spoken woman who favors Tom, aids the course of true love by letting drop to each of them what the other feels. Tom's scruple about his responsibility to Molly is removed when he visits her and finds the worthy moral philosopher Square hidden away in a corner of her bedroom, and also when he finds that a famous local gallant who had first seduced Molly is just as likely as he to be the father of her child. Molly's infidelity with Square is in itself not enough to make Tom feel free of his responsibility for Molly; he requires this additional evidence to clear his conscience.

Book V, Chapter 6, is a wonderful presentation of Tom's newly released feelings and his unsuccessful attempt to conceal them from Sophia, who is quite aware of what is going on in him. The declaration of love takes place by the canal in which Tom had nearly drowned trying to rescue Sophia's pet bird when they were children. She leads the conversation into a discussion of his demonstrated and brave devotion to her, and he in a trembling and indirect way expresses his feelings while she as tremblingly and indirectly accepts. She begs him not to say any more, and they totter back to the house.

The next chapter begins a series of events that alter Tom's position disastrously and send him out on the road. This is a climactic portion of the novel that is referred to frequently in later chapters. Allworthy, apparently mortally ill, makes his will and says good-by to his relatives and friends, for whom he has provided generously. Tom is plunged into a profound grief, which turns into boundless joy when he finds that Allworthy will recover. He is so overjoyed and drinks so much wine at dinner that he gives vent to extravagant expressions of joy (kissing the doctor and shouting loudly his love for Allworthy). Blifil, who has just learned that his mother, Allworthy's sister, has died, is offended at Tom's conduct in what should be a house of mourning and rejects Tom's contrite apology with the insulting remark that he, Blifil, unlike the foundling Tom Jones, "had the misfortune to know who his parents were, and consequently must be affected with their loss." A scuffle between the two young men is broken up, and Tom leaves after making peace with Blifil.

While walking in a grove, amid all the lovely sights and sounds of the evening, he meditates on his love for Sophia and vows constant love to her, even though cruel fortune and the gulf in their social positions would separate them forever. At this moment he comes upon Molly Seagrim, clad in a coarse, dirty shift, and smelling of her agricultural labors—a great contrast with the delicate and accomplished Sophia. But after a few minutes' conversation, Tom accompanies Molly "into the thickest part of the grove." Fielding explains this seemingly strange conduct "by suggesting, that Jones probably thought one woman better than none, and Molly as probably imagined two men to be better than one" (p. 93c). He also notes that Tom was quite drunk by now, and unrestrained by reason and moral principles. Parson Thwackum and young Blifil, who are passing by at the moment, see the couple retiring into the bushes and attempt to apprehend them. Tom gallantly gives battle to the two intruders, so that Molly may get away and her identity will not be revealed. Squire Western, passing by with a party, rushes to Tom's aid, and helps him beat up the two moralists. The earthy squire, far from being shocked at Tom's conduct, thinks it is admirably natural and will help increase the dwindling population. This scene ends happily, with Tom going off with Squire Western and his party, including the fair Sophia, who fainted dead away at the sight of blood on the combatants.

But a new factor has entered upon the scene in the person of Mrs. Western, the squire's sister. Having lived in high social and political circles and having acquired a knowledge of worldly matters, she considers herself an authority on love, although she has no personal experience of her own in that line. She is an expert on stratagems and affectations, but knows nothing of "the plain simple workings of honest nature." It is obvious to her from Sophia's fainting at the scene of the fight and from certain other signs that the girl is deeply in love with young Blifil. Mrs. Western retails this startling information to her brother, whom she patronizes as a member of the inferior male sex, and also as a crude bumpkin, with no knowledge of politics, love, and other worldly matters. The squire considers it a good match, since it will join the two neighboring estates into the greatest estate in the county, and he proceeds to propose the marriage to Allworthy. The later, however, thinks they should first consult the two persons immediately involved.

Blifil, unlike Tom, finds it easy to subdue his animal passions, and is too self-centered to feel anything like love for another person. However, he is possessed by the social passions of avarice and ambition, and finds the Western fortune very attractive. Hence he consents to begin the courtship of Sophia Western. How that young lady receives the news from her aunt is told with great effectiveness in Book VI, Chapter 5. Under the impression that Mrs. Western is aware of her feeling for Tom, and that the match she is talking about is with him, Sophia blurts out her secret.

"Nay, I will own," says Sophia, "I know none with such perfections. So brave, and yet so gentle; so witty, yet so inoffensive; so humane, so civil, so genteel, so handsome! What signifies his being base born, when compared with such qualifications as these?" "Base born? What do you mean?" said the aunt, "Mr. Blifil base born!" Sophia turned instantly pale at this name, and faintly repeated it. Upon which the aunt cried, "Mr. Blifil—ay, Mr. Blifil, of whom else have we been talking?" "Good heavens," answered Sophia, ready to sink, "of Mr. Jones, I thought; I am sure I know no other who deserves—" "I protest," cries the aunt, "you frighten me in your turn. Is it Mr. Jones, and not Mr. Blifil, who is the object of your affection?" "Mr. Blifil!" repeated Sophia. "Sure it is impossible you can be in earnest; if you are, I am the most miserable woman alive." Mrs. Western now stood a few moments silent, while sparks of fiery rage flashed from her eyes. At length, collecting all her force of voice, she thundered forth in the following articulate sounds:
    "And is it possible you can think of disgracing your family by allying yourself to a bastard? Can the blood of the Westerns submit to such contamination? If you have not sense sufficient to restrain such monstrous inclinations, I thought the pride of our family would have prevented you from giving the least encouragement to so base an affection; much less did I imagine you would ever have had the assurance to own it to my face." (p. 106a-b)

Mrs. Western thereupon forces Sophia to accept Blifil as her suitor under the threat of informing Squire Western of her passion for Tom if she does not. Indeed, that worldly lady decides that in view of Sophia's "base passion," the marriage, however disagreeable to her, must be hastened, to preserve her honor and that of the family. Thus the author introduces the problematic situation that the hero and his girl must work their way out of through the rest of the novel.

After Sophia's first meeting with Blifil, she tells her father that she detests the man and will not marry him. He flies into a rage, insisting that she must do as he says; and his rage becomes murderous when he learns from his sister about Sophia's passion for Tom, for whom he has had a great fondness but whom he cannot consider a suitable match for his daughter. Western tells Allworthy the shocking news and asserts his unshaken resolve that Sophia shall marry Blifil. The latter, out of spite against Tom for winning Sophia's love and frustrating his own plans, tell Allworthy of Tom's drunken behavior on the night Allworthy was recovering from his illness. Blifil paints Tom as a shameless sot who, at a time of sickness and death in the family, caroused and beat up those virtuous souls Thwackum and Blifil. This sudden revelation, together with Western's news of the relation between Sophia and Tom—the "attempt to steal away the young lady . . . so base and barbarous an action"—leads Allworthy to condemn Tom as an utterly worthless person and to banish him permanently from his household and from all communication.

Tom, having lost the five-hundred pound "stake" Allworthy had given him on parting, sets out on the road to Bristol to go to sea, a profession which requires no preparation and no capital. Sophia, aided by her maid Mrs. Honour, runs away from home, in order to put a stop to her family's project of marrying her off to Blifil. Her destination is London, where she can stay with a relative, who she feels will be sympathetic.

IV

In the first of the three stages of action into which we have divided the book, Fielding has presented the major characters of the story and the situation out of which the ensuing events of the novel develop. In the second of our three stages, he unfolds the events that center around Tom and Sophia on their separate roads to London, and which contribute to the additional problems and final solution in the last part of the story. In this second stage (beginning with Book VII, Chapter 10 and ending with Book XII, Chapter 14) we get an interesting picture of the life and times of eighteenth-century England, somewhat like the journey of Don Quixote through sixteenth-century Spain. And though Tom Jones is by no means the same type of character as Don Quixote, he acquires the equivalent of the Don's companion, Sancho Panza.

Constantly in the background through this section of the book is the attempt of Charles Edward, the Stuart Pretender, to regain the English throne in his final, desperate campaign of 1745-1746. Fielding tells us that "this was the very time when the late rebellion was at the highest; and indeed the banditti were now marched into England, intending, as it was thought, to fight the king's forces, and to attempt pushing forward to the metropolis" (p. 140b). The journeys of both Tom and Sophia are complicated by this crisis. (For the details of the campaign see "Charles Edward," *Encyclopædia Britannica*, Vol. 5.)

At the beginning of his journey, Tom falls in with a company of soldiers marching to fight the "rebels," and he decides to join them instead of going to sea. However, a barroom brawl with one of the officers puts him out of action at the very start. A most interesting barber-surgeon attends him during his convalescence, an apparently erudite fellow who constantly peppers his talk with Latin citations. This barber is "one of the pleasantest barbers that was ever recorded in history, the barber of Bagdad, or he in Don Quixote, not excepted" (p. 158a). To Tom's astonishment, the barber turns out to be Partridge, the disgraced schoolmaster who is supposed to be his father. Partridge assures Tom that the report is false and notes that this erroneously bestowed "honour" has been his ruin. He begs Tom to take him along on his journey (in hopes that Tom will soon be restored to Allworthy's favor, and that he, Partridge, will be able to profit by it). As a result, Partridge becomes Tom's companion through the rest of the story, contributing his humor, simple-mindedness, indiscreet garrulity, and a prudential cowardice that reminds us of Sancho Panza. Along the road, the dialogues between Tom and Partridge add greatly to the tone and color of the story.

The main scene of this section is the inn at Upton, where occur the events that are decisive for the course of the action. (See Book X.) Tom has just rescued a half-naked lady in distress, and he fights the innkeeper at Upton to get her a room. Tom has an intimate dinner with the lady (an army captain's woman by the name of Mrs. Waters), and spends the night with her. Their repose is interrupted by the farcical and nearly serious intrusion of a Captain Fitzpatrick (the husband of a niece of Squire Western), who bursts in on Tom and the lady under the impression that the lady is his wife. No sooner has this contretemps been smoothed over, than Sophia and Mrs.

Honour appear at the inn. Partridge's loose babling reveals that Tom is in bed with another woman, and the irate Sophia leaves the inn at once, vowing to have nothing more to do with Tom. Just to make him smart she has her muff—a prized thing for Tom—put in the empty bed in Tom's room, with a piece of paper pinned to it bearing her signature. Tom, of course, is mad with disappointment when he finds the muff and discovers what has happened. At the moment, however, he has to contend with the crusty Squire Western, who has also arrived at the inn, in pursuit of his daughter, and who gets the mistaken impression that it is Sophia whom Tom has slept with. The squire soon gives up the chase of Sophia for the chase of a fox, joining a hunting party in the vicinity, conscientious lest he let a glorious day for fox hunting get away from him. (See Book XII, Ch. 2.)

Fielding interrupts at this point, where the characters involved in this scene have all taken to the road again, to give us a backward glance at Sophia's escape (Book X, Ch. 8-9), and then recounts the events that she experiences on the road from Upton to London (Book XI). The most important event is her encounter with her cousin, Mrs. Fitzpatrick, who is running away from her husband (the gentleman who made the embarrassing intrusion into Mrs. Waters' bedchamber). Mrs. Fitzpatrick's "history" affords another interesting digression. In a ludicrous scene, Sophia is mistaken by an innkeeper for the Pretender's mistress. Ultimately, Sophia and her cousin get to London in the coach of an Irish peer who is a friend of Mrs. Fitzpatrick. Sophia finds asylum in the house of her relative Lady Bellaston, who welcomes her most cordially.

In Book XII we pick up Tom's trail again, which at first is directed toward joining the forces fighting the Pretender, and then at following Sophia. En route, he picks up her pocketbook, containing a hundred-pound note, which a poor beggarman has found. Tom enjoys the touch of it, kisses it, and intends to restore it to her himself. Colorful scenes with a company of puppet-players and a group of gypsies occur along this stretch of the journey. So also does a conversation between Tom and Mr. Dowling, who has appeared briefly in previous passages of the story. Dowling first appears in the story at the time of Allworthy's illness, as the attorney from Salisbury with an important message, which is delivered to Blifil, after which he rushes off in a tremendous hurry. (See pp. 88a-b, 90c.) He next appears in the dining room of the inn at Gloucester, where he eats at the same table as Tom and protests some remarks made about Tom's character and antecedents by another lawyer who knows the Allworthy family. He says "that the gentleman looked like another sort of man." (See pp. 165d-167a.)

Now again they meet at an inn, shortly after Tom's departure from Upton, and Mr. Dowling invites Tom to share a bottle of wine with him. He tells Tom that when he brought the news of Blifil's mother's death to Blifil on the night of Allworthy's illness, "he looked so like a very honest gentleman, and behaved himself so prettily, that I protest I never was more delighted with any gentleman since I was born." When Tom paints Blifil as a base character, Dowling protests that "it is a pity such a person should inherit the great estate of your uncle Allworthy." Tom is quick to reply, "I assure you, sir, I am no relation of Mr. Allworthy," and he explains to Dowling why people make this mistaken supposition. After listening to his story, including the account of his rejection by Mr. Allworthy, Dowling says it seems a hard thing to do to someone who is almost an adopted son, although "by law you cannot claim as heir." Tom protests he is not interested in Allworthy's estate and would not accept what rightfully belongs to Blifil even if it were given to him. The scene ends at this point, with an indication that we shall probably meet Dowling again. The way Fielding handles his appearance here indicates that he has an important role to play in the story, that he "knows something." (See pp. 261b-264a.)

V

The second stage of the action has brought the main characters through an interesting and complicated series of events from Somersetshire to London. In the very first chapter of the book, Fielding has promised, like a good cook, to start with plain food, and then gradually rise to fancier and spicier fare. "In like manner, we shall represent human nature at first to the keen appetite of our reader, in that more plain and simple manner in which it is found in the country, and shall hereafter hash and ragoo it with all the high French and Italian seasoning of affectation and vice which courts and cities afford" (p. 2a). In the London scene, Tom and Sophia encounter much more sophisticated and shocking pitfalls than was the case in the earlier sections of the book. In this section (Books XIII-XVIII) Tom, through his indiscretions and various accidents, almost completely alienates Sophia and comes close to fulfilling the prophecy that he was born to be hanged.

To understand Sophia's attitude toward Tom, which is so important for the action of this section, we must recognize that it is not based on simple jealousy or moral shock. In the earlier sections of the book, Sophia is portrayed as no prude. She recognizes that Tom is a natural man, a passionate, affectionate young fellow who is very attractive to women. His affair with Molly did not anger or hurt Sophia very much. And even in the case of his sharing Mrs. Waters' bed in the inn at Upton, she was more angry at the bruiting about of her name in public than his temporary physical infidelity. At various inns where she happens to follow Tom's road on the way to London, she finds that her name and her relation to Tom have been given wide publicity. This is due mainly to the irrepressible and garrulous Partridge, but the angry Sophia is unaware of that. "Sophia was much more offended at the freedoms which she thought (and not without good reason) he had taken with her name and character, than at any freedoms, in which, under his present circumstances, he had indulged himself with the person of another woman . . ." (p. 259d).

The action of the third stage begins with Tom's arrival in London and his search for Sophia. He finds Sophia through a series of accidents. Lady Bellaston, the relative with whom Sophia is staying, is attracted to him and decides to have him for herself, keeping Sophia's presence a secret from him. Tom readily succumbs to Lady Bellaston's desire to have him as her lover, partly in the hope that she may lead him to Sophia, and partly out of the "gallantry" that is part of his character. "Jones had never less inclination to an amour than at present; but gallantry to the ladies was among his principles of honour; and he held it as much incumbent on him to accept a challenge to love, as if it had been a challenge to fight" (p. 286a). This affair, however, is a bit different from Tom's previous simple amours, for this is London, and the woman is a sophisticated society lady. When Tom starts the affair he does not have a shilling in his pocket; after his first night with Lady Bellaston he has a fifty-pound bank note, and soon, through her largess, he becomes "one of the best-dressed men about town . . . raised to a state of affluence beyond what he had ever known (p. 289d).

Fielding observes wryly that though the lady was not noted for giving to the usual worthy causes, she considered this penniless young fellow for whom she had conceived a "violent fondness" a proper object for the Christian virtue of charity. Although Tom has no ardent passion for her, he feels compelled to make love to her because he feels obligated to her for supporting him, and he needs her support. "He knew the tacit consideration upon which all her favours were conferred; and as his necessity obliged him to accept them, so his honour, he concluded, forced him to pay the price" (p. 290b).

This affair takes surprising and amusing turns, often descending to the incidents of stage farce, but through it all is the poignant fact that the aging lady has a real passion for the indifferent youth and is willing to suffer all kinds of humiliation to fulfill it. Through accident, Tom meets Sophia at Lady Bellaston's, proceeds to return her pocketbook, and defends himself from her accusations. As for what happened that night at Upton, he insists, "my heart was never unfaithful to you. That had no share in the folly I was guilty of; it was even then unalterably yours" (p. 293a-b). His amour with Mrs. Waters was not serious, he insists, and he has never seen her since. As for Sophia's name being traduced in public, he convinces her that this is entirely the fault of Partridge, and he is completely innocent. The two lovers are reconciled, but at that moment Lady Bellaston appears, and Sophia pretends that Tom is just an unknown man who has returned her pocket-book.

Lady Bellaston is furious with Tom, but she is so madly in love with him that she overlooks his meeting with Sophia and imprudently comes to his lodgings. At almost the same moment Mrs. Honour arrives with a message from Sophia, and Lady Bellaston is forced to hide behind the bed and listen to slanderous gossip about herself by Sophia's maid. Jones succeeds in mollifying her, and it is arranged that he visit her at her home on the pretext of visiting Sophia (which for Tom is the real incentive). The lady is sure that Tom will not reveal their relationship to Sophia, and she is satisfied, under the circumstances, to take second place in his affections. "She was, indeed, well convinced that Sophia possessed the first place in Jones's affections; and yet, haughty and amorous as this lady was, she submitted at last to bear the second place; or, to express it more properly in a legal phrase, was contented with the possession of that of which another woman had the reversion" (p. 300a).

She takes steps, however, to get Sophia out of the way through a proper marriage to a highborn peer, Lord Fellamar. When Sophia rejects his suit, Lady Bellaston induces him to assure himself of winning Sophia's hand by raping her and thus making marriage to him necessary for her. The peer is on the point of accomplishing what Fielding calls "his villainy" when the loud voice of Squire Western comes bellowing through the house, demanding to see his daughter. The squire, drunk as well as angry, bursts into the room, not noticing the "amazed, affrighted, vexed, and ashamed" Lord Fellamar, and proceeds to a profane scolding of his daughter and the demand that she marry Blifil. Fellamar fatuously thinks it is he that the squire has in mind, but the choleric and profane father, who detests city peers, soon disabuses him of that notion. " 'You are a son of a b——,' replied the squire, 'for all your laced coat. You my son-in-law, and be d——n'd to you! . . . I'll teach you to father-in-law me' " (p. 323c). Sophia again becomes a prisoner, this time in her father's lodgings in London.

Mrs. Honour rushes to Tom to tell him about this new turn of events, and now it is she who has to hide behind the bed, as Lady Bellaston comes to visit Tom and sits down on the bed. It is a very embarrassing situation for Tom as the lady wants to make love and he is not free to respond, with Mrs. Honour ensconced behind the bed. At this moment Nightingale, a fellow lodger of Tom's, intrudes, and Tom rushes to the door and escorts him to his own room so that he will not see Lady Bellaston sitting on the bed. When he gets back, there is the devil to pay, for the alarmed Lady Bellaston has hidden behind the bed, to find her hiding place already occupied by Mrs. Honour. Despite insults exchanged between the two women in the heat of the moment, they come to an amicable understanding, and Mrs. Honour, just discharged as Sophia's maid by Squire Western, enters the employ of Lady Bellaston, who wants to keep her silent about what she has discovered.

Lady Bellaston, in spite of her deep embarrassment and humiliation, sends Tom tender love letters begging him to come to see her, but he is moved to disgust with her by Nightingale's portrait of her as a loose woman who habitually "debauches" and supports young men whom she finds attractive. Nightingale provides him with the "handsome pretence" he needs to put an end to the affair, so that he may devote himself solely to the pure and perfect Sophia. This pretense is to propose marriage to the lady, the one price she is unwilling to pay for love. (See p. 352d.) Tom, with some trepidation lest she accept, writes her a letter proposing marriage. She is deeply offended and breaks off all relations with him. Her last note says: "I see you are a villain! and I despise you from my soul. If you come here I shall not be at home" (p. 332d). So inspired is Tom by this heroic action of giving up a good provider that he politely rejects an offer of marriage from a well-to-do widow who is attracted to him. (See Book XV, Ch. 11.)

Sophia is now living with her aunt, Mrs. Western, who has given her freedom on condition that she not try to see Tom. Sophia writes to Tom to tell him that she will not marry against her father's wishes and to recall her promise that she will never marry any other man. Tom, in spite of his declaration that all he wants is Sophia's happiness, is very glad to hear this, for he is no Platonic lover, and he does not want anyone else to have her. (See p. 346d.)

Events mount to a climax, as Mr. Allworthy comes to town with Blifil who still seeks Sophia's hand. Lady Bellaston is set on ruining Tom and preventing Sophia from having him—"a woman who hath once been pleased with the possession of a man, will go above halfway to the devil, to prevent any other woman from enjoying the same," observes Fielding (p. 353a). She induces Mrs. Western to urge Fellamar's suit now instead of Blifil's, and she presents Mrs. Western with Tom's letter of proposal to turn Sophia against Tom.

At this moment, when his enemies are scheming for his frustration and downfall and Tom needs all his luck, he is undone by an accident. He visits Mrs. Fitzpatrick, Sophia's cousin, in the hope of getting some aid in his pursuit of Sophia, and is attacked by her jealous husband as he steps outside her door. Captain Fitzpatrick is badly injured in the ensuing sword fight and Tom is imprisoned, facing possible murder charges and hanging. At this dark moment, Tom gets a letter from Sophia telling him she has just seen his letter proposing marriage to Lady Bellaston, and she cannot forgive his deceit— "All I desire is, that your name may never more be mentioned to [me]." Fielding remarks that "his misery was such that even Thwackum would almost have pitied him" (p. 356d).

Our genial author announces that he is now faced with a difficult task which he cannot promise to accomplish: "to bring our favourites out of their present anguish and distress, and to land them at last on the shore of happiness" (p. 357b). On Tom's side are Partridge, Nightingale, and Mrs. Miller, Tom's landlady in London, who is an old friend and beneficiary of Allworthy. Allworthy, with Blifil, is staying at her place in London, and she constantly proclaims Tom's virtues, attested by many good deeds he has done for her, her daughter, Nightingale, and others. She also brings a letter of Tom's to Sophia and pleads on his behalf. Squire Western, however, dances with joy at the news that Tom has committed murder and is likely to hang. Thus he will no longer be able to frustrate the squire's plans to marry off Sophia to Blifil.

Mrs. Waters, the lady with whom Tom spent the night at Upton, now turns up again. She visits him in prison, to bring him the good news that Fitzpatrick, with whom she has been consorting, is out of danger, and admits that he was the aggressor in the fight. It seems certain now that Tom will be cleared, and despite Sophia's apparent resolution to have nothing more to do with him, things seem bright again—but not for long. Through Mrs. Waters he has received the information necessary for legal acquittal; through her also he comes to feel deep moral guilt. Partridge—who through various accidents had never seen Mrs. Waters at Upton—has just seen her exit from Tom's cell. Pale as a ghost, hair standing on end, and trembling in every limb, Partridge enters and asks Tom,

. . . "was that woman who is just gone out the woman who was with you at Upton?" "She was, Partridge," cried Jones. "And did you really, sir, go to bed with that woman?" said he, trembling.—"I am afraid what past between us is no secret," said Jones.—"Nay, but pray, sir, for Heaven's sake, sir, answer me," cries Partridge. "You know I did," cries Jones. "Why then, the Lord have mercy upon your soul, and forgive you," cries Partridge; "but as sure as I stand here alive, you have been a-bed with your own mother." (p. 375b-c)

Tom is horrified and crushed by the news. Partridge has recognized that Mrs. Waters is Jenny Jones, his former maid-servant and Tom's acknowledged mother.

Here the center of action shifts to Allworthy, around whom the final denouement of the story takes place. Things begin to fall into place. A deathbed letter from the philosopher Square reveals to Allworthy what really happened the night of his illness, when Tom got drunk and went into the bushes with Molly, and it extols Tom's real character. Dowling, engaged in various affairs for Allworthy and Blifil, enters the story again. Blifil hired Dowling to cook up false evidence against Tom in the expected murder case, but this does not become clear to Allworthy until he has his conversation with Mrs. Waters in which everything is cleared up. (See Book XVII, Ch. 7.)

She reveals to Allworthy that the real father of Tom Jones was a university student named Summer, a protégé of All-worthy's who is now dead, and that Tom's mother was Allworthy's sister, Bridget. Bridget had paid Jenny Jones to take the blame and thus had been able to have her baby in her own home without incurring suspicion. Mrs. Waters also reveals that Dowling has visited her with the offer to finance the prosecution of Tom, should Fitzpatrick die. Allworthy exclaims on the wonderous ways in which "the blackest and deepest villainy sometimes [is] discovered!" Dowling, who admits to Allworthy that he has been Blifil's agent in this matter, also tells how he delivered the deathbed message from Bridget, informing Allworthy that Tom Jones was her son, to Blifil on the night of Allworthy's illness. Mr. Allworthy finally admits that Tom Jones has been wronged and complains that he has been deceived by one who is "the worst of villains." The "discovery" passage ends with this remark by Allworthy to Blifil as he leaves the house, " 'Harkee, sir, do you find out, before my return, the letter which your mother sent me on her death-bed.' Allworthy then departed, and left Blifil in a situation to be envied only by a man who is just going to be hanged" (p. 391b).

The story ends with a complete "reversal." Tom is installed as Allworthy's heir and Blifil is repudiated, owing his income to Tom's generosity. Squire Western now accepts Tom as a worthy and desirable match for his daughter, and even presses the match upon her when she tries to put Tom through an agony of delay in requital for his escapades; "I took thee for another person," he assures Tom. This is also Lord Fellamar's explanation when he finds that the young man whom he was going to press into service at sea at Lady Bellaston's suggestion is of "good" connection. Sophia, despite her reprobation of Tom as a "good-natured libertine," accepts his protestation of reform and sole fidelity to her henceforth. So Tom and Sophia are married and the history of Tom Jones ends in consummate happiness, greater than he possessed before the malevolence of others and his own weaknesses brought him down.

All were happy, but those the most who had been most unhappy before. Their former sufferings and fears gave such a relish to their felicity, as even love and fortune, in their fullest flow, could not have given without the advantage of such a comparison. (p. 403d)

VI

Before we enter into a discussion of the manner in which Fielding has told this story, let us see what Fielding himself has to offer in the way of literary criticism.

In the first chapter of the book, Fielding tells us that the subject of the novelist is human nature, and that discerning judgment and great art are required to find true human nature and set it forth properly. Fielding compares the skillful writer with the good cook who knows how to prepare food invitingly. And the writer, not the critic, he insists, is the best judge of how to do this. Indeed, Fielding claims to be "the founder of a new province of writing," where he alone makes the laws, without being "accountable to any court of critical jurisdiction" (p. 20a). He insists on the selectivity that emphasizes those events which are most interesting or important for the story, summarizing the events of years in a few words and taking whole chapters to describe the events of a day or an hour. (See Book II, Ch. 1.) The titles of Books IV-VXIII inform us of the amount of time covered in each book. Fielding also points out how actions may be foreseen from character, and the acute penetration required on the part of the reader in order to infer action from character. (See p. 35d.) To go further, we may see men as actors on life's stage, playing the role of villain, hero, or fool, sometimes alternating these roles like actors in a repertory group. (See Book VII, Ch. 1.)

The novelist must keep within the limits of possibility and probability. The historian who narrates public events that actually took place must record them, even when they are improbable. The novelist must not only depict actions that are generally possible for human beings, but actions that are fitting and probable for the particular characters in his story. Fielding objects to dramas in which characters who have been rogues and hussies through four acts suddenly change into virtuous gentlemen and ladies in the fifth act. Within the limits of faithfulness to character, however, it is proper and good for the novelist to deal with extraordinary events that arouse interest, " 'to join the credible with the surprizing.' " (See Book VIII, Ch. 1.)

This kind of writing, "one of the most useful as well as entertaining of all kinds of writing," requires the highest and most unusual mental qualities. The novelist must have the natural gifts of invention (which for Fielding is discovery rather than origination) and judgment (the discerning of distinctions). To these he must add the widest learning in history and belles-lettres and a good deal of experience of the world and men, for the writer's best source for his depiction of human nature is life and not books. Finally, the novelist must have "a good heart, and be capable of feeling." He must feel the distressing or ridiculous scene he is portraying, in order to make the reader weep or laugh. (See Book XIV, Ch. 1; Book IX, Ch. 1.)

Fielding carries on a running fight with literary critics all the way through the book, calling them "reptiles," "slanderers," and worse. His main complaint is that they are ignorantly setting themselves up as judges and legislators in a realm where they are not competent to judge. They claim to set up laws for writers instead of describing the laws to be found in actual writings. The critic should be a mere clerk transcribing the laws that great literary geniuses proclaim in their works. Otherwise he falls into the absurd role of prescribing what the writer must or must not do, concocting rules about the unities of time, place, etc., which no sensible author pays the least attention to. (See Book V, Ch. 1; Book X, Ch. 1; Book XI, Ch. 1.)

Parodies of Homer run all through the book. A wonderful instance of this is the story of the battle royal between Molly and other women, "sung by the muse in the Homerican stile," in Book IV, Chapter 8. See also the invocation in Book XIII, Chapter 1, which includes the list of comic writers—among them are these contributors to our Reading Plans, *Imaginative Literature I* and *II:* Aristophanes, Cervantes, Rabelais, and Shakespeare. Fielding sees himself as a "comic" novelist, that is, a novelist, of "low" rather than of "high" society, for the simple reason that low society is much more interesting, humorous, and entertaining.

One of the most memorable passages on the enjoyment of literature is the scene where the naïve Partridge attends a performance of *Hamlet*. The opening scene where Hamlet en-

counters his father's ghost holds Partridge spellbound; he partic-
ipates wholly in what takes place on the stage, "the same
passions which succeeded each other in Hamlet, succeeding
likewise in him." He explains to Tom that he is not really
frightened by the actor playing the ghost, but partakes sym-
pathetically in the feelings portrayed by the actor playing
Hamlet—"when I saw the little man so frightened himself, it
was that which took hold of me." Partridge believes that the
fear and sorrow of the stage Hamlet are real emotions, not
merely put on, for they are the same emotions he would feel
in such a situation. He advises and cautions Hamlet as the
play goes on. In order not to panic at his own fright of the
ghost, he keeps saying, "I know it is only a play." But in the
scene where Hamlet confronts his mother, Partridge urges
him to shake the life out of that adulterous woman. Indeed,
because he identifies so completely with Hamlet, he believes
that the role requires little acting ability—for he, Partridge, or
any good man would have acted the same in his situation. He
considers the actor with the clear, loud diction, who plays the
king, by far the best performer.

VII

Is Tom Jones worthy of being the hero?

Thackeray, the English novelist and critic, said: "A hero
with a flawed reputation, a hero sponging for a guinea, a hero
who cannot pay his landlady, and is obliged to let his honor out
to hire, is absurd, and the claim of Tom Jones to heroic rank is
quite untenable." Is Tom Jones so morally unworthy that you
cannot accept him as a hero, identify with him, and espouse
his cause? Is he "an accomplished blackguard," as Lord Byron
called him? Or is he a good man, with obvious weaknesses, the
type of character Fielding has suggested in his critical passages?

For Fielding, Tom Jones is a hero and Blifil a villain. What
is there about the characters of these two persons, as he portrays them, that justifies Fielding's attitude? What virtues does
Tom possess that Blifil lacks? What vices does Blifil have that

Tom is free from? Sophia in a moment of exasperation calls Tom "a good-natured libertine." Could either the adjective or the noun apply to Blifil? How can "a good-natured libertine" be a hero?

We must go on to inquire what the hero of a story like this— a "comic novel" or "prosai-comi-epic writing"—must be like. Must he be a model of virtue, a heroic figure in the old tragic and epic sense? Or should he be a man on the ordinary level of humankind with common failings? What kind of defects would alienate you from Tom so that he could not be your hero? If Tom were habitually cruel, malicious, and vindictive, could he still be a hero? Does Tom's acceptance of Lady Bellaston's payments for his making love to her—his becoming a "gigolo" or "kept man," in effect—shock and alienate you? Or do you accept it as in character for Tom in the circumstances?

We must also raise once again the question of whether the hero must be the initiator of action and decisive in the resolution of the problems he faces. How does Tom come out on this score? Is it he or the force of circumstance, accident, and other people's actions that spins the plot and brings it to its conclusion? Does Tom take the initiative in his amorous episodes or, rather, merely respond to the lady's desires?

Fielding expounds openly on the role of accident in this story, as in life, "where the greatest events are produced by a nice train of little circumstances" (p. 376a; see also pp. 377c, 387c). Does accident, "Fortune," or circumstance play the same role in this novel, and affect its hero in the same way, as does Fate, Destiny, or the will of the gods in the old Greek epics and tragedies? Is a hero who both acts and is acted upon closer to the real life that Fielding claims he is describing?

Note that although Fielding shows accidents or feminine wiles as the causes of Tom's amorous missteps, he also ascribes a "gallant" quality to Tom's masculine responses. He says about Tom's reaction to Molly's seductiveness, "the youth must have had very much or very little of the heroe if her endeavours had proved unsuccessful" (p. 58d). Tom himself continually regards it as a principle of honor or gallantry to respond ardently to a willing lady's advances. Does Fielding want us to take this form of virility as a virtue in a healthy, normal young man?

Can you see Squire Western or Allworthy or Partridge as the hero of a novel? Could Mrs. Western, Mrs. Waters, or Lady Bellaston be heroines?

Does the interest of this novel depend on the mystery of Tom's parentage?

Many serious critics have asserted that *Tom Jones* is a great mystery story, in which the puzzle of Tom's parentage is raised at the very beginning and not solved until the final chapters. They see the story as a masterful composition in which the original problem becomes more and more complicated, its solution is successfully concealed, and interest continually mounts until the explanation is revealed in the final chapters.

Is the "mystery" the main interest of the story for you? Does Fielding make it central to the unfolding of the story? Is this the subject of the "history" of Tom Jones? Is Tom himself concerned about the identity of his parents? Is it shown as of interest to the other characters, except insofar as it is dubious and probably "base"? Finally, is the story enjoyable and interesting to you, once the "mystery" is solved? Would you enjoy reading it again, knowing the "solution"?

What part does the mystery play in the plot of *Tom Jones?* Is the mystery of Tom's parentage essential to the story, so that the plot could not stand without it? Suppose the mystery were solved early in the book. Would Tom have had the adventures and trials that make up the story? Suppose it were never solved at all or not solved in the way it is; would the story hang together, with all its parts contributing to the effect of the whole? Suppose Fielding had constantly maintained our interest in the mystery, making it a central concern throughout the book. What would the effect be on our appreciation of the story?

Is Fielding playing fair in setting up the details of the mystery and its solution? The mystery throughout the book, once Partridge has been eliminated as a candidate, is the identity of Tom's father. Jenny Jones confesses that she is the mother, and the reader is persuaded by the author to leave it at that. In the end, his father turns out to be someone who has never figured in the novel, even in retrospect, conversation, or the narrator's hint. Would this be "fair play" in a mystery novel? Of what significance is it to bring in a character of whom the reader could not possibly have been aware?

What can we say about the identity of Tom's mother? Does Bridget Allworthy play an important role in the early books of the novel? Are there any hints there that she has other than a distant attitude toward the foundling? Is it necessary for the story that she be an Allworthy? What purpose is served by Bridget's marriage to Captain Blifil? This complicates things immeasurably for Tom and raises up an enemy and a rival in young Blifil. The story depends on this complication. But why does Bridget make this error and enter into a marriage with a person whom she does not really like, as it turns out? In Fielding's own terms, is it probable? Is it in character? Does he give us any hint of why she may have taken this ill-advised step?

Does the action flow from the characters?

Fielding tells us in one of his critical passages in the book that character determines action. Is this true of the characters and events of *Tom Jones?* Suppose Tom were prudent, sensible, careful, and discreet in his words and actions. Could this novel have the plot it does? Would he have gotten drunk the night of Allworthy's illness and recovery? Would he have naïvely trusted in Blifil's good intentions? Would he have gotten into all his troubles with women? What of Blifil? Does his cold, egotistical character affect the course of events? And what of Allworthy's combination of sweet benevolence and blind judgment? Is this kind of character essential to starting the "history" of Tom Jones, and making the plot go? Can you imagine a thoughtful and sensitive Squire Western in this story? Is his bullheaded insensitivity essential to Sophia's troubles?

We take for granted the importance of the members of the Allworthy and Western families in the story, but what is there in Partridge's character that makes him loom so large in the story? Does Fielding give him so much attention because he plays an essential, functional, and dynamic role in the development of the plot? Or is there something of inherent value in Partridge's character, aside from any role he may play in the incidents of the story? Does he add something akin to what the fools add in Shakespeare's plays? Is the analogy with Cervantes' Sancho Panza really accurate here? Is Partridge a foil to Tom —a timid good nature versus a wild good nature? Or does the value lie in the bubbling humor and delightfulness of the character?

Does the value of characters like Squire Western, Mrs. Western, and Mrs. Honour lie in their contribution to the comic quality of *Tom Jones* as well as to the development of the plot?

What part, if any, does the Man of the Hill play in the story? Why does Fielding devote six chapters to him and to his "history"? Is it merely a relapse into the traditional digression of earlier fiction writers? Or is it a play within the play, with some significance for the main story?

What is the role of social structure and manners in the story?

The characters in *Tom Jones* are not only individual persons. They are, as Fielding himself points out, social types as well. How does this affect the story? What is the social significance of the fact that Tom Jones is a foundling? How does it affect his prospects of a union with Sophia Western? Is the anger of her father or the shock of Allworthy at the news of the love between Tom and Sophia merely an individual reaction? What, then, makes Squire Western and Lord Fellamar change their views of Tom's "person" when his parentage becomes known? But does Allworthy change his views of Tom only because of Tom's newly discovered lineage?

Could the story of *Tom Jones* be set in present-day American society? Or are American attitudes toward ancestry and social status more fluid and relaxed? Suppose the Allworthy and Western families were well-to-do farmers in the Middle West. Would the foundling Tom Jones have the same problem in winning consent to a marriage with Sophia? Or do we have to put the Allworthys and the Westerns on adjoining estates on Long Island to maintain the leisure-class analogy? Would Tom have a problem on Long Island or on Chicago's North Shore?

For a possible analogy in American fiction with the history of Tom Jones, see Saul Bellow's novel, *The Adventures of Augie March.*

Do you resent or welcome the author's entering into the story?

One of the major tendencies among novelists in the twentieth century has been to take the author out of the story; that is, to tell the story solely through objective narration, dramatization, and dialogue, obtaining the desired effect through skillful craftsmanship and style, but without letting the author "intrude" to speak in his own person. Fielding, however, purposely intrudes and insists it is his right to do so. He takes the role of the omniscient narrator who will point out things that the reader cannot discern for himself—not only events but also motivations. Fielding goes into detailed analyses and explanations of why Tom, Sophia, Blifil, and the other characters act as they do on certain occasions. He continually advises us, gives us "tips" on the events and characters. He often makes statements, amounting to little essays, rather than present what he has to convey in action and dialogue—he states rather than dramatizes.

Do Fielding's "intrusions" add or detract from your appreciation and enjoyment? Would you rather have a "purer" method of storytelling, in which we listen and watch the characters, without being aware of the author's presence? Is there any other way of presenting what is going on in a character's mind, besides direct statements and analytical essays? Can it be suggested in action and dialogue? Is it possible to present a character's mental processes directly from the character's viewpoint rather than indirectly through an omniscient narrator's statements?

Obviously Fielding uses both dramatic presentation and narrative statements through the book. Is there any discernible principle in his variation between the two methods in particular passages? Does he ever resort to subtle hints and allusions to convey implications of the story?

Do the introductory chapters at the beginning of every book add something essential to the book, or do you think they are out of place in a work of fiction?

What do you think of Fielding's style? Is it enjoyable to read? Does it illuminate meanings? Does it add to your appreciation of the uses and virtues of the English language? Is it archaic, anachronistic, too "dated" for the present-day reader?

The following questions are designed to help you test the thoroughness of your reading. Each question is to be answered by giving a page or pages of the reading assignment. Answers will be found on page 248 of this Reading Plan.

1 Who makes the "great discovery" that Jenny Jones is the foundling's mother?

2 How does Captain Blifil act on the devil's maxim to "kick the stool from under you," once you are up in the world?

3 To what famous painting does Fielding refer to describe the appearance of Mrs. Partridge and Parson Thwackum?

4 How does young Tom's association with the gamekeeper get him into trouble?

5 Whose sentiments are these—"I had rather be anything than a courtier, and a Presbyterian, and a Hanoverian too"?

6 Who picked up Tom's pocketbook with the five-hundred-pound "stake"?

7 How does Ensign Northerton figure in the affairs of Tom Jones and Mrs. Waters?

8 What is the story of Mrs. Fitzpatrick?

9 Who is Jenny Cameron?

10 Who is Mr. Anderson?

GOETHE

Faust

Vol. 47

Goethe is for the world of the nineteenth and twentieth centuries what Homer, Dante, and Shakespeare were for the Western world of earlier ages. He is one of those giants of the poetic art who have created masterpieces of universal significance and enduring enjoyment. He is also a great national poet, with a preeminent value for the German people and for German literature. Goethe's work is a rare combination of the entertaining and the profound, of gay humor and heavy seriousness. In *Faust*, this great master of lyric poetry devoted his talents to an ambitiously broad and deep portrayal of the human condition and destiny.

But Goethe the man is as important as Goethe the poet. To be or become himself was for Goethe his primary creative activity, as salient or even more so than writing books. This many-sided genius has been called the last "universal man" of the Western world. Poet, novelist, prime minister, scientist, artist, critic, theatrical director, lover, philosopher, conversationalist extraordinary—he bestrode his age like a colossus. He was the great figure of his time, a kind of "Olympian" personage, to whom men journeyed from all over Europe to pay homage. The late Thomas Mann said that in the old days German schoolboys learned about Goethe's love affairs as if he were Zeus. Wilhelm von Humboldt noted that Goethe's main influence and importance lie in his existence, in his being Goethe, "entirely apart from his creative work as a thinker and writer."

Goethe's works expressed his experience and thought in the various phases of his life. He lives for us now in these works. And into his masterwork, *Faust*—which took sixty years to complete—he put all that he wanted to say about the depths and heights of human existence, based on the experience and thought of a lifetime. This tremendous pageant of the journey of the human soul through life seems to have everything in it: tender romance, slapstick comedy, philosophic wisdom, religious piety, mordant cynicism, scientific theory, the experience of evil and suffering, and ultimate joy and salvation. Goethe welds the Greek, the Gothic, and the modern phases of Western culture into a poetic whole, which unites the past and the present and points to the future.

This vast, many-faceted work has had a great influence on the modern mind. From its celebration of the ever aspiring and struggling spirit of man has come the term "Faustian" for ages, cultures, and personalities. It has provided man with a new image of himself. Jacob Burckhardt says that "*Faust* is a genuine myth, *i.e.*, a great primordial image, in which every man has to discover his own being and destiny in his own way." To understand *Faust* each reader must open his heart and mind to the vision of the world and man that Goethe created in this work.

Fourth Reading

I

Johann Wolfgang von Goethe was the greatest writer of the golden age of German literature. The great creative spurt in German imaginative writing came in the eighteenth century, after three hundred years of religious conflict, including the devastating Thirty Years' War. German literature, which had been skipped by the Renaissance, now had its own Renaissance and became a central element of European and world literature.

This fresh, new national literature combined the seemingly polar elements of Classicism and Romanticism, embodying ancient ideas and values with those of the modern age. Romanticism, the great new creative force in European literature in the eighteenth and nineteenth centuries, was a reaction against a modern form of Classicism, called Neoclassicism (new classicism). Neoclassicism, which arose in France in the seventeenth century, aimed to imitate the clarity and simplicity of the ancient Greek and Latin classics. It sought a literature in which decorum and correctness according to fixed rules prevailed. Inspired by the rationalism of the new science and philosophy of the age (Newton, Descartes, etc.), it emphasized intellectual perfection—the witty thought perfectly expressed in an elegant phrase—rather than imaginative color or feeling. In form, Neoclassicism fostered formally correct, elegant, urbane expression. In thought, it emphasized an 'unsentimental realism, which viewed certain characteristics of human nature as permanent and universal, and did not consider the individual variations important or interesting. (The French Neoclassical tragedians put the ancient Greeks into seventeenth-century French clothing.)

The great Neoclassical literature was that of the French writers of the seventeenth century—Molière, Racine, Corneille, La Fontaine, etc.—and their influence extended to the latter half of the eighteenth century. In England, the Neoclassical period came in the eighteenth century and was represented by Alexander Pope, Addison and Steele, Samuel Johnson, and other writers of the so-called Augustan Age of English letters. It was in England that the reaction against Neoclassicism, called Romanticism, originated among such poets as James Thomson, Thomas Gray, William Cowper, Robert Burns, and William Blake. From England the revolt spread to France, Germany, and Italy. The French philosopher Jean Jacques Rousseau was the greatest single intellectual influence on the Romantic movement.

The Romantics espoused imagination, feeling, passion, vitality, nature, and individuality, as against the decorum, rules, and universality of the Neoclassicists. The Romantics emphasized the inner depths of the human soul and the immensities of the natural world, the expression of intimate personal experience, of joy, and especially of melancholy and suffering. For the Neoclassicists the dominating attitude was rational detachment; for the Romantics it was sensitive involvement. The Neoclassicists stressed the values and forms of European civilization and urban, advanced, Western society. The Romantics stressed the natural, the primitive, the medieval, the oriental, the ancient, and remote.

Romanticism played a key role in the development of the new German literature. The so-called Storm and Stress period in the 1770's was marked by the Romantic tendencies of the great trio of young writers who were to dominate the literature of their time—Herder, Goethe, and Schiller. But the rise of the new German literature was also characterized by an appreciation and understanding of the ancient classical writers —of the original classics, especially the Greeks, rather than of the modern Neoclassicists, who had formulated a doctrine and rules about them.

Thus the new German literature was heir to the ancient Greco-Roman culture and at the same time influenced by all the new literatures of Europe, at first those written in the Romance languages—Italian, French, and Spanish—and then by English literature, for which the Germans felt an instinctive affinity. Shakespeare, who was considered a "barbarian" by French Neoclassic critics, was a venerated, inspiring figure to the great German writers—"our Shakespeare," they called him.

Goethe, the greatest of the new German writers, illustrates this openness to many varied influences. He believed that paganism and Christianity, ancient and medieval culture, all the creative achievements of artists, scientists, and philosophers were valuable and meaningful, and that they should be assimilated and welded into the culture and thought of the modern world. He aimed at universality in his life and in his work. He considered this assimilative capacity as essential to creative genius. In his last letter, written two weeks before his death, he said:

The best genius is that which absorbs and assimilates everything without doing the least violence to its fundamental destiny—that which we call character—but rather improving and enhancing it as far as possible . . . Through training, instruction, contemplation, success, failure, advancement, hindrance, and ever more contemplation, the organs of man, in their instinctive, free activity, unite the acquired with the innate to produce a harmonious unity that astonishes the world.[1]

This openness to all forms of culture and experience was a Romantic characteristic, as opposed to the Neoclassical sense of limits and concentration on the single, developed line of European culture in a "modern" urban setting. It characterizes Goethe's masterpiece *Faust*.

Goethe practiced this universality and many-sidedness in his life as well as in his writing. This great poet was the main administrator of the petty state of Weimar, dealing with its natural resources, finances, arms, and education. He engaged in serious research in the biological and physical sciences, contributing works on plant metamorphosis and a new theory of colors. And this serious, dedicated man, for whom produc-

[1] *The Permanent Goethe*, ed. Thomas Mann (New York: Dial Press, 1948), pp. 613-614.

tive genius meant the taking of infinite pains, was also a great lover of women. His love affairs marked significant high points or low points in his life, and they were often reflected in his works.

Indeed, all these interests, all these activities, all these aspects of life were expressed in his work. Goethe's work is more intimately connected with his life history than that of any of the other major writers of the past—including Dante and Milton. Not only did he strive to make his life a work of art—his greatest work of art—but he regarded the particular forms in which genius takes shape as of secondary importance to the life and source from which it arises. Goethe said, "Whether a man expresses his genius in science or in war, or in government, or whether he composes a song, it is all the same; the only thing that matters is that the idea, the formulation, the act must live and continue to live."

The best sources for a knowledge of Goethe's life are Eckermann's *Conversations with Goethe* and Goethe's autobiography, *Poetry and Truth from My Own Life*. For a modern version of the Faust story see Thomas Mann's novel *Dr. Faustus*. For an application of Goethe's idea of Faust to the history of culture, see Oswald Spengler's *The Decline of the West*.

II

The great work into which Goethe poured his experiences, thoughts, and vision of the human condition was based on the legend of a wandering magician, Dr. Johann Faust (or Faustus). According to the legend, Faust had secured his magical powers through a pact with the Devil, who carried him away to Hell in the end. Apparently such a scholar-magician actually existed in Germany about 1480-1540. Melancthon, the great Lutheran humanist, claimed to have known him personally and witnessed his magical acts.

The original literary source of the Faust legend is a chapbook, or pamphlet, entitled *The History of Dr. Johann Faustus*, published in 1587 at Frankfurt am Main. It describes Faust's erudition, his pact with the devil Mephistopheles (a life of power and pleasure in return for his soul), his magical acts, including the summoning up of Helen of Troy, her bearing him a son, and his being snatched away to Hell.

There were many attempts before Goethe's to put the Faust story into a dramatic form. The most famous of these was Christopher Marlowe's *Doctor Faustus* (about 1588), based on the original Faust chapbook, and one of the gems of English dramatic poetry. In Germany, the Faust story became the subject of folk plays and puppet plays, which were current in Goethe's time. Many eighteenth-century German writers wrote dramas or fiction on the Faust theme, among them the great writer and thinker Gotthold Lessing, Goethe's older contemporary.

Thus the story which Goethe chose as the theme for his crowning work was familiar to the German people of his time. Through his imaginative and intellectual powers, Goethe made of this well-worn plot of wandering players and puppet shows one of the great works of world literature. Goethe's *Faust* became the great national literary work of the German people. Its lines were memorized, its phrases passed into common speech, and its characters became as well known as living acquaintances.

Goethe's *Faust* was the work of a very long lifetime. He conceived the work in his early twenties and finished it just before he died, at the age of eighty-three. He began writing the First Part about 1774 and published the final completed version in 1808. Most of the First Part was completed before 1800. By that time he had already started on the Second Part, which he completed in 1832.

What Goethe put into his work of sixty years becomes evident only through reading it. It contains Goethe's basic notions about man and existence, and is often considered a great philosophical poem ranking with Dante's *Divine Comedy*. Goethe could hardly deny the aesthetic seriousness of his sixty-year work, but he often denied the philosophical or edifying quality that was ascribed to it. He resented the dull seriousness that seeks for weighty themes or abstract ideas in poetry. Speaking in 1827, he said,

They come and ask what idea I meant to embody in my Faust; as if I knew myself, and could inform them. *From heaven, through the world, to hell,* would indeed be something; but this is no idea, only a course of action. And further: that the devil loses the wager, and that a man continually struggling from difficult errors towards something better, should be redeemed, is an effective—and, to many, a good enlightening —thought; but it is no idea at the foundation of the whole, and of every individual scene. It would have been a fine thing indeed if I had strung so rich, varied, and highly diversified a life as I have brought to view in Faust upon the slender string of one pervading idea.

It was, in short, [continued Goethe] not in my line, as a poet to strive to embody anything *abstract*. I received in my mind impressions, and those of a sensuous, animated, charming, varied, hundredfold kind— just as a lively imagination presented them; and I had, as poet, nothing more to do than to round off and elaborate artistically such views and impressions, and by means of a lively representation so to bring them forward that others might receive the same impression in hearing or reading my representation of them.[2]

But, speaking in his eightieth year, Goethe pointed to a fundamental human experience as the theme of Faust:

The commendation which the poem has received far and near may be perhaps owing to this quality, that it permanently preserves the period of development of a human soul which is tormented by all that afflicts mankind, shaken also by all that disturbs it, repelled by all that it finds repellent, and made happy by all that it desires. The author is at present far removed from such conditions; the world likewise has to some extent other struggles to undergo; nevertheless the state of man, in joy and sorrow, remains very much the same, and the latest born will still find cause to acquaint himself with what has been enjoyed and suffered before him in order to adapt himself to that which awaits him.

III

Goethe's *Faust* consists of two parts. Part I deals with Faust's compact with Mephistopheles and his tragic love affair with Gretchen (Goethe's own addition to the Faust story). Part II deals with Faust's exploits in the great world of politics and culture, through a highly complex and symbolic presentation which covers the main stages of Western civilization. Part I consists of twenty-five scenes (not numbered in our edition). Part II is divided into five acts.

[2] Johann Peter Eckermann, *Conversations with Goethe* (New York: Everyman's Library, 1931), pp. 205-206 (May 6, 1827).

Two short scenes precede the beginning of Part I—the Prelude on the Stage and the Prologue in Heaven.

In the Prelude, Goethe deals with the problem of the theatrical producer who wants to present a drama that will have a meaning and at the same time please the audience. (Goethe was himself a theatrical director.) This is a very delightful scene, with the manager, poet, and jester presenting their clashing viewpoints and hinting at a few of the themes in the drama. It ends with the manager's call to stage this cosmic drama of *Faust*.

> Thus in our narrow house of boards preside
> And on through all Creation's circle stride;
> And wander on, with speed considered well,
> From Heaven, through the world, to Hell! (p. 6a)

The second preliminary scene, in imitation of the Book of Job, shows Mephistopheles wagering that he can tempt the Lord's servant Faust to follow evil. The Lord agrees to the wager, pointing out that man needs "the spirits of negation" to stir him to creative activity. The Lord is not disturbed at Faust's present confused and restless state. "Man errs as long as he doth strive," and yet, if he is good, "Remains aware that there is one right way." This notion that human striving and error lead to ultimate rightness is a basic theme of *Faust*.

As Part I opens, Faust is seen in his musty chamber, proclaiming his frustration at his state of ignorance despite his long pursuit of scientific knowledge. He has now turned to magic arts in order to learn the ultimate structure of the universe. But here too he encounters disappointment. When he contemplates the sign of the Macrocosm (the "great world," or the universe, as contrasted with the "little world," or man), he sees into the very essence of things, but he turns away, frustrated anew. What he sees through contemplation is a mere show, "pageantry," with which he can have no intimate contact. He feels hemmed in by his narrow, musty room, full of dusty books and instruments, with "each impulse to live . . . repressed," and longs for "Nature's living sphere."

Hoping to fulfill his need, he now calls on the Earth-Spirit, which stands for the ever fluctuating forces of the physical universe, "An infinite sea." But again he is disappointed, for the Earth-Spirit, which appears in response to his summons, rejects his claim to kinship: "Thou art like the spirit thou canst comprehend,/Not me!" Faust is depressed to the point of despair at the realization that he who has presumed to see into ultimate things and to be at one with nature is a mere puny human being, lacking the power and the constancy to attain what his mind conceives.

> I am not like the gods! Feel it I must.
> I'm like the worm that burrows through the dust, (p. 17b)

Convinced that the only rational and dignified act remaining is to commit suicide, he puts a goblet of poison to his lips, when he hears the bells and hymns announcing Christ's resurrection and His victory over corruption and death. It is Easter Day, and the unbelieving Faust is called back to life by these "heavenly tones," which remind him of his childhood faith and joy.

The gloom and seriousness of this first scene of the First Part is broken halfway by a humorous conversation between Faust and his "famulus" or attendant, Wagner. Wagner is a dull, plodding fellow who pursues the arts and sciences without any depth of understanding or imagination. He is a caricature of the narrow, pedantic, German culture-vulture, and also of the Hegelian type of philosopher of history. (See Hegel's *Philosophy of History,* Vol. 46.) Faust, his complete spiritual opposite, makes fun of his attempt to gain wisdom through critical scholarship and parchment reading, instead of from his own soul.

In the next scene, outside the town gate, we see and hear the common folk taking their ease on a Sunday-holiday afternoon. Faust enters with Wagner and comments on how the people, like Christ, have risen—they from their slums and factories and narrow streets to the fields and the pleasure boat. He appreciates and envies the common man's joys. Looking on the lovely landscape and the setting sun, Faust is seized with an ardent longing to soar above the earth, but the human condition prevents it.

> Alas! To wings that lift the spirit light
> No earthly wing will ever be a fellow.
> Yet 'tis inborn in everyone, each fancies
> His feeling presses upward and along, (p. 27a-b)

Wagner confesses that he has never had such a feeling when in the presence of nature, but soon gets bored and would rather be reading a good book, especially a rare parchment. Faust retorts,

> By one impulse alone are you impressed.
> Oh, never learn to know the other!
> Two souls alas! are dwelling in my breast;
> And each is fain to leave its brother.
> The one, fast clinging, to the world adheres
> With clutching organs, in love's sturdy lust;
> The other strongly lifts itself from dust
> To yonder high, ancestral spheres. (pp. 27b-28a)

He calls on the spirits to lead him "to new and varied life," and a moment later notices a black poodle running in ever narrowing circles around him and Wagner. Faust fears a magic noose, but the common-sensical Wagner soon convinces him that the poodle is no specter, but only a well-trained dog.

Two scenes in Faust's study follow, and they present the central situation and theme of the drama. Faust enters his study, accompanied by the poodle. Faust is calmed by contact with nature, filled with hope and love, and then plunged into depression again. He turns to the New Testament for consolation, and tries to translate the opening words of the Gospel of John: "In the beginning was the Word." He is not satisfied with the term "Word." He tries "Thought," then "Power," finally hits on "Deed." "In the beginning was the Deed." The primacy of action is a basic notion of *Faust*.

Faust then turns his attention to the poodle, who distracts him with his whining and howling, and suddenly begins to grow and change shape. Through magic incantations Faust brings forth Mephistopheles, dressed as a traveling scholar, who has been "the kernel of the brute." To Faust's question of his identity, he answers that he is

> Part of that Power which would
> The Evil ever do, and ever does the Good . . .

> I am the Spirit that denies!
> And rightly too; for all that doth begin
> Should rightly to destruction run;
> 'Twere better then that nothing were begun.
> Thus everything that you call Sin,
> Destruction—in a word, as Evil represent—
> That is my own, real element. (p. 33a)

He proclaims that he is part of the original nothingness and darkness that existed before anything was created. But he admits that he has had a difficult time annihilating "This Something, this your clumsy world," because of ever-renewed creativity that brings forth new beings. Faust remarks,

> So to that Power never reposing,
> Creative, healing, you're opposing
> Your frigid devil's fist with might and main.
> It's clenched in spite and clenched in vain! (p. 34a)

Mephistopheles wants to continue the argument some other time, but he is caught fast in the magic pentagram on the floor of the study. He puts Faust to sleep through a sensuous song, chanted by spirits, and, as "lord of all the rats and mice," calls on them to gnaw away the point that holds him bound. When Faust awakes, he thinks the appearance of the Devil has been a dream or illusion.

But Mephistopheles returns in the next scene, dressed like a noble squire, and invites Faust to come out with him and enjoy life. Faust complains that he is too old to play and too young to accept renunciation. He is bitter over the frustration of human hopes and strivings, and utters

> A curse on Hoping! on Believing!
> And cursed be Patience most of all! (pp. 38b-39a)

A chorus of spirits and Mephistopheles, too, urge him to throw off his sadness and despair and enter into active life again. Faust and Mephistopheles make a contract, whereby Faust will have a life of pleasure on earth in return for service to Mephistopheles hereafter, on one condition—that a moment will come in which Faust will find complete fulfillment. Says Faust:

> If to the moment I shall ever say:
> "Ah, linger on, thou art so fair!"

> Then may you fetters on me lay,
> Then will I perish, then and there! (p. 41a)

But there are limits to what Faust may experience, even when he has the Devil as an aide. He cannot know all the experience of mankind, expand his self to include all selves. This is a divine capacity, beyond human power, Mephistopheles warns. He advises Faust to seek this from a poet, who through his imagination is "Mr. Microcosm," rather than from diabolic powers. He stresses that Faust is what he is, and nothing more —a particular, finite human being.

Mephistopheles appeals to Faust to leave dry reflection for the richness of concrete life. In a soliloquy he reveals to the audience what is behind his appeal, and his judgment of Faust's character.

> Humanity's most lofty power,
> Reason and knowledge, pray despise!
> Let but the Spirit of all Lies
> With works of dazzling magic blind you;
> Then, absolutely mine, I'll have and bind you!
> To him has Fate a spirit given
> That, uncurbed, ever onward sweeps,
> Whose striving, by too hasty impulse driven,
> The joys of this earth overleaps.
> Him will I drag through wild life whirling past,
> Through all that is unmeaning, shallow stuff; (p. 44a-b)

In an amusing passage, Mephistopheles dons Faust's professorial garb and advises a student on his course of studies. He exposes the main subjects of the university curriculum to biting satire, portraying logic, metaphysics, law, theology, and medicine as useless, shallow, or dangerous disciplines. He concludes his advice thus:

> Dear friend, all theory is grey,
> And green the golden tree of life. (p. 48a)

And he writes this verse in the grateful student's album: "Ye shall be as God, know good and evil."

IV

The above scene ends with Mephistopheles taking Faust off on his cloak, which is to carry them through the air to "the little world" and "the great." The rest of Part I is for the most part a journey through "the little world" of ordinary human interests and centers on the love affair between Faust and Gretchen. Two extraordinary events occur: Faust's youth is restored through a magic elixir, and he has a vision of Helen of Troy, the image of ideal beauty.

The first stop on the journey is Auerbach's Cellar in Leipzig. (This was an actual inn, which contained murals of the Faust legend.) Faust finds no satisfaction in the coarse drunkenness going on there. The next stop is the witch's kitchen, where Faust is transformed into a youth through a disgusting witch's brew. Apes stir the caldron, roll around a great globe (the world?), and break a crown (reason?). Faust sees in the magic mirror a perfectly beautiful women (Helen?). Mephistopheles says that now he will see a Helena in every girl he meets.

Sure enough, when he meets the maiden Margaret, or Gretchen,[3] on the street, he falls deeply in love with her and insists that Mephistopheles help him to win her. Mephistopheles puts rare jewels in Margaret's room to indicate her admirer's attraction and affects knowledge of the death of her friend Martha's husband in order to bring Faust into contact with her. In a charming scene in Martha's garden, Faust courts Margaret while Mephistopheles attends to Martha. The idealism and tenderness of the young couple are set off by the practicality and cynicism of the older pair.

Faust is in a moral dilemma, for he wants the love of this lovely and virtuous girl, but he is winning it through the aid of evil powers; if he takes advantage of her love, he will ruin her. His predicament is dramatized in a soliloquy and a dialogue with Mephistopheles in the natural setting of forest and cavern. He thanks the "Spirit sublime" which has granted him intimacy with the depths of nature and of his own soul, but his ecstasy in nature is impaired by his consciousness of corruption.

---

[3] "Gretchen" is the familiar for "Margaret" in German. Our translator notes that Goethe usually calls her "Margaret" in the happy scenes and "Gretchen" in the sad scenes, save for the tragic prison scene where she is "Margaret" again. Faust's first name is "Henry."

Oh, that for man naught perfect ever is,
I now do feel. Together with this rapture
That brings me near and nearer to the gods,
Thou gav'st the comrade whom I now no more
Can do without, though, cold and insolent,
He lowers me in my own sight, transforms
With but a word, a breath, thy gifts to nothing.
Within my breast he fans with busy zeal
A savage fire for that fair, lovely form.
Thus from desire I reel on to enjoyment
And in enjoyment languish for desire. (p. 79b)

Mephistopheles rails at him for his withdrawal into gloomy solitude, and pours scorn on his grandiose feelings.

It's more than earthly, such delight!
To lie in night and dew on mountain height,
Embracing earth and heaven blissfully,
Puffing one's self and deeming one a deity;
To burrow through earth's marrow, onward pressed
By prescient impulse, feel within one's breast
All six days' work, in haughty power enjoy and know
I can't tell what, soon all creation overflow
In rapturous love, lost to all sight the child of clay,
And then the lofty intuition
Ending—I dare not say in what fruition! (p. 80b)

He ridicules Faust's moralistic prudishness at the disclosure of his underlying desires. Mephistopheles' talk and the sexual images which he evokes impel Faust to surrender to his passion, even if it means the ruin of Gretchen and himself. He detests himself for what he is about to do.

How am I, in her arms, by Heaven blessed?
Though I grow warm upon her breast,
Do I not always feel her need?
Am I not still the fugitive? unhoused and roaming?
The monster without goal or rest
That like a cataract from rock to rock roared foaming
To the abyss, by greed and frenzy headlong pressed?
She at one side, still with her childlike senses furled,
Upon the alpine meadow in the cottage small,
With all her homely joys and cares, her all,
Within that little world;
And I, the God-detested,

> Not enough had I
> That all the rocks I wrested
> And into pieces made them fly!
> Her did I have to undermine, her peace!
> Thou, Hell, didst have to have this sacrifice!
> Help, Devil, make it brief, this time of agony!
> What must be done, let it at once be so!
> Then may her fate plunge crushing down on me,
> And she with me to ruin go! (pp. 81b–82a)

Gretchen's readiness to give herself to him is revealed in her song at the spinning wheel. But first she questions Faust on his religious belief (which is a kind of pantheism) and expresses her aversion to his companion Mephistopheles, into whose character she sees very acutely.

> For nothing has he any real sympathy;
> It's written on his forehead, one can see
> That in his sight no soul can be dear. (p. 85a)

Faust passes her feeling off as mere "antipathy" toward a "queer bird." So that he may spend the night with Gretchen, he induces her to administer a sleeping potion to her mother.

The next scene reveals that Gretchen is pregnant, regretful for her sin and the public condemnation that will follow, but joyous for the feeling that led her to it. She prays to the Virgin Mary for mercy and salvation. Her brother Valentine is furious at Gretchen's pregnancy, because it will make him the butt of scorn and he will be dishonored by her shame. He tries to kill Faust, but the latter, aided by Mephistopheles' diabolic powers, runs him through mortally before Gretchen's door.

This scene ("Night") conveys a growing sordidness. Just before the duel with Valentine, Faust seeks more jewels to please his mistress, while Mephistopheles, "a sentimental tom-cat," suggests that it would not hurt Faust "To have some pleasure gratis too." Mephistopheles then sings a bawdy song warning maidens not to give in to their lovers until they put a ring on the finger. After the duel, the dying Valentine coarsely curses the sorrowing Gretchen as a common whore, who will soon be the convenience of all the men of the town and end up a pariah "Among beggars and cripples." He also calls Martha a "coupling pimp," then commends himself to God as "a soldier brave," and dies.

In the next scene, at the cathedral, Gretchen is overcome by her sense of guilt at the death of her brother and her mother, who died from the sleeping draught—"Through thee to long, long torment fell asleep."

Preceding the tragic conclusion of the First Part come the Walpurgis Night scenes, at the annual festival of the witches on Mount Brocken in the Hartz Mountains. These scenes are the wildest in the work, throwing together a horde of spirits from legend and from Goethe's imagination, and combining obscene humor, wonderful fantasy, and engaging verse rhythms. Goethe also includes satirical references to contemporary figures, such as Nicolai, the "rump-visionary"—the dry rationalist who advocated getting rid of ghosts by applying leeches to one's rump.

Apparently, Mephistopheles' purpose in bringing Faust to this Witches' Sabbath is to distract him from the tragic reality of human existence—from the results of his affair with Gretchen. But as Faust is dancing with a beautiful young witch, a red mouse jumps out of her mouth, and his pleasure turns to disgust. In that moment he has a vision of Gretchen in chains. When he gets back to the lowlands, in the dismal light of day, he berates Mephistopheles for distracting him with "insipid diversions" while Gretchen languishes in prison. There is a bitter exchange between Faust and Mephistopheles, who regards Gretchen as just one more fallen soul among thousands, and who reproves Faust for now trying to renounce the compionship with the powers of evil into which he had freely entered. Mephistopheles agrees, however, to help Faust free Gretchen from prison. Notice that this scene is in prose, symbolizing the sudden change from the mood of Walpurgis Night.

In the prison Faust finds Gretchen in an insane state, possessed with guilt and remorse, for she has drowned their child. Her sad, mad songs give a poignancy to the scene that reminds us of Ophelia in Shakespeare's *Hamlet*. "Torn lies the wreath," she laments, "scattered the flowers are." When she comes to her senses and recognizes Faust, she is overjoyed and full of love for him. But she feels too fettered by her bonds of sin and guilt to flee with him. "I dare not go," she says, "for me there's no hope any more." The images of her child drowning and of her mother falling into eternal sleep torment her. "I have done all for love of you," she tells Faust. She foresees the scene of her execution (by beheading).

When Mephistopheles comes to take Faust away, she urges that the evil one be thrust out from "this holy place." She calls on the heavenly hosts to protect her and to express her aversion for Faust, who is profaned by his contact with Mephistopheles.

> *Margaret.* . . . Henry! I shrink from you!
> *Mephistopheles.* She is judged!
> *A Voice [from above].* She is saved!
> *Mephistopheles [to* FAUST]. Here to me!
> *He disappears with* FAUST.
> *A Voice [from within, dying away].* Henry! Henry! (p. 114b)

V

In Part I, Faust has journeyed through the "little world" of private life and love. In Part II, he enters the world-historical stage of civilization and culture. Acts I-III of Part II deal with the fusion of the Classical and Romantic spiritual attitudes, of the ancient Greek and the modern German cultures, symbolized in the marriage of Faust and Helen. Acts IV-V deal with the productivity of man and his conquest of nature, symbolized by Faust's project of draining the marshes and reclaiming the land from the sea. Compared to the unity, simplicity, and singleness of theme of Part I, the Second Part is extremely complex and rich with symbolic meanings.

As Part II opens, Faust is sleeping in a pleasant landscape. Beneficent spirits or elves soothe Faust's wounded soul, attempting to raise him from despair and remorse to bold and intelligent action. Faust awakens, filled with joy in nature and imbued with the resolve for "Unceasing strife." He recognizes his limits now, symbolized by his turning away from the fierce flame of the sun to gaze on the waterfall with its thousand streams and the rainbow that emerges from its foam and mist. "The many-coloured rainbow's changeful being . . . mirrors human aims and action . . . Life is but light in many-hued reflection" (p. 117b).

The scene shifts to a meeting of the State Council with the Emperor. Mephistopheles, appearing as the new court fool, suggests that mining for hidden gold will solve all political problems, providing it is directed by "A man endowed with Mind's and Nature's might." Next there is a gay masquerade party, at which Faust appears as Plutus, the god of wealth, and Mephistopheles as Avarice. They arrive in a chariot driven by a boy who symbolizes Poetry. The Emperor's beard catches fire when he gets too close to Faust's magic treasure chest, and Faust proves his magic powers by putting the fire out. The Emperor is so sure of Faust's magical capacity that he issues paper money which is backed by the gold that has not yet been mined. The people meet the inflationary measure with shallow and greedy eagerness.

Faust's next commission from the Emperor is to summon up Paris and Helena as the ideal models of man and woman. To do so he must first descend to "the Mothers"—the primeval sources of all things—to the boundless void beyond existence, out of which come continual formation, transformation, re-creation. Faust shudders at the mention of "the Mothers." Mephistopheles remarks offhandedly as Faust goes down, "Will he come back? I'm curious to see." Faust does return with Paris and Helena, whom he presents in a pageant to an audience that is carping and critical, instead of appreciative of the ancient archetypal ideal. Faust, trying to take Helena for himself, causes an explosion which fells him and dissipates the ancient archetypes.

Act II continues Faust's quest to attain the Classical spirit. It starts out with a scene in Faust's former room, "a high-vaulted, narrow, Gothic chamber," in which the academic life is again held up to ridicule. The green bumpkin whom Mephistopheles lectured in Part I is now a cocksure young Bachelor of Arts, who scorns the wisdom of the ages and thinks that wisdom and understanding began with him. Mephistopheles explains to the audience that the brash collegian will ripen and "wise up" with age.

We also meet Wagner again, now a famous scholar and

scientist engaged in fashioning a Homunculus—an artificial man. In an amusing scene, Wagner argues against Mephistopheles in favor of this new and higher, more rational way of making men, compared with the old chance method of love-making between a man and a woman. "Well, Daddy! how are you?" the new-made man greets Wagner from within the test tube, and he begs to be put to work right away. Homunculus prepares to lead Faust to a *Classical* Walpurgis Night festival. He scorns the Romantic, Northern, Gothic era to which Mephistopheles belongs.

> Of course. You from the North,
> In ages dark and drear brought forth,
> In all the murk of knighthood and of papistry,
> How could your vision, then, be clear and free?
> Only in gloom are you at home.
>
> . . . .
>
> Only romantic ghosts are known to you;
> A ghost that's genuine must be classic too. (pp. 169b-170a)

Mephistopheles admits as much:

> The Greeks were never worth much, it is true,
> Yet their free play of senses dazzles you,
> The heart of man to happy vices winning.
> Gloomy will always seem our ways of sinning. (p. 170b)

The Classical Walpurgis Night scene follows, peopled by the figures of Greek mythology and occurring in Thessaly. It is Goethe's own invention, commemorating the Battle of Pharsalus in 48 B.C., in which Caesar conquered Pompey, thus assuring the empire which Augustus was to rule and which was to transmit Classical culture to the West. Faust wanders up and down the beautiful Peneus River, searching for Helena, amid sphinxes, sirens, nymphs, and other figures of ancient imagination. "Where is she?" are his first words on touching the soil of ancient Greece. Chiron, the learned centaur who educated many Greek heroes and who once bore Helena on his back, warns Faust that his ideal woman is a poetic myth. He carries Faust to Manto, the daughter of Aesculapius, who symbolizes healing power, to cure him of his madness. Faust protests,

> I'm sound in mind. A cure is not my aim;
> Else, like to others, I'd be base and tame. (p. 182b)

The wise Manto, approving of his sublime yearning, says, "Who yearns for the impossible I love" (p. 183a). Hailing him as the "audacious one," she takes him down to Hades, where he must begin his journey to union with Helena.

The next scene dramatizes Goethe's conviction that creativity must take place gradually and peacefully, not suddenly and violently. It also dramatizes his theory of geologic change. Sudden violence is personified in Seismos, who creates great mountains through an earthquake and occasions the greedy grasping of the valuable metals thus exposed, by the Ants, Griffins, and Pygmies—symbolizing base and small-minded peoples. Thales and Anaxagoras, ancient Greek philosophers, debate the issue of the modes of creation, Thales upholding the view that the earth's surface was created by water (through alluvial deposits) and Anaxagoras holding the view that it was created by fire (through volcanic eruptions). Homunculus, who is striving to come into corporeal existence, listens to the debate and sides with Thales. A meteor falls and destroys the mountain and the little beings created by Seismos' violence. Thales takes Homunculus to the Aegean Sea.

In the next scene, by the rocky coves of the Aegean Sea, the sea-god Proteus changes into a dolphin and carries Homunculus out to sea, so that he may begin his corporeal existence in the water, as the early forms of life did. Homunculus sees the sea nymph Galatea approaching on a sea-borne chariot and, smitten with love for her, he throws himself into the sea, to become a flame of new life coming to birth in the water. Love is the original creative force: "Now Eros be ruler who all hath begun!" the Sirens sing. Act II and the Classical Walpurgis Night end with a hymn to all four elements:

> Hail, ye waves! Hail, sea unbounded,
> By the holy fire surrounded!
> Water, hail! Hail, fire's glare!
> Hail to this adventure rare!
>
> Hail, thou gently blowing breeze!
> Hail, earth rich in mysteries!
> Hail, fire, sea, whom we adore,
> Hail, ye elements all four! (p. 206b)

During the Classical Walpurgis Night, Mephistopheles assumes the shape of Phorkyas, a hideous figure of ancient Greek mythology, to counter Helena's perfect beauty with utter ugliness.

(George M. Priest, the translator of this version of *Faust*, suggests in his notes to the original edition that the reader who is bewildered by the various scenes and themes of the Classical Walpurgis Night proceed thus: First read the lines dealing with Faust (7005-79, 7181-7213, and 7249-7494); then read those dealing with Mephistopheles (7080-7180, 7214-48, 7676-7850, and 7951-8033); then the lines dealing with Homunculus (7825-7950, 8082-8159, and 8219-8487); and finally all the other lines. Then, he suggests, read the section as a whole. We would suggest reading it as a whole first and then following Priest's suggestion.)

Act III presents the fulfillment of Faust's quest for Helena. The whole of the Classical Walpurgis Night has been a preparation that develops Faust to the stage where he is ready for union with Helena. Act III is modeled in form on Greek tragedy, opening with a prologue by Helena and using a chorus to present the action.

As the act opens with a chorus of Trojan women, Helena appears before the palace of her husband, Menelaus. Apparently Faust, through the aid of Manto, has obtained her release from Hades, and she re-enacts her return from Troy. She has, at Menelaus' command, preceded him to prepare a sacrifice. Mephistopheles, appearing in the ugly form of Phorkyas, informs the lovely woman that she and the Trojan women are to be the victims of her husband's sacrifice, and that a barbarian lord in a northern province will save her. During the dialogue with Helena, Mephistopheles utters cynical remarks about the immorality and destructiveness of beauty.

In the next scene, Helena and the chorus appear in the courtyard of a medieval castle, somewhere in Arcadia (the blissful land), north of Sparta. Faust is a conquering Germanic or Gothic lord, who welcomes and wins the ideal classic beauty. Out of this union between classic Greek and medieval Gothic comes Euphorion, the personification of poetry, of the imaginative re-

sponse to the world. He is an impulsive boy, wild and rebellious, constantly aspiring to reach ideal beauty and also inspired to help others. But his lack of moderation leads to his
death, and he accomplishes nothing. Helena, realizing that
"bliss and beauty never lastingly unite," returns to Hades.
Euphorion leaves his lyre behind, Helena leaves her mantle
and veil. The chorus chooses to become part of living nature.
At the end of the scene and the act, Mephistopheles reappears
in his own form to sum up Faust's Grecian journey (a summary
which Goethe never wrote).

For Goethe, Euphorion had a general allegorical significance
and also stood for an actual poet. He told Eckermann that
"Euphorion is not a human but only an allegorical being. He is
a personification of poetry that is not bound to any time or place
or person." In this sense he is identical with the Boy Charioteer
in Act I. But Euphorion is also symbolic of Lord Byron, as the
epitome of the modern poet, and Goethe intended this scene as
a memorial elegy for the great British Romantic poet, who had
died in the Greek struggle for independence, three years before this scene was written. (See Eckermann's *Conversations
with Goethe,* July 5, 1827, and December 20, 1829.)

In Act III Goethe uses the meters of ancient Greek tragedy
and modern meters to convey the meeting of Helena and Faust,
of the Greek and modern spirits. Our translator notes how
dramatically Goethe uses the alternation of rhythm from the
scene in the castle courtyard to the end of the act.

Goethe's use of metre and rhyme from this point on to the end of
the Act presents in highly artistic and at the same time symbolical
fashion both Helena's organic development and her adjustment to Faust.
The metres—at first Greek, then modern—always remain in keeping with
the nature and mood of the speaker and with the situation. For example,
Faust speaks first (9192-9212) in modern blank verse to which Helena
at once conforms. She then hears rhyme for the first time and it charms
her so much that she requests Faust to teach her how to speak in
rhyme. She learns her lesson thoroughly, speaking in rhyme thence-
forth in perfect formal as well as spiritual harmony with Faust until she
feels herself recalled to the lower world (9939-44) when she voices and
thus symbolizes her farewell in Greek iambic trimeter.[4]

[4] Johann Wolfgang von Goethe, *Faust,* trans. by George Madison
Priest (New York: Alfred A. Knopf, 1941), p. 406.

VI

After the pursuit of ideal beauty in its classic Greek form, presented in Acts II and III, Faust returns to his own place and time. The quest for Helena has been an ennobling and uplifting phase in Faust's development, but he realizes that he must direct his energies, will, and vision to productive activity in the actual world. This productive activity is the theme of Acts IV and V, the concluding portions of the drama.

As Act IV opens, Faust is seen on a high mountain range, encircled by clouds. A vision of his youthful love for Gretchen appears to him briefly (p. 245, lines 10055-66). When Mephistopheles, who appears in seven-league boots, asks him what more he wants after surveying "The kingdoms of the world and all their glory," Faust says he aims at "a great work." Scorning Mephistopheles' images of sensual enjoyment and fame, he proclaims, "The deed is everything, the glory naught." The sight of the ocean waves constantly pounding away on the land has aroused in him the desire to conquer and dominate nature.

> Here dares my soul above itself to soar;
> Here would I fight, of this be conqueror.
>
> . . . .
>
> "Win for thyself great joy, a costly store:
> Push back the lordly ocean from the shore;
> Limit the bounds of that vast, watery deep
> And force it, far away, within itself to keep." (p. 249a-b)

But before he can accomplish this project, he has to save the Emperor from the civil war and anarchy that threaten his rule. Mephistopheles' paper-money scheme in Act I has worsened rather than helped matters. Now Mephistopheles proposes that he aid Faust with his magical powers to lead the Emperor's forces to victory, and thus gain Faust "a boundless strand" of seashore as his fief. He summons the Three Mighty Men—Fight-hard, Get-quick, and Hold-fast—to help Faust as the original mighty trio helped David against the Philistines. (See II Sam. 23:8-9.) Here the three seem to stand for various virtues required for successful activity, or for the three ages of man—youth, maturity, and old age. With their help, and

Mephistopheles' magic arts—which produce floods and lightning—Faust wins a victory for the Emperor.

The Emperor tries to convince himself that the victory is the result of valor and chance rather than of magic arts. In a parody of the formal pomp of the court of the Holy Roman Empire, he invests his chief generals with the choicest fiefs of the realm, reserving to Faust the strip of seashore he desires. The scene of the investiture in the rival Emperor's tent was the last Goethe wrote—having finished the later scenes before—and is not quite filled out. Apparently he was too old and tired to do all he wanted to in this scene. In his final letter, written shortly after he finished this scene, he said, "I developed only the places that were individually most interesting to me, so that gaps remain in the second part, to be connected with the rest of a uniform interest."[5]

As Act V opens we learn that Faust has been successful in conquering the sea and in creating a thriving, heavily populated area out of marshes and sand bars. But there is a note of foreboding about the calloused amorality that goes with his power and effectiveness. An old couple—Philemon and Baucis —fear that he will wrest their cottage and land from them. Their fear is well grounded. We glimpse Faust in the splendid garden of his palace, an old man (a hundred years old, according to Goethe's notes), at the height of power and achievement, yet racked with desire to have the old couple's land and trees. He must have their little plot to build an observation tower where he may look out on his great work,

> The masterpiece of human thought,
> Which made a fact shrewd wisdom's plan
> And won broad dwelling-place for man. (p. 273b)

He summons to his aid Mephistopheles and the Three Mighty Comrades who have been performing deeds of piracy on the high seas and bringing their loot back to Faust's palace by the canal which joins it to the ocean. Their amoral spirit is intoned by Mephistopheles:

> The free sea sets the spirit free.
> Who'll stop to think when he's at sea!

[5] Thomas Mann, *op. cit.*, p. 614.

What helps is suddenness of grip.
You catch a fish, you catch a ship,
And when you're once the lord of three,
You hook the fourth one easily;
Then is the fifth in sorry plight,
You have the Power and so the Right.
You ask not *How* but *What* it be.
I know not how the sea is charted
If war and trade and piracy
Are not triune and can't be parted. (p. 272a-b)

Faust sends this piratical crew to move the old couple from their land to a pleasant farm he has selected for them. Mephistopheles points out to the spectators the resemblance of this deed to Ahab's seizure of Naboth's vineyard in I Kings 21:1-16. In the process of eviction, the old couple fall dead of fright and are burned to ashes when their house catches fire accidentally in the fracas. Faust is horrified and curses "This unconsidered, savage blow" and those who have perpetrated it.

At midnight four gray women enter—Want, Guilt, Worry, and Distress. Want, Guilt, and Distress cannot enter the home of a rich man, but Worry can slip in anywhere. Worry stays, and the other three go away, sighting their brother Death coming in the distance. Faust, disturbed by these gloomy presences and portents, tries to shake off this superstitious dread and his dependence on magical powers.

Could I all magic from my pathway banish,
Could quite unlearn its spells and bid it vanish
Nature, could I face thee, in thy great plan,
Then were it worth the pain to be a man.
    Such was I once ere I the gloom explored
And cursed me and the world with impious word. (p. 277b)

When challenged by Worry, who claims to be where she belongs, Faust responds,

Through the world I have but flown.
Whatever I craved, I seized it by the hair,
Whatever sufficed not, I let fare.
Whatever escaped, I let it go.
I've but desired and but achieved, each hour,
And then again have wished, and so with power
Stormed through my life; at first with power and greatness;
But now life moves with cautious, wise sedateness.

> Well do I know the sphere of earth and men.
> The view beyond is barred to mortal ken;
> A fool! who thither turns his blinking eyes
> And dreams he'll find his like above the skies.
> Let him stand fast and look around on earth;
> Not mute is this world to a man of worth.
> Why need he range through all eternity?
> Here he can seize all that he knows to be.
> Thus let him wander down his earthly day;
> When spirits spook, let him pursue his way;
> Let him find pain and bliss as on he stride,
> He! every moment still unsatisfied. (p. 278a-b)

But Worry claims that whoever she possesses finds all endeavor worthless, is pessimistic, dilatory, futile, indecisive, unfit for living, and on the verge of Hell. Faust defies Worry to do her worst: "Thy power I shall not acknowledge ever." Worry breathes on him and blinds him before she leaves. The blinded Faust is firmer than ever in his will to accomplish his plans, and as the scene ends he is commanding his workers to apply their shovels and other tools. Says Faust,

> To consummate the greatest enterprises
> *One* spirit for a thousand hands, suffices. (p. 280a)

In the next scene, the Lemurs—spirits of the wicked dead—are digging Faust's grave. Faust, hearing their spades, thinks they are working on his project. He urges then on, looking forward to the day when the poisonous marshes will be drained and a free, happy, productive people will be living in "a land like Paradise." His final words and vows are these:

> Yes, to this thought I hold unswerving,
> To wisdom's final fruit, profoundly true:
> Of freedom and of life he only is deserving
> Who every day must conquer them anew.
> Thus here, by danger girt, the active day
> Of childhood, manhood, age will pass away.
> Aye! such a throng I fain would see,
> Stand on free soil among a people free.
> Then might I say, that moment seeing:
> 'Ah, linger on, thou are so fair!'
> The traces of my earthly being
> Can perish not in æons—they are there!

That lofty moment I now feel in this:
I now enjoy the highest moment's bliss. (pp. 281b-282a)

Thus, having spoken the words that were a condition of his original contract with Mephistopheles, he dies. Mephistopheles has contempt for this mere mortal who followed the call of pleasure and power and now winds up as dust—"here the old man lies in sand."

While the Lemurs bury Faust's body, Mephistopheles summons up devils from Hell to secure his claim to Faust's soul. But a chorus of angels, imbued with forgiving love, descends and frustrates Mephistopheles' design. While the latter is distracted by a perverted sexual lust for the angels, they bear Faust's soul away. Mephistopheles is utterly crestfallen at having been circumvented through his own "vulgar lust, an absurd, lovesick passion."

The final scene of the drama presents Faust's rise to Heaven. It starts in forests, rocks, and desert, with holy anchorites scattered around. Three Paters (Fathers)—Ecstaticus, Profundus, and Seraphicus—represent various modes or stages of attaining intimacy with God: physical martyrdom or mortification, understanding of God's immanence in nature, and endless loving's revelation. Faust's spirit, borne by the angels, ascends to the higher atmosphere, in company with the Blessed Boys—the souls of children who died unbaptized. Stages of purification are implied and symbolized in the upward journey. The angels sing

> Lo! rescued is this noble one
> From evil machination;
> 'Who e'er aspiring, struggles on,
> For him there is salvation.' (p. 290b)

Dr. Marianus, the holy teacher of the worship of the Virgin, appears "in the highest, purest cell" to plead Faust's cause to the Virgin, who soars into view as the Mater Gloriosa, the Glorious Mother and patron of love. Three sinning women—Mary Magdalene, the Woman of Samaria, and Mary of Egypt (indicated by Latin terms here)—plead to the Virgin for pardon to Gretchen. Gretchen sings her bliss at forgiveness and her joy at the return of Faust.

> My early lover,
> His troubles over,
> Comes back to me. (p. 293b)

The Blessed Boys sing of him as higher than they, for

> Early were we removed,
> Life did not reach us;
> But he has learned and loved
> And he will teach us. (p. 294a)

Faust drops off his earthly bonds, takes on his heavenly form. The Virgin urges Gretchen,

> Come, rise to higher spheres! Conduct him!
> If he feels thee, he'll go thy way. (p. 294a)

The scene and the drama end on the mystical chorus:

> All earth comprises
> Is symbol alone;
> What there ne'er suffices
> As fact here is known;
> All past the humanly
> Wrought here in love;
> The Eternal-Womanly
> Draws us above. (p. 294b)

What takes place in the world reaches ultimate fulfillment in eternity. Human striving and loving aspire toward the heavenly love which is embodied in the Eternal-Womanly—on earth in Gretchen, in Heaven in the Virgin.

VII

Is Faust *a tragedy?*

Goethe calls *Faust* a "tragedy"; yet, unlike Marlowe's *Dr. Faustus,* Goethe's drama ends with the salvation, not the damnation of his hero. Goethe signals in the Prologue in Heaven, before the action begins, that the drama will have a happy ending. Man, striving and aspiring, errs, but through his striving and despite his erring, he comes to ultimate rightness and salvation. This is the obvious and proclaimed theme of Goethe's *Faust.* Where, then, does the tragedy lie? Does not Goethe, like Dante in his *Divine Comedy,* take his hero from the depths of despair and evil to the purity and light of the heavenly realm?

Or does the tragic quality of *Faust* lie not in its ending, but in the seriousness of the action, its portrayal of the dangers and perils of the human soul in its journey through life, its handling of the evil and negative aspects of existence? Perhaps works such as these require us to expand the ancient notion of tragedy to apply to any deep and serious imaginative presentation of significant human action and concerns.

But is not coarse humor and wild fantasy as much a part of Goethe's *Faust* as deep seriousness? Think of Mephistopheles' ironic wit and crude obscenities throughout the drama, and of such things as the German Walpurgis Night scenes in Part I. Is *Faust* a hybrid form of the tragic and comic, rather than a tragedy? Is the same true of Shakespeare's tragedies? Does the comic play the same role in *Hamlet* and *King Lear* as it does in *Faust*?

Can you envisage *Faust* as a stage play? Part I was staged at Weimar during Goethe's lifetime. Gounod's opera presents the portions of Part I dealing with the love story of Faust and Gretchen. Could Part II be presented as a whole in an actual theatrical performance? Which scenes of Part II do you think would be especially fitted for the stage? Which scenes would be difficult to present?

What is Gretchen doing in the story of Dr. Faustus?

There is no Gretchen in the original story of Faust. Helen of Troy, the ideal ancient Greek beauty, played a key role in Marlowe's drama about Faust, and was also an obsessive motif with Goethe when he first conceived his version of the story. But he saved his Helena for Part II and concentrated on what is often called "the Gretchen tragedy," or "the Gretchen episode," in Part I. Why this stress on an ordinary love affair in a drama concerned with the deepest and most basic concerns of human existence? Perhaps there was a "real" basis for the Gretchen story in Goethe's own youthful love affairs, as the commentators tell us. But why does he use it here, in this story? What is the artistic function of the Gretchen story in

Goethe's *Faust?* What does he see in his love affairs that he wishes to express in the Gretchen story?

How does Goethe present the love between man and woman in *Faust?* Does he see such love as ennobling or degrading? Gretchen is ruined, at least in an earthly sense, by her love affair with Faust. Is that the essential meaning of her love, as Goethe presents it here? Does the love affair, with its tragic ending, have a decisive effect on Faust? Does it affect his restless striving for experience and power? Is Faust a different kind of person in Part II, as a result of his tragic love affair with Gretchen in Part I? Does his love develop him ethically or enlighten his understanding of existence?

What is Goethe saying about the womanly and man's love of woman when he brings back Gretchen at the end of Part II? Does such a love as that of Faust for Gretchen ultimately connect with the eternal love at the heart of creation and salvation? Is there any intimation of this at the end of Part I? Does the Gretchen theme of Part I connect with the Gretchen motif of Part II?

Is the Gretchen episode in Part I a tragedy, despite the promise of salvation in the last lines? Erich Heller, a distinguished critic of German literature, suggests that Goethe may have created a new kind of tragedy in this section of *Faust*—"sentimental tragedy, or the tragedy of human *feelings*," as if Ophelia had been the protagonist of *Hamlet*. How does such a form of tragedy differ from the kind Aristotle discusses in the *Poetics?* (For Aristotle's view of tragedy, see *Imaginative Literature I*, pp. 29-30.)

Does this work celebrate the Romantic spirit?

Undoubtedly the Faust of Part I is a Romantic hero. He aspires to partake of infinite and eternal things in his own immediate experience. He scorns formal conventions, academic rules, the petty pace of ordinary life. He wants to be at one with nature and with the depths of his own spirit. He wants his own personal existence to be rich and full, with all kinds of knowledge, power, and pleasure. He wants to do and be everything. He is undeterred by any ethical or religious scruples, and resorts to black magic and a pact with the devil to attain his ends. He is never satisfied, but always looks forward to new experiences and new activities.

Do the events of Part II indicate a basic change in Faust, or does he still remain a Romantic hero? Is Faust's Romantic spirit altered by his encounter with Classical culture in the Classical Walpurgis Night and the Helena scenes? Does Goethe point to a welding of the Classical and Romantic spirits as the ideal for modern man? Or does the tragic ending of the Helena episode indicate that such a fusion is impossible? What, then, is the meaning of Helena's mantle and veil and Euphorion's lyre being left behind when they depart for Hades—that modern man can partake in Greek culture, or that he should fashion his own? Is the yearning after the Classical ideal itself a Romantic attitude, a straining for contact with the past and the remote?

This brings us finally to the engineering activities that crown Faust's career. Is this emphasis on productive activity in the actual material and social world the fruition of his experience of Classical beauty? Or is it simply a new stage in Faust's development? Does this new orientation of Faust's energy mean that he is finally cured of his Romantic aspiration? Is this new stage a disappointing, pedestrian, philistine dénouement of Faust's quest, as some critics think? Or is Faust still striving, aspiring, seeking to exercise his will and gain power, to feel great and strong? Is there an essential difference involved in his looking at his work as laying the foundation for the good life and freedom of a whole people, of future generations? Or is this just a modern way of playing the Romantic hero?

Do the passages directed against Romanticism—such as those uttered by Mephistopheles, the Earth-Spirit, and Faust himself in Part I—indicate the viewpoint from which Goethe wants us to see Faust's quest? Or are we to identfy ourselves with Faust and his quest, nevertheless? What can we say about the ending, when the angels themselves bless Faust's continual aspiration and struggle as an indication that he is worthy of salvation? Is this a heavenly blessing for the Romantic spirit?

Whose side is Goethe on, anyway—the Romanticists', the anti-Romanticists', or neither?

What does Mephistopheles represent?

In the Prologue in Heaven, Mephistopheles is portrayed as being on speaking terms with God, who is fond of his wit and willingly lets him be man's companion so that he may stir man to creative activity. In the scene in Faust's study, Mephistopheles announces that he is the spirit of negation and destruction, part of the original Nothing and Chaos that preceded creation. He also describes himself as always aiming at evil and always accomplishing good. Just what does he mean by this?

Is Mephistopheles, like Milton's Lucifer, a diabolical power that wills evil but accomplishes ultimate good, who unwittingly furthers the divine plan for creation and even makes the ultimate result better through his diabolical action? Or is evil (negation and destruction) Mephistopheles' good, and is *nothing* better than something for him? Or is Goethe hinting that, from a cosmic viewpoint, destruction is a necessary element in creation or the evolutionary process?

What negative or unpleasant aspects of human character and mentality does Mephistopheles represent? Is he perfectly consistent in his evil pattern or does he ever side with right and reason? If so, is he in character in such instances and motivated by his essential negativity, or is he merely a spokesman for the author's own views? How does Mephistopheles affect Faust ethically—in Part I?—in Part II?

What is the meaning of identifying Mephistopheles with the spirit of restlessness, the spur to creativity, the impulse that receives angelic blessing? Is not Faust inspired by restlessness long before he meets Mephistopheles? Does not Mephistopheles try to cast scorn on Faust's idealistic aspirations and to satisfy him with common pleasures and powers? Is restlessness and striving a divine or diabolical quality? Do any and all aspirations and struggle tend to eternal salvation, according to Goethe's *Faust*?

What is the underlying religious view in this work?

Does the ending of *Faust* indicate an essentially Christian viewpoint, such as provides the framework for Dante's *Divine Comedy* and Milton's *Paradise Lost?* Does the final scene fit in with the spirit of the rest of the poem? Think back to the references to religious themes in the previous parts of the work. How are orthodox Christian ideas and attitudes viewed—by Faust? by Gretchen? by Mephistopheles? in the scenes in ancient Greece? Is Christianity just one of the elements in Goethe's view of existence, or is it central and dominating? Does Goethe's *Faust* have a Christian ending? Or does Goethe use Christian symbols and images to express a different point of view?

In this work there are many expressions of the reverence for Nature. What kind of religious viewpoint underlies these expressions? Is such a religious attitude compatible with the Christian view of God and of man's relation to God? Does this reverence for the God or Spirit that is present in Nature, as expressed in *Faust*, imply any particular moral principles? If so, are the implicit ethics of Faust at variance with the Judaeo-Christian ethical doctrines? Is the view of human nature in *Faust* similar to or different from the Christian view? Is the handling of the problem of evil in the world the same as or different from the Christian treatment of it?

The following questions are designed to help you test the thoroughness of your reading. Each question is to be answered by giving a page or pages of the reading assignment. Answers will be found on page 248 of this Reading Plan.

1 Is Mephistopheles mainly interested in the living or the dead?

2 What German city does Frosch compare to Paris?

3 What does Margaret do with the starflower in the courtship scene?

4 Who is the "Proctophantasmist" in the Walpudgis Night scene in Part I?

5 What are the two castes which, according to the Chancellor, uphold the Empire?

6 How does Faust view "the thrill of awe"?

7 Who are the Phorkyads?

8 What causes Lynceus the warder to forget his duty?

MELVILLE

Moby Dick

Vol. 48

H erman Melville's *Moby Dick* is the only work of imaginative literature by an American writer to be included in *Great Books of the Western World*. The selection of this work indicates once again that the greatness of a writer may not be recognized in his own time. For Melville, after a brief moment of popularity, faded into obscurity and insignificance. It is extremely unlikely that *Moby Dick* would have been included in this set if it had been published shortly after the First, instead of the Second, World War. The revival of Melville and the recognition of his genius has occurred only in the last generation. Perhaps a new time, with a new experience and a new awareness, was required to recognize the depth and scope of Melville's work.

Moby Dick was the masterwork of this master American writer. He himself called it "the Whale"; and it is a whale, a Leviathan, of a work. It has everything in it—some critics say too much. It is the story of the hunt for a malignant white whale, a hunt which culminates in one of the most exciting chases in literature.

It is also an account of the whaling industry, and includes much historical and nonfictional material. It contains a "cetology," or natural history, of the whale, based on the works of naturalists and Melville's own experience and interpretation.

Moby Dick is all these things and something more. For the white whale that Captain Ahab hunts not only is the beast that bit off his leg, but also symbolizes all the evil and negative aspects of existence. It is a primal, demonic force in the universe against which Ahab, like a modern Prometheus, hurls his defiance and struggles to the bitter end. Thus *Moby Dick* is not only a sea story, an account of the whaling industry, and a natural history of the whale; it is also heavily freighted with metaphysical and theological meanings, for it deals with the problems of evil, providence, and free will.

All of these elements are conveyed in magnificent language that at times achieves a Shakespearean eloquence. And the work is peopled with characters that reveal various facets of human nature. The monomaniac "king" Ahab heads a motley company, including Starbuck, a man of virtue and understanding, who lacks the strength of will to oppose his demonic leader; Stubb, an unreflective man, who just takes things as they come, foul or fair; and Flask, who acts the role of a clown in the face of the perils of the deep. And there is Ishmael, the outcast, the "Isolato," through whose genial, profound, and enigmatic personality Melville tells his story, and who may indeed be the literary body and voice of Melville himself.

Fifth Reading

I

At the time of the Revolution, American literature was an imitation of English literature, reflecting the Neoclassical attitude and manner of the contemporary Augustan age in England. The era of political and social change ushered in by the Revolution was also an era of literary change. American writers responded to the new Romantic writers of England and France, and the wide political and social vistas of the new nation provided a home-grown inspiration for the Romantic mood.

Washington Irving (1783-1859), the first of the new American writers to win world recognition, combined an elegant style and comic wit with a romantic interest in the past, particularly the European past. In the later part of his career Irving also found romance in the new Western frontier. It was James Fenimore Cooper (1789-1851), however, who was the first of the new writers to fashion romances out of the struggle between settlers and Indians. His "Leatherstocking Series," centering around the remarkable Natty Bumppo, emphasized the conflict between primitivism and civilization on the new frontier. Nathaniel Hawthorne (1804-1864), on the other hand, found food for the imagination in the crises and corruption of the Puritan soul of New England, which he narrated in a searching and symbolic fashion in such tales as *The Scarlet Letter*.

Herman Melville had perhaps the hardest and most adventurous existence of all the notable new American writers. He quit school at the age of fifteen and went to work as a bank clerk, hat salesman, farm laborer, and schoolteacher. His wanderlust soon sent him out to sea as a cabin boy on a merchantman bound for Liverpool (1837). He experienced the hard life of the merchant seaman and saw the sordidness of English slums and water-front dives. On his return he became a schoolteacher again and began his first, amateurish attempts at writing (1837-1841). But this kind of life proved too tame for him, and he set out for sea again in January, 1841, as a seaman on a whaling voyage to the South Seas. A year and a half later, he jumped ship in the Marquesas and for several weeks lived a life of happy captivity among the cannibals of the valley of Taipi (or Typee). Perhaps because he feared his genial captors might eat him some day, he escaped on a passing Australian whaling vessel, signing on as a seaman but deserting when the ship docked at Tahiti. Because of a mutiny which had broken out on the ship, he spent his first few weeks in Tahiti in the brig of a French warship and in a British jail on land. After his release, he worked as a field laborer and studied the depressing social conditions of the local islands. When he became bored, he went to sea again on a whaler bound for the North Pacific and got off at Honolulu. Here he worked as a clerk and then shipped out as a seaman on a United States warship, passing through the Polynesian islands again, and finally docking at Boston (October, 1844).

Melville later called these years at sea "My Yale College and My Harvard" (p. 82a). But now he felt that he had graduated, and he tried to make his way in the landlubbers' world. He turned to writing as the only profession he was fitted for, using his experiences in the South Seas as the material for his first books.

Typee (1846) and *Omoo* (1847), dealing with his adventures in Taipi and Tahiti, won popular and critical acclaim. Although he antagonized some people by his satirical comments on the corruption of "civilization" and on the evil effect of Christian missions on the idyllic native existence, he was hailed by most critics and readers as another Daniel Defoe, telling the adventures of a new Robinson Crusoe. Melville's sudden fame, however, came at a price—that of being stereotyped as "the man who had lived among cannibals," a writer of Robinson Crusoe-type stories.

In his third novel, *Mardi* (1849), he attempted a highly symbolic, allegorical, and enigmatic fiction, combining satire on contemporary institutions with a quest for transcendental reality. This work met a cool and cruel reception. The public was disappointed that he had not given them another *Typee* or *Omoo*. The critics were scornful of what they considered a wild farrago of romance, satire, philosophy, and abstruse allegory. Melville was deeply hurt by the harsh criticism of this work—"driven forth like a wild mystic Mormon into shelterless exile," he wrote of himself. Yet in *Mardi* he first demonstrated the peculiar genius that was to flower in *Moby Dick*.

Melville wrote his next book, *Redburn* (also 1849), frankly to make money. This work deals with his first voyage, and gives a realistic account of life at sea and in England. In *White-Jacket* (1850) Melville dealt with life on board a United States warship, based partly on his own experience. It is a vivid criticism of the conditions and treatment of the seamen, and especially of the use of flogging. Writing to his father-in-law about these two books (October 6, 1849), Melville said:

They are two *jobs* which I have done for money—being forced to it, as other men are to sawing wood. And while I have felt obliged to refrain from writing the kind of book I would wish to; yet, in writing these two books, I have not repressed myself much—so far as *they* are concerned; but have spoken pretty much as I feel.—Being books, then, written in this way, my only desire for their 'success' (as it is called) springs from my pocket, & not from my heart. So far as I am individually concerned, & independent of my pocket, it is my earnest desire to write those sort of books which are said to 'fail'—pardon this egotism.

It was also in 1850 that Melville moved from New York and its literary set to a farm in Pittsfield, Massachusetts. Here he wrote *Moby Dick* and enjoyed the friendship of Nathaniel Hawthorne, whom he had long admired and who was now his neighbor. When he finished his masterpiece, Melville dedicated it to Hawthorne—"In token of my admiration for his genius."

Melville recognized that in *Moby Dick* (1851) he had reached the fulfillment of his promise. At the age of thirty-one he had published his literary masterpiece, the great work of his career. It had taken a tremendous toll in literary energy and emotional tension—"the hell-fire in which the whole book is broiled." Now, after "this hardest possible day's work," he had to face the unfavorable reaction of the critics, which he took as cruel derision and blind misunderstanding. The book was almost universally condemned for its structure and style, earning such epithets as "Bedlam literature" and "intellectual chowder." Despite the warm response of Hawthorne and a few others to his great effort, Melville felt crushed by the hostile criticism. In this mood of black despair he wrote his next novel, *Pierre* (1852), which further alienated the critics and the public by its pessimism, subtheme of incest, and main theme of the misery arising from the doing of good.

Raymond Weaver has presented the harsh facts and figures about Melville's take-home pay from his writings in his Introduction to *The Shorter Novels of Herman Melville:*

Whereas before *Pierre,* Melville and Harpers had shared, half-and-half, cost of manufacture of books and profit from sales, with *Pierre* Harpers agreed to pay Melville twenty-five cents on the sale of any volumes after the first 1,190 copies. Melville's first royalties on *Pierre* were $58.25: an amount greater than the sum of royalties that *Pierre* accumulated during all the years that were to follow. During 1853—the year after the publication of *Pierre,*—54 copies of *Typee* were sold; 56 of *Omoo*; 42 of *Redburn*; 49 of *Mardi*; 29 of *White-Jacket*; 48 of *Moby-Dick*; and 27 of *Pierre.* After his initial burst of popularity, it was a miraculous year, indeed, that brought him $100 in royalties.

Despite the success of *Israel Potter* (1855), an adventure story of the American Revolution, Melville's disheartenment was permanent. He was never again able to complete a full-length novel on a serious theme, although he did write some excellent short stories and novelettes. His novelette *Billy Budd,* first published in 1924, won him fame long after his death. Because of the almost complete obscurity into which he had fallen and the problem of making a living, the last half of his life (1855-1891) was increasingly difficult. A fire at his publishers in 1853 destroyed the plates and most of the unsold copies of his books. He tried to earn his living by lecturing. In 1866, he secured a lowly post as an outdoors customs inspector in New York, and held this post until 1885. In his last years he was completely neglected and unknown by the public.

The bitterness of the man whom Raymond Weaver called "the most disillusioned of American writers" is revealed in his later poems, in such lines as these from "Camoens":

> What now avails the pageant verse,
> Trophies and arms with music borne?
> Base is the world; and some rehearse
> How noblest meet ignoble scorn.
> Vain now thy ardor, vain thy fire,
> Delirium mere, unsound desire:
> Fate's knife hath ripped the chorded lyre.
> Exhausted by the exacting lay,
> Thou dost but fall a surer prey
> To wile and guile ill understood;
> While they who work them, fair in face,
> Still keep their strength in prudent place,
> And claim they worthier run life's race,
> Serving high God with useful good.

The neglect of Melville persisted for a generation after his death, although he was appreciated by such choice readers as Robert Louis Stevenson, Sir James Barrie, and John Masefield in the days of his greatest neglect.

The literary resurrection of Melville began about 1920, inspired by Raymond Weaver, Lewis Mumford, and other American literary scholars and critics. By the forties and fifties, Melville was regarded as one of the great giants of American and world literature. Today his fame no longer derives from his having lived among the cannibals and recreated "true adventures" at sea and in the South Sea Islands. He is noted now for having transmuted into great art his vision of the human condition and of man's relation to the core of reality. Lewis Mumford said of Melville: "In depth of experience and religious insight there is scarcely any one in the nineteenth century, with the exception of Dostoyevsky, who can be placed beside him."

II

As Melville indicates in *Moby Dick*, a large body of literature on the whaling trade was available to him. (See the "Extracts" on pp. xi-xx and the passages discussed in Section VII below.) An article entitled "Mocha Dick or the White Whale," which appeared twelve years before the publication of *Moby Dick*, may have made an impression on Melville. The article contained a story of an extraordinary, fierce whale which wrought much havoc among whaling ships and their crews in the early nineteenth century. But probably the most essential sources of Melville's work were his own experiences on a whaling ship and his aim to write a great "whale" of a work on the evil or "dark" aspect of existence. Indeed, in his correspondence while he was writing the book, he often calls it "the Whale" and expresses his creative difficulties in seagoing terms.

Writing to Richard Henry Dana, Jr. on May 1, 1850, he remarked:

It will be a strange sort of a book, tho', I fear; blubber is blubber you know; tho' you may get oil of it, the poetry runs as hard as sap from a frozen maple tree;—& to cook the thing up, one must needs throw in a little fancy, which from the nature of the thing, must be ungainly as the gambols of the whales themselves. Yet I mean to give the truth of the thing, spite of this.

And to Nathaniel Hawthorne, about June 1, 1851, he says:

But I was talking about the 'Whale.' As the fishermen say, 'he's in his flurry' when I left him some three weeks ago. I'm going to take him by his jaw, however, before long, and finish him up in some fashion or other. What's the use of elaborating what, in its very essence, is so short-lived as a modern book? Though I wrote the Gospels in this century, I should die in the gutter.

And to Hawthorne again, on June 29, 1851:

Shall I send you a fin of the 'Whale' by way of a specimen mouthful? The tail is not yet cooked—tho' the hell-fire in which the whole book is broiled might not unreasonably have cooked it all ere this. This is the book's motto (the secret one), Ego non baptiso te in nomine—but make out the rest yourself.

In September, 1851, he warns a woman friend:

Dont you buy it—dont you read it, when it does come out, because it is by no means the sort of book for you. It is not a piece of fine feminine Spitalfields silk—but is of the horrible texture of a fabric that should be woven of ships' cables & hawsers. A Polar wind blows through it, & birds of prey hover over it. Warn all gentle fastidious people from so much as peeping into the book—on risk of a lumbago & sciatics.

Again to Hawthorne, about November 17, 1851:

I have written a wicked book, and feel spotless as the lamb. Ineffable socialities are in me. I would sit down and dine with you and all the gods in old Rome's Pantheon. It is a strange feeling—no hopefulness is in it, no despair. Content—that is it; and irresponsibility; but without licentious inclination. I speak now of my profoundest sense of being, not of an incidental feeling.

And this letter to Hawthorne's wife, on January 8, 1852:

. . . your allusion for example to the 'Spirit Spout' first showed to me that there was a subtle significance in that thing—but I did not, in that case, *mean* it. I had some vague idea while writing it, that the whole book was susceptible of an allegoric construction, & also that *parts* of it were—but the speciality of many of the particular subordinate allegories, were first revealed to me, after reading Mr. Hawthorne's letter, which, without citing any particular examples, yet intimated the part-&-parcel allegoricalness of the whole.

III

Moby Dick has one of the best beginnings any novel ever had. The rhythmic beat and freighted meaning of the first five syllables, along with the themes of wanderlust and the sea-going impulse in the very first paragraph, launch us on our voyage through 135 chapters.

Call me Ishmael. Some years ago—never mind how long precisely—having little or no money in my purse, and nothing particular to interest me on shore, I thought I would sail about a little and see the watery part of the world. It is a way I have of driving off the spleen, and regulating the circulation. Whenever I find myself growing grim about the mouth; whenever it is a damp, drizzly November in my soul; whenever I find myself involuntarily pausing before coffin warehouses, and bringing up the rear of every funeral I meet; and especially whenever my hypos get such an upper hand of me, that it requires a strong moral principle to prevent me from deliberately stepping into the street, and methodically knocking people's hats off—then, I account it high time to get to sea as soon as I can. This is my substitute for pistol and ball. With a philosophical flourish Cato throws himself upon his sword; I quietly take to the ship. There is nothing surprising in this. If they but knew it, almost all men in their degree, some time or other, cherish very nearly the same feelings towards the ocean with me. (p. 1a)

We listen to the narrator's evocation of the irresistible lure of the waters—"the image of the ungraspable phantom of life."

He tells us in good, meaty, warm, living, genial language that he abominates "all honourable respectable toils, trials, and tribulations of every kind whatsoever," and hence always ships out as a common seaman. He admits the role of fate and his own needs in sending him out on a whaler this time instead of the usual merchant vessel. "Those stage managers, the Fates" have worked with his inner "springs and motives" to assign him "this shabby part." The lure of the remote and the mysterious is overwhelming for him.

> Chief among these motives was the overwhelming idea of the great whale himself. Such a portentous and mysterious monster roused all my curiosity. Then the wild and distant seas where he rolled his island bulk; the undeliverable, nameless perils of the whale; these, with all the attending marvels of a thousand Patagonian sights and sounds, helped to sway me to my wish. With other men, perhaps, such things would not have been inducements; but as for me, I am tormented with an everlasting itch for things remote. I love to sail forbidden seas, and land on barbarous coasts. Not ignoring what is good, I am quick to perceive a horror, and could still be social with it—would they let me—since it is but well to be on friendly terms with all the inmates of the place one lodges in. (pp. 4b-5a)

Ishmael tells a leisurely tale, but one that is always moving forward, voyaging outward, filling with meaning, building up in interest, and steadily heightening the reader's appreciation —if he has the creative patience to follow every step of the way. Ishmael begins his tale with his journey from New York to Nantucket to find a whaling ship. Stopping off at New Bedford, he spends a night in the Spouter Inn, whose proprietor is ominously named Coffin. Because of crowded conditions, he is forced to sleep two in a bed with some unknown harpooner, who turns out to be a multicolored South Sea savage, equipped with a wooden idol, a shrunken human head, and a tomahawk that also serves as a pipe. But amiable relations are soon established, and Ishmael wakes up the next morning to find the savage "Queequeg's arm thrown over me in the most loving and affectionate manner," as if they were man and wife. Ishmael soon grows to love this goodhearted "cannibal with a tomahawk," who crawls under the bed to put on his shoes. He recognizes that Queequeg is "a creature in the transition . . . just enough civilised to show off his outlandishness in the strangest possible manner." The noble savage—a prince in his native land—shaves with his harpoon and uses it to reach for beefsteaks and other viands at the breakfast table.

It is Sunday morning, and Ishmael goes to the Whaleman's Chapel, consecrated to the memory of those who go out to sea in ships to hunt the great Leviathan. Marble tablets on the wall commemorate men lost at sea in the whale hunt. Ishmael meditates on the "speechlessly quick chaotic bundling of a man into Eternity" that is the lot of such men. Now the pastor, Father Mapple, mounts to his pulpit, shaped like a ship's bow and reached by a rope ladder that the pastor pulls up after him, in token of his withdrawal from earthly ties. "Yes," comments Ishmael, "the world's a ship on its passage out, and not a voyage complete; and the pulpit is its prow."

Father Mapple's sermon (Ch. 9) is on the little book of Jonah, "that canticle in the fish's belly!" The sermon is a magnificent example of the homiletical art, creating a vivid and graphic image of Jonah's experience, and cogently emphasizing the lesson taught in the biblical story. For Father Mapple, the lesson is that no man can foil God's will or escape God's presence, no matter where he flees. Jonah could not escape his duty and his God, for God is everywhere: "God came upon him in the whale, and swallowed him down to living gulfs of doom . . . and all the watery world of woe bowled over him." But when he cried "out of the belly of hell," God heard him and caused the whale to vomit Jonah out upon the dry land, to do His will and preach the truth. As against the Eternal, the world and its praise or honor are nothing. "Woe to him who seeks to please rather than to appal!"

After listening intently to this good Protestant sermon, Ishmael comes home to the comradeship of his heathen roommate. Their friendship ("marriage") is sealed by smoking Queequeg's tomahawk-pipe. Ishmael accepts the gifts the savage generously presses on him and joins him in worshiping his little wooden idol, on the principle that it is the intention that determines the rightness of forms of worship. Ishmael explains:

I was a good Christian; born and bred in the bosom of the infallible Presbyterian Church. How then could I unite with this wild idolater in worshipping his piece of wood? But what is worship? thought I. Do you suppose now, Ishmael, that the magnanimous God of heaven and earth —pagans and all included—can possibly be jealous of an insignificant bit of black wood? Impossible! But what is worship?—to do the will of God —*that* is worship. And what is the will of God?—to do to my fellowman what I would have my fellowman do to me—*that* is the will of God. Now, Queequeg is my fellowman. And what do I wish that this Queequeg would do to me? Why, unite with me in my particular Presbyterian form of worship. Consequently, I must then unite with him in his; ergo, I must turn idolater. (p. 39a-b)

Lying in bed that night, the two chat like husband and wife, keeping each other warm in the cold night. Queequeg tells how he left his island in the South Pacific ("It is not down in any map" Ishmael notes; "true places never are.") and became a harpooner on Yankee whaling ships. He had hoped "to learn among the Christians the arts whereby to make his people still happier than they were; and . . . still better than they were." But his experiences in New England harbors have taught him that Christians are far more miserable and wicked than his own people. "Thought he, it's a wicked world in all meridians; I'll die a pagan. And thus an old idolater at heart, he yet lived among these Christians, wore their clothes and tried to talk their gibberish" (p. 42a). Indeed, he feels too defiled by Christianity, that is, by Christians, to ascend his pure pagan throne.

Queequeg and Ishmael agree to ship out on a whaler together, and the next morning they take the boat to Nantucket. There they stop at the Try Pots Inn, before which there is a gallows-like structure, holding two big pots, and with hanging place for two men. Ishmael is momentarily disturbed.

It's ominous, thinks I. A Coffin my Innkeeper upon landing in my first whaling port; tombstones staring at me in the whalemen's chapel; and here a gallows! and a pair of prodigious black pots too! Are these last throwing out oblique hints touching Tophet? (p. 48a)

But the buckets of savory chowder he stows away at the inn soon put these morbid thoughts out of his mind.

Queequeg's little black god Yojo tells him that Ishmael should select their whaling ship. Leaving Queequeg to observe "some sort of Lent or Ramadan, or day of fasting, humiliation, and prayer," Ishmael goes to the docks alone the next morning. He picks out the "Pequod," an old-fashioned ship, with "venerable bows" and "ancient decks," steered by a tiller instead of a wheel, garnished with trophies of the whale hunt—the tiller itself is made of a whale's jawbone. "A noble craft," Ishmael comments, "but somehow a most melancholy! All noble things are touched with that" (p. 51b).

Ishmael is signed on the crew by the two captains aboard, Peleg and Bildad, crusty old veterans of the whaling hunt, now retired and part owners and agents of the "Pequod." Whaling crew members are paid a certain share of the profits of the voyage, according to their value and their bargaining ability. Ishmael gets a three-hundredth part, which will hardly pay for the clothing he will wear out in the three-year voyage.

Captain Peleg refuses Ishmael's request to see Captain Ahab, who is to command the vessel. Ahab is too sick to see anyone. "He's a grand, ungodly, god-like man . . . been used to deeper wonders than the waves; fixed his fiery lance in mightier, stranger foes than whales" (p. 59b). Ahab has been in a dark mood "ever since he lost his leg last voyage by the accursed whale." But Peleg insists that Ahab is essentially a good man— "Ahab has his humanities!" That he bears the name of a wicked king (see I Kings 16-22) is not significant. Ishmael is moved by sympathy, awe, and impatient curiosity toward this mysterious character.

A snag develops when Queequeg comes to sign on, for Peleg insists that he must first prove he is a Christian convert. Ishmael insists that Queequeg is a member and deacon of "the first congregational Church," and explains,

"I mean, sir, the same ancient Catholic Church to which you and I, and Captain Peleg there, and Queequeg here, and all of us, and every mother's son and soul of us belong; the great and everlasting First Congregation of this whole worshipping world; we all belong to that; only some of us cherish some crotchets noways touching the grand belief; in *that* we all join hands." (p. 66a)

That and a demonstration of Queequeg's pinpoint accuracy with the harpoon earn him a post with a ninetieth share.

As Ishmael and Queequeg leave the ship they encounter a shabby stranger, who makes ominous comments on their sailing aboard the "Pequod" and drops disturbing innuendoes about Captain Ahab. Finding that they have already signed on, he remarks, "Well, well, what's signed, is signed; and what's to be, will be; and then again, perhaps it won't be, after all. Anyhow, it's all fixed and arranged a'ready; and some sailors or other must go with him, I suppose" (p. 69b). The name of this prophet turns out to be Elijah, the same as that of the biblical figure who opposed King Ahab and the devotees of Baal.

Elijah is on the dock in the dim gray of dawn on the morning that they ship out. He asks if they have noted some men going aboard and to see if they can find them now. He goes away with the ominous farewell, "Shan't see ye again very soon, I guess; unless it's before the Grand Jury." The "Pequod" sails at noon, with Captain Ahab aboard, but "invisibly enshrined within his cabin." After piloting the ship to the point where it can take to the open sea, Bildad and Peleg get into their boat to go ashore, Bildad uttering various household admonitions and a warning to "beware of fornication" if they touch on the islands.

Ship and boat diverged; the cold, damp night-breeze blew between; a screaming gull flew overhead; the two hulls wildly rolled; we gave three heavy-hearted cheers, and blindly plunged like fate into the lone Atlantic. (p. 78a)

IV

The description of the voyage into the open sea begins with an elegy for the helmsman Bulkington that may remind us of that for the helmsman Palinurus in the *Aeneid*. (See *Imaginative Literature I*, p. 94.) Bulkington plays no further role in *Moby Dick,* but he embodies here the irresistible, restless, seagoing impulse that sends a man out almost immediately after he has returned from a long, arduous voyage—"The land seemed scorching to his feet." The narrator compares him to "the storm-tossed ship, that miserably drives along the leeward land," but must avoid the land and seek "the lashed sea's landlessness again; ..."

> ... all deep, earnest thinking is but the intrepid effort of the soul to keep the open independence of her sea; while the wildest winds of heaven and earth conspire to cast her on the treacherous, slavish shore?
> But as in landlessness alone resides the highest truth, shoreless, indefinite as God—so, better is it to perish in that howling infinite, than be ingloriously dashed upon the lee, even if that were safety! For worm-like, then, oh! who would craven crawl to land! Terrors of the terrible! is all this agony so vain? Take heart, take heart, O Bulkington! Bear thee grimly, demigod! Up from the spray of thy ocean-pershing—straight up, leaps thy apotheosis! (p. 78b)

In Chapters 26-27, the "knights and squires" of Ahab are introduced to the reader. These are the mates and the harpooners—the aristocracy of whaling ships. First is Starbuck, the chief mate, a serious, brave man, whose courage is part of his professional equipment.

> Starbuck was no crusader after perils; in him courage was not a sentiment; but a thing simply useful to him, and always at hand upon all mortally practical occasions ... For, thought Starbuck, I am here in this critical ocean to kill whales for my living, and not to be killed by them for theirs ... (p. 84a)

Stubb, the second mate, has a calm matter-of-fact attitude toward his dangerous work, keeping his boat comfortable, humming "old rigadig tunes while flank and flank with the most exasperated monster. Long usage had, for this Stubb, converted the jaws of death into an easy-chair" (p. 85b). Where Starbuck is keenly aware of the perils and horrors of whaling, Stubb regards them with an "almost impious good-humour" and fearlessness. Flask, the third mate, is gayest and most fearless of all, treating the great Leviathan of the seas as if it were "a species of magnified mouse," and the hunting of it as a big joke. "Little Flask" is called "King-Post," after the short, square timber that braces the Arctic whaler "against the icy concussions of those battering seas."

These three are the headmen, or commanders, of each of the whaling boats—"knights" equipped with "lances," their long whaling spears. Next in rank come their boat steerers or harpooners. Queequeg is Starbuck's harpooner. Tashtego, a Gay-Header Indian from Martha's Vineyard, is Stubb's "squire." Daggoo, "a gigantic, coal-black negro-savage, with a lion-like tread," is Flask's harpooner.

The rest of the crew, as on most American whalers, are foreigners from various islands. "*Isolatoes* too, I call such, not acknowledging the common continent of men, but each *Isolato* living on a separate continent of his own. Yet now, federated along one keel, what a set these Isolatoes were!" (p. 88a-b). And there is also Pip, the little black boy from Alabama, who goes mad with terror during the whale hunt.

Finally, there is Captain Ahab, the "supreme lord and dictator" of the vessel, crew, and voyage. His appearance startles Ishmael when he suddenly appears after days of isolation in his cabin. "He looked like a man cut away from the stake," and yet "made of solid bronze, and shaped in an unalterable mould." Strangest of all, there is "a slender rod-like mark, lividly whitish," running up one side of his face, as if he had been struck by lightning. The whole aspect of the man is grim, and this is heightened by "the barbaric white leg" made of the jawbone of a whale, which compensates for the leg he lost to another whale. Auger holes are bored into the plank of the quarter-deck, so that he may stand firmly and look out to sea.

There was an infinity of firmest fortitude, a determinate, unsurrenderable wilfulness, in the fixed and fearless, forward dedication of that glance . . . moody stricken Ahab stood before them with an apparently eternal anguish in his face; in all the nameless regal overbearing dignity of some mighty woe. (p. 90b)

There has been a foreshadowing of this startling person in Chapter 16, as Ishmael meditates on the type of character that sometimes emerges from among the Nantucket Quaker seamen:

. . . a mighty pageant creature, formed for noble tragedies. Nor will it at all detract from him, dramatically regarded, if either by birth or other circumstances, he have what seems a half wilful over-ruling morbidness at the bottom of his nature. For all men tragically great are made so through a certain morbidness. (p. 55a)

Hence the narrator treats "a poor old whale-hunter like

him . . . in all his Nantucket grimness and shagginess" as a royal personage. "For a Khan of the plank, and a king of the sea, and a great lord of Leviathans was Ahab" (pp. 93b-94a). But the tragic dramatist must go beneath the externals to reveal Ahab's greatness. "Oh, Ahab, what shall be grand in thee, it must needs be plucked at from the skies, and dived for in the deep, and featured in the unbodied air!" (p. 107b). The narrator drops the hint that Ahab is using the rigid hierarchical forms and usages that govern relations between a sea captain and his subordinates to serve his own ends. "That certain sultanism of his brain, which had otherwise in a good degree remained unmanifested; through those forms that same sultanism became incarnate in an irresistible dictatorship" (p. 107a).

In Chapter 34, "The Cabin-Table," we get a wonderful, humorous picture of "the punctilious externals" that are observed when the captain and his mates—here treated as the Sultan and his Emirs—eat dinner. First Ahab must go in and sit down, then Starbuck, then Stubb, and finally Flask. The latter, unseen by his superiors, goes into a ludicrous hornpipe before going into the captain's cabin, pausing to put on a serious face and enter "King Ahab's presence, in the character of Abjectus, or the Slave." The captain serves the mates as if they were children, each passing up his plate to him for the food. "And poor little Flask . . . the youngest son, and little boy of this weary family party" gets the shinbones of the salt beef. According to protocol he may not help himself, he gets the worst cuts, he must be the last man down and the first up; and if the second mate is in a hurry and wants to leave early, Flask must precede him and go hungry. Indeed, he claims that he has been hungry ever since he became an officer. On the other hand, the harpooners, just below him in the "pecking order," dine like kings, stowing away vast quantities of viands, and, unlike the officers who dine in grim silence, they make as much noise as comes naturally while eating.

The narration of the early portion of the voyage is climaxed by Ahab's declaration of his hidden purpose and the compact, sealed with vivid symbolism, between him and the crew. (See Ch. 36.) The narrator has constantly remarked on Ahab's mono-

maniacal aspect, "the footprints of his one unsleeping, ever-pac-
ing thought" on his brow, the "intense bigotry of purpose in his
aspect." That one idea is revealed, when Ahab calls all hands up
to the quarter-deck and tells them that whoever "raises me a
white-headed whale with a wrinkled brow and a crooked jaw"
shall receive a golden Spanish coin worth sixteen dollars. He
nails the gold piece to the mainmast amid the cheers of the men.
The harpooners recognize the whale he has described as Moby
Dick, and Ahab admits to Starbuck that this is the whale that bit
off his leg.

> "Aye, aye! and I'll chase him round Good Hope, and round the Horn,
> and round the Norway Maelstrom, and round perdition's flames before
> I give him up. And this is what ye have shipped for, men! to chase
> that white whale on both sides of land, and over all sides of earth, till
> he spouts black blood and rolls fin out . . ." (p. 119b)

Starbuck objects that he "came here to hunt whales, not my
commander's vengeance," and that "Vengeance on a dumb
brute that simply smote thee from blindest instinct" is madness
and blasphemy. Ahab answers:

> ". . . All visible objects, man, are but as pasteboard masks. But in each
> event—in the living act, the undoubted deed—there, some unknown but
> still reasoning thing puts forth the mouldings of its features from behind
> the unreasoning mask. If man will strike, strike through the mask! How
> can the prisoner reach outside except by thrusting through the wall?
> To me, the white whale is that wall, shoved near to me. Sometimes I
> think there's naught beyond. But 'tis enough. He tasks me; he heaps
> me; I see in him outrageous strength, with an inscrutable malice
> sinewing it. That inscrutable thing is chiefly what I hate; and be the
> white whale agent, or be the white whale principal, I will wreak that
> hate upon him. Talk not to me of blasphemy, man; I'd strike the sun
> if it insulted me. For could the sun do that, then could I do the other;
> since there is ever a sort of fair play herein, jealously presiding over
> all creations. But not my master, man, is even that fair play. Who's
> over me? Truth hath no confines . . ." (p. 120a-b)

Ahab now leads the ritual of the compact, "an old custom
of my fishermen fathers before me." First the crew drink the
hot grog from a brimming pewter flagon. Then the mates cross
their lances before Ahab, and he grasps the lances at their
axis, looking at his mates with a "strong, sustained, and mystic
aspect," as if to shock into them "the same fiery emotion ac-

cumulated within the Leyden jar of his own magnetic life."
(Melville apparently has in mind the universal power mani-
fested in extraordinary events and beings, which the South
Sea Islanders call mana.) Ahab is aware of "the full-forced
shock" of "mine own electric thing," which he might lose by
transmitting it, and which might kill the others.

He appoints the mates "three cupbearers to my three pagan
kinsmen,"—the harpooners—and while the mates hold the de-
tached iron parts of the harpoons, he pours the liquor into the
sockets. The three harpooners drink from "the murderous
chalices" and join in an "indissoluble league" to "hunt Moby
Dick to his death." The cup is passed around to "the frantic
crew" again, and the ceremony ends.

The ensuing chapters give the reaction of Ahab, the mates,
and the crew to this weird event. (See Ch. 37-40.) They include
three prose soliloquies—by Ahab, Starbuck, and Stubb—and a
dramatic scene of songs and dialogue among the crew, along
with stage directions. Ahab's soliloquy exults over his bend-
ing the wills of the others to serve his own "demoniac" fixed
purpose. Starbuck laments his submission to a will he opposes,
his sailing with a heathen, demonic crew, and the "latent horror" that he has just discovered in life. Stubb, on the other
hand, considers "a laugh's the wisest, easiest answer to all
that's queer," and finds "unfailing comfort" in the thought that
"it's all predestinated."

V

It is at this point (Ch. 41-42) that the title character is introduced—introduced in prospect and interpretation, and in relation to Ahab's monomaniacal purpose, for Moby Dick does not
enter the action until the final three chapters. Ishmael tells
how the terrible reputation of this "unaccompanied, secluded
White Whale . . . of uncommon magnitude and malignity" has
grown among whaling men, based on the actual havoc he has
wrought and on superstitious "rumours and portents" which
fitted in with their beliefs about sperm whales in general.
Moby Dick is believed to be ubiquitous, appearing on opposite sides of the world at the same time. He is also believed

to be immortal (" for immortality is but ubiquity in time"), escaping certain death time and time again. But aside from such beliefs, his very appearance is enough to strike terror— his immenseness, the "shrouded hue" which gives him the name White Whale, and his deformed, sickle-shaped lower jaw, but, above all, his "unexampled, intelligent malignity," his "infernal forethought of ferocity," the apparent purposefulness of his actions. It was this "seeming malice" that drove Ahab, mutilated by Moby Dick, to his monomaniacal vengefulness.

. . . ever since that almost fatal encounter, Ahab had cherished a wild vindictiveness against the whale, all the more fell for that in his frantic morbidness he at last came to identify with him, not only all his bodily woes, but all his intellectual and spiritual exasperations. The White Whale swam before him as the monomaniac incarnation of all those malicious agencies which some deep men feel eating in them, till they are left living on with half a heart and half a lung. That intangible malignity which has been from the beginning; to whose dominion even the modern Christians ascribe one-half of the worlds; which the ancient Ophites of the east reverenced in their statue devil;—Ahab did not fall down and worship it like them; but deliriously transferring its idea to the abhorred white whale, he pitted himself, all mutilated, against it. All that most maddens and torments; all that stirs up the lees of things; all truth with malice in it; all that cracks the sinews and cakes the brain; all the subtle demonisms of life and thought; all evil, to crazy Ahab, were visibly personified, and made practically assailable in Moby Dick. He piled upon the whale's white hump the sum of all the general rage and hate felt by his whole race from Adam down; and then, as if his chest had been a mortar, he burst his hot heart's shell upon it. (pp. 135b-136a)

As for himself, Ishmael is moved by the mystical whiteness of Moby Dick. He contends that whiteness, especially when "coupled with any object terrible in itself," arouses awe and horror. He points to the polar bear, the white shark, the albatross, dead human bodies, ghosts, and the albino as manifestations of "this crowning attribute of the terrible." Ishmael proceeds to evoke the meaning of various "imaginative impressions" to illuminate the horror that whiteness arouses in the soul, and he concludes:

Is it that by its indefiniteness it shadows forth the heartless voids and immensities of the universe, and thus stabs us from behind with the thought of annihilation, when beholding the white depths of the milky way? Or is it, that as in essence whiteness is not so much a colour as the visible absence of colour, and at the same time the concrete of all colours; is it for these reasons that there is such a dumb blankness, full of meaning, in a wide landscape of snows—a colourless, all-colour of atheism from which we shrink? And when we consider that other theory of the natural philosophers, that all other earthly hues—every stately or lovely emblazoning—the sweet tinges of sunset skies and woods; yea, and the gilded velvets of butterflies, and the butterfly cheeks of young girls; all these are but subtile deceits, not actually inherent in substance, but only laid on from without; and when we proceed further, and consider that the mystical cosmetic which produces every one of her hues, the great principle of light, for ever remains white or colourless in itself, and if operating without medium upon matter, would touch all objects, even tulips and roses, with its own blank tinge—pondering all this, the palsied universe lies before us a leper; and like wilful travellers in Lapland, who refuse to wear coloured and colouring glasses upon their eyes, so the wretched infidel gazes himself blind at the monumental white shroud that wraps all the prospect around him. And of all these things the Albino whale was the symbol. Wonder ye then at the fiery hunt? (pp. 144b-145a)

As for the crew, he does not claim to have plumbed "their unconscious understandings," but he suggests that to them Moby Dick represents "the gliding great demon of the seas of life" (p. 138a).

VI

These are the characters and the forces that enact the story of *Moby Dick*. The basic pattern of the story is the voyage of the "Pequod," punctuated by its various lowerings for whales, meetings with other ships, and the incidents of life and work on board. A new set of characters appears at the first lowering (Ch. 48)—a picked crew to man Ahab's boat, which he had signed on secretly and kept hidden in the hold in order not to alarm the ship's owners about his intentions. They are yellow men, from "the Manillas," led by Fedallah, a tall, swart figure with a turban. The narrator often hints that they are diabolical creatures. Fedallah especially is singled out for his demonic qualities. Stubb thinks that Fedallah is the devil, has his tail rolled up and hidden away in his jacket, and aims at swapping Moby Dick for Ahab's soul. Fedallah's fate is tied up with

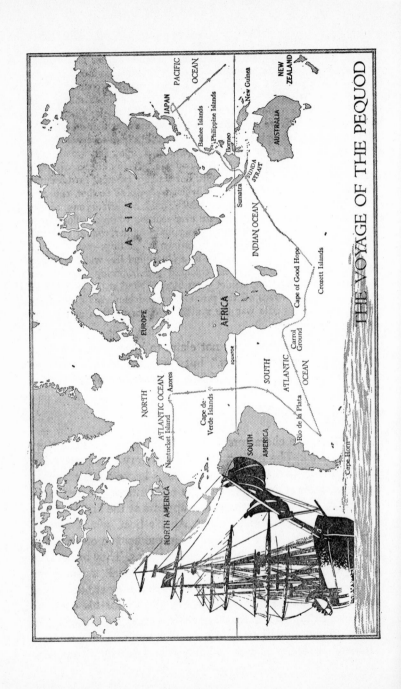

THE VOYAGE OF THE PEQUOD

Ahab's, for it is ordained, so Fedallah prophesies, that he must die before Ahab.

As the voyage progresses, Ahab discards the ordinary human activities and interests. He throws his pipe into the sea (p. 94a); regrets his inability to enjoy the world anymore (p. 123a); gives up his razors, "for now I neither shave, sup, nor pray" (p. 359a; also p. 391a); destroys his quadrant as a "vain toy" of cursed science (p. 366 a-b; also p. 375b and Ch. 124). In Chapter 119 Ahab contends with the lightning from heaven. He glories in his nickname "Old Thunder" and claims descent from the lightning, his "fiery father," whom he addresses as "unbegotten" and "omniscient" (though recognizing an eternal "unsuffusing thing" beyond the lightning). He has the steel razors he has discarded made into barbs, tempered with the blood of pagan harpooners, and howls *"Ego non baptizo te in nomine patris, sed in nomine diaboli!"* ("I do not baptize you in the name of the Father, but in the name of the devil"; p. 359b). These barbs, intended for Moby Dick, are struck by lightning, and thus are tempered both by blood and lightning. (See pp. 371f., 393.) Ahab loses his hat to a sea hawk, which snatches it from his head as he sits perched in a basket at the top of the mast, searching for Moby Dick. The narrator implies that the incident is ominous.

So hardhearted and immune to human appeals does Ahab become that he refuses the desperate plea of the captain of the ship "Rachel" to help him pick up a boat missing after an encounter with the White Whale. Even the revelation that the captain's own son, a twelve-year-old boy, is among the missing does not dissuade the monomaniacal Ahab, who does not want to incur a moment's delay in his hunt, now close to fruition, "after so long and wide a preliminary cruise." There is a final poignant picture of the "Rachel" zigzagging across the ocean, seeking the missing. "But by her still halting course and winding, woeful way, you plainly saw that this ship so wept with spray, still remained without comfort. She was *Rachel*, weeping for her children, because they were not" (p. 388b). (See Jer. 31:15 and Matt. 2:18.)

Before the chase begins, Ahab has a moment of common

human feeling. It is a lovely day, and this time Ahab enjoys to the fullest the sky and water and breezes.

That glad, happy air, that winsome sky, did at last stroke and caress him; the stepmother world, so long cruel—forbidding—now threw affectionate arms round his stubborn neck, and did seem to joyously sob over him, as if over one, that however wilful and erring, she could yet find it in her heart to save and to bless. From beneath his slouched hat Ahab dropped a tear into the sea; nor did all the Pacific contain such wealth as that one wee drop. (pp. 394b–395a)

He talks to Starbuck about his forty years at sea, the solitude of command, his marriage at fifty to a young girl whom he made in effect a widow, and the madness and dangers of the whale hunt. He is thankful to look into Starbuck's eyes, into a human eye which alone can be the "magic glass" whereby he sees his wife and child—it is better to gaze into a human eye than into the sea or sky or on God. Starbuck begs him to give up the hunt for the White Whale and keep himself safe for his wife and child.

But Ahab's glance was averted; like a blighted fruit tree he shook, and cast his last cindered apple to the soil.

"What is it, what nameless, inscrutable, unearthly thing is it; what cozening, hidden lord and master, and cruel, remorseless emperor commands me; that against all natural lovings and longings, I so keep pushing, and crowding, and jamming myself on all the time; recklessly making me ready to do what in my own proper, natural heart, I durst not so much as dare? Is Ahab, Ahab? Is it I, God, or who, that lifts this arm? But if the great sun move not of himself; but is as an errand-boy in heaven; nor one single star can revolve, but by some invisible power; how then can this one small heart beat; this one small brain think thoughts; unless God does that beating, does that thinking, does that living, and not I. By heaven, man, we are turned round and round in this world, like yonder windlass, and Fate is the handspike. And all the time, lo! that smiling sky, and this unsounded sea! Look! see yon Albicore! who put it into him to chase and fang that flying-fish? Where do murderers go, man? Who's to doom, when the judge himself is dragged to the bar? But it is a mild, mild wind, and a mild-looking sky; and the air smells now, as if it blew from a faraway meadow; they have been making hay somewhere under the slopes of the Andes, Starbuck, and the mowers are sleeping among the new-mown hay. Sleeping? Aye, toil we how we may, we all sleep at last on the field. Sleep? Aye, and rust amid greenness; as last year's scythes flung down, and left in the half-cut swathes—Starbuck!" (pp. 396b–397a)

The book ends magnificently with the pursuit of Moby Dick, which takes three days and three chapters. The White Whale proves to be all that rumor has forecast. He is a malign and awful force, turning to dash boats to pieces, flailing his tail among the men and wreckage. Ahab, though thrown into the water the first two days, his whalebone leg smashed, and Fedallah gone, is intransigent. After the "morn" and the "noon" —the first two days—comes the "night"—the third day. Ahab, sensing that he is embarking on his final conflict, sets off in a sea full of sharks to meet Moby Dick "Forehead to forehead." The whale circumvents all attempts to kill him and ends up by charging the "Pequod" head-on and sinking it. Ahab makes a last desperate attempt to harpoon the whale, but he is caught by the line and suddenly strangled and shot out into the water. His boat and crew go down in the concentric circles formed by the sinking "Pequod." Tashtego, the Indian harpooner, has been hammering at the top of the mast, and as he goes down, his hammer catches the wing of a sky hawk.

. . . and so the bird of heaven, with archangelic shrieks, and his imperial beak thrust upwards, and his whole captive form folded in the flag of Ahab, went down with his ship, which, like Satan, would not sink to hell till she had dragged a living part of heaven along with her, and helmeted herself with it.
Now small fowls flew screaming over the yet yawning gulf; a sullen white surf beat against its steep sides; then all collapsed, and the great shroud of the sea rolled on as it rolled five thousand years ago. (p. 419b)

Ishmael alone is saved, and keeps afloat with a coffin Queequeg had made for himself and which now serves as a life buoy. In the end he is picked up by *the devious-cruising* Rachel, *that in her retracting search after her missing children, only found another orphan.*

VII

Melville's tale of the pursuit of the White Whale includes a factual account of whales and whaling. Chapter 32 presents Melville's "cetology," or science of whales, which he does not claim to be complete, precise, or perfectly systematic—"because any human thing supposed to be complete, must for that very reason infallibly be faulty," and he is "the architect, not the builder" (p. 97a-b). His sources range from the Bible and Aristotle to the writers of his own time. (See also the "Extracts"—supplied by a sub-sub-librarian—pp. xi-xx.) He stresses the supreme importance of the sperm whale, the family to which Moby Dick belongs, as against the attention given to the Greenland or right whale by other writers. And, as against biologists like Linnaeus, he asserts that the whale is a fish, the one fish with lungs and warm blood, and finally defines a whale as "*a spouting fish with a horizontal tail.*" The sperm whale he describes as "the largest inhabitant of the globe; the most formidable of all whales to encounter; the most majestic in aspect; and lastly, by far the most valuable in commerce; he being the only creature from which that valuable substance, spermaceti, is obtained" (p. 99a).

Being a literary man, Melville presents his systematic division of whales or cetaceans in terms of the size of pages in books—folio, octavo, duodecimo—from the largest to the smallest. These three main "books" are divided into "chapters"; for instance, Book I (Folio) is divided into six chapters, ranging from the sperm whale to the sulphur-bottom whale. The sperm whale of Chapter I is the representative type of Folio I; similarly, the grampus whale is the typical whale of Book II (Octavo), and the porpoise is the typical type of Book III (Duodecimo). Melville considers the porpoise the smallest of the whales, and hence concludes that any genuine whales hereafter discovered will fit into his system. He insists again at the close on its imperfections and incompleteness.

Heaven keep me from ever completing anything. This whole book is but a draught—nay, but the draught of a draught. Oh, Time, Strength, Cash, and Patience! (p. 105b)

In Chapter 45, "The Affidavit," the narrator substantiates his account of Moby Dick by historical evidence of individual sperm whales of marked maliciousness and power. "So ignorant are most landsmen of some of the plainest and most palpable wonders of the world, that without some hints touching the plain facts, historical and otherwise, of the fishery, they might scout at Moby Dick as a monstrous fable, or still worse and more detestable, a hideous and intolerable allegory" (p. 152a). Indeed, shortly after *Moby Dick* appeared, Melville learned that a whale had just sunk a whaling ship near Panamá. "Ye Gods!" he wrote his informant, "what a Commentator is this . . . whale. What he has to say is short & pithy & very much to the point. I wonder if my evil art has raised this monster."

In Chapters 55-57, he attacks the erroneous pictures of whales by artists, but points to some that are close to "the true form of the whale as he actually appears to the eye of the whaleman when in his own absolute body the whale is moored alongside the Whale-ship." Subsequent chapters present a graphic picture of the equipment and technique of hunting whales. Chapter 60, "The Line," deals with "the magical, sometimes horrible whale-line," which plays such a dramatic role in the culmination of the story. We learn the details of its composition and how it lies coiled dangerously around the crew of each boat and how it may strangle a man and pull him overboard if anything goes amiss. But this, Melville points out, is the situation of every man in everyday existence—"born with halters around their necks," but it is only when caught in the swift, sudden turn of death that mortals realize "the silent, subtle, ever-present perils of life" (p. 209b). In Chapters 62-63, the narrator informs us of the use of the dart and the crotch, in order "to elucidate several most important, however intricate passages, in scenes hereafter to be painted."

Chapters 67-69, 74-80, 85-86, 95-98, and 102-105 deal with the various organs and structures of the whale, and the processes of dismemberment and extraction of valuable substances that the crew perform on the body of the whale. Whole chapters are devoted to the whale's spout, head, tail, genital organ, skeleton, and dimensions. And in Chapters 82-83 Melville throws in material from pagan mythology and a critical comment on the biblical story of Jonah. The narrator, perhaps in self-defense, points out to the reader: "There are some enterprises in which a careful disorderliness is the true method" (p. 267a).

VIII

Why is the narrator called "Ishmael"?

Ishmael, in the Old Testament, is the son of Abraham and the bondwoman Hagar. (See Genesis 16:11-16.) The name means "God hears (or will hear)." It has come to mean "social outcast," following the role assigned to Ishmael by the angel of the Lord—"And he will be a wild man; his hand will be against every man, and every man's hand against him" (Gen. 16:12).

Why does Melville give this name to his narrator? Is the Ishmael of the story an outcast from society because of his wanderlust and his quest for the remote? Is he one of those men who do not belong to the common life and ways of men—an "Isolato"? Was Melville also such an outcast? Does he identify himself with Ishmael? Why does he choose an "Ishmael" to tell his story? Does Ishmael ever play a part in the story in accordance with his name? Is there any particular significance in having the ship that rescues him called the "Rachel"?

Is the inclusion of factual and historical material a defect in this novel?

It has been pointed out as far back as Aristotle's *Poetics* that conformity with actual events or persons is irrelevant to the quality and effect of a work of fiction. Plausibility in imaginative works, according to this view, does not rest on their conformity with the reports of common experience. Even an utterly unlikely event may be made impressively plausible by the poet's skill. Why, then, does Melville, who displays such great poetic powers, insist on putting so much nonfictional material into a work of fiction?

Let us put it the other way around. What difference does it make for you, the reader, that Melville proceeds in this way? Let us suppose that Melville's white whale were as fictitious a creature as the centaur or other imaginary creatures of mythology. Would that make *Moby Dick* a better story? Or is the imaginative effect of this story enhanced by the fact that it is about an actual creature, a sort of archetype of the actual whales described in Melville's "cetology"? Do the realistic details add meaning, substance, and depth to the story, or would you just as soon have them omitted? Do the factual sections hinder your absorption and appreciation of the story, or do you take them in your stride, once you get used to them?

Is the factual, empirical material one of many "levels" of the story? If so, what are the other levels, and how is the factual level related to the others?

Who is the hero of Moby Dick?

Who is the predominant figure or force in the action? Is it Captain Ahab? Moby Dick? The Sea? The evil in the universe? Fate? The human spirit?

If Ahab is the hero, whom does he resemble most among the heroes in our previous readings—Ulysses, Orestes, Aeneas, Othello, Lear, Macbeth, Tom Jones, or Faust? Is Ahab a tragic hero in the Aristotelian sense—a man above the ordinary who falls from happiness to misery through a defect in character? Is he merely "the Fates' lieutenant" enacting "under orders" what has been immutably decreed for billions of years? (See p. 410a.) Or is he a modern Prometheus hurling his defiance at the divine or demonic power at the core of things? (See Vol. 5, pp. 40-51, and the First Reading in the *Religion and Theology* Reading Plan.) Is he a Faustian hero, who has mortgaged his soul to demonic powers to accomplish obsessive ends? Is Ahab a romantic hero, yearning for infinite power and knowledge? Does he have an irresistible impulse to understand as well as to fight the evil in the universe? Is he overwhelmed in the end, or do his defiance and his insight transcend his death? (See his final words, p. 418b.)

What is the theme of Moby Dick?

The fictional action of this novel centers around Ahab's quest for vengeance against the white whale that bit off his leg. Moby Dick is a whale like those actually experienced and recorded by whaling men, and the "Pequod" and her voyage are much like the ships and voyages that took place at the time. But is Moby Dick a whale like any other? Is Ahab concerned only with vengeance against a brute beast, as Starbuck charges? If Moby Dick is not merely a whale, what does he stand for? For the evil, fault, suffering, and contradiction in the universe of man's experience? Does *Moby Dick,* like the Book of Job, deal with the problem of evil? Where, then, is God in *Moby Dick*? Or what sort of God is assumed, if any? Is he the predestinating God of Father Mapple's sermon? Is Moby Dick serving some inscrutable divine purpose? Or is it just that Ahab is fighting so intransigently against him? Is Moby Dick the symbol or agent of the ultimate power in the universe? If so, is that power conceived as good or bad, so far as human happiness is concerned?

Is *Moby Dick* ultimately hopeful or pessimistic concerning human aspiration and striving? Do Ahab's last words contain the final meaning of the book? Or is it contained in the narrator's words at the end of the last chapter—"and the great shroud of the sea rolled on as it rolled five thousand years ago" (p. 419b)? What does the final incident of "a living part of heaven" going down with the ship signify?

Is Moby Dick *defective in formal structure?*

This work includes various literary genres—travel, history, saga, drama, epic, natural history, philosophy, mythology, and fictional narrative. This nineteenth-century American author often borrows language, images, and dramatic devices from Shakespeare. The work is extremely episodic in form, jumping from one scene and event to another in 135 chapters, some of them only a page or less in length. Also, the work is said to have very little plot, in the sense of a logical progression of events to a climax and conclusion. Melville uses little if any of the narrative devices of the conventional novelist, merely introducing subjects and events as he sees fit, as the voyage of the "Pequod" proceeds. He jumps frequently from the first-person account by Ishmael to the third-person account of an omniscient narrator. For these and other reasons, many readers consider *Moby Dick* confusing or dull.

Does this work confuse or bore you? Do you accept Melville's unique manner of narration with interest and enjoyment, or does it annoy and hamper you? Does this work have a unity? If so, where does the unity lie—in its form, its mood, its style, its theme, or its general over-all effect? If we do not have the traditional plot, as a definite line of action, what sort of plot do we have here? Is this a plot centered on characters, ideas, or something else?

Is Melville expressing his own feelings and experiences in this story?

Is this book, from the first to the last words, an expression of Melville's frustration, isolation, and pessimism? Is the "outcast" Ishmael the literary body and voice of Melville? Does the author identify himself with the "Isolatoes" that go down to the sea in whaling ships? Is the frustrated old blacksmith, Perth, an expression of Melville's state or a prophetic insight of his future lot in life?

Does our knowledge of the author's life add to our appreciation and understanding of the work before us? Or is an awareness of the biographical reality out of which the author wrote irrelevant to what a work of fiction communicates to us? Should we just concentrate on the work and forget the writer, or is this impossible? Can we turn the biographical interpretation around and learn something about the author from his work? Is all writing self-revelatory, especially fiction writing? Can a writer succeed in concealing himself and keeping himself completely out of the story?

Rainer Maria Rilke, a great German poet of our time, said that the poet should write out of his experience and suffering—*with* them, so to speak, but not *about* them. Which does Melville do in *Moby Dick?* Is he writing *about* his personal state and experience or *with* them? Has he fashioned an objective work of art? Does his personal slant and tone distort and detract from the aesthetic qualities of the work or add to them?

The following questions are designed to help you test the thoroughness of your reading. Each question is to be answered by giving a page or pages of the reading assignment. Answers will be found on page 248 of this Reading Plan.

1 What are the sights of New Bedford?

2 What is the menu at the Try Pots Inn?

3 What do the upper classes in Queequeg's country use for sofas?

4 What is a Specksynder?

5 Does Ahab retain his intellectual power in his madness?

6 What is a "gam"?

7 What is a "brit"?

8 What is the difference between a Fast-Fish and a Loose-Fish?

9 What is the "cassock"?

10 What led the blacksmith to his ruin?

TOLSTOY

War and Peace

Vol. 51

About a hundred years ago, a Russian aristocrat, in the bliss of his early married life and the peace of his country estate, started to write what was to be the greatest war novel of all time. It turned out to be a titanic task, requiring many years, and the finished book ran over a thousand pages. What was originally intended as a story of family life, set against the background of the conflict between Russia and Napoleonic France, became a great historical novel, including a philosophy of history.

This unique combination of fiction, history, and philosophy in the form of a novel was put together by a unique writer. Not since Goethe had such a many-sided figure appeared in Western literature. Soldier, hunter, magistrate, aristocrat, anarchist, educator, religious reformer, aesthetic critic—he commanded world-wide attention in his time by his very being and character as well as by his writings. In his own lifetime, his estate became a shrine to which people journeyed from all parts of the world to come into contact with his person and spirit.

War and Peace, however, was written before Tolstoy had become a world figure and attained prophetic or saintly status. It is the work of his literary prime, when writing was his sole vocation, and he could pour all his creative powers into this single channel. Moreover, he set out to write a great work, to take advantage of this peaceful pause in his turbulent life, to satisfy his urge toward literary creation. When he had finished his task, he was convinced that he had written one of the masterpieces of world literature.

Generations of readers have shared this opinion. They have been enthralled by his lifelike re-creation of common human experience, by the constructive power with which he handles hundreds of characters and events, by the magnificent and realistic portrait of battles and the men who fight them. In the twentieth century, when war has played so large a role in the lives of individuals and nations, Tolstoy's novel has drawn an enthusiastic response, for it has answered to the experience and condition of millions of people.

It also answered to the experience of millions of men in Tolstoy's own day. The year in which he started to write this book was also the year of Gettysburg, marking the mid-point of the bloodiest war in history up to that time. At the end of that war, Abraham Lincoln, the American plebeian, came to a conclusion somewhat similar to that which Tolstoy, the Russian aristocrat, arrived at a few years later in his philosophy of history—that men do not control and decide historical events. But where Lincoln appealed to the traditional doctrine of Divine Providence, Tolstoy appealed to the idea of historical inevitability.

Sixth Reading

I

Until the reign of Peter the Great (1672-1725), Russia had little contact with the history and culture of the West. The Russian tsars considered themselves the successors of the emperors of the eastern half of the Roman Empire. Russian Christianity was derived from the Greek or Eastern sector of the early Catholic Church, which separated from the Roman or Western sector in the Great Schism of 1054. (See Fourteenth Reading, *Religion and Theology*.) The Russian language, originally a Slavonic tongue, was transformed into a written language, using a partly Greek alphabet (the Cyrillic) and Greek syntax, by monks in the ninth century. This so-called "Church Slavonic" was used mainly for religious writings, and a secular literature arose very slowly. But there was an immense oral folk "literature," rich in fables, fairy stories, sagas, proverbs, and folk tales, which demonstrated the fertility of the Russian imagination.

Western influence began to seep into Russian culture about 1650, with the introduction of a new Latinized scholasticism. Peter the Great, interested in opening "a window on Europe," encouraged the inroads of Western culture and the development of a new secular language and literature. The great culture of the age was French, and French language and literature became the central concern of the Russian intellectual and social élite. Russian literature reflected the Neoclassical modes and attitudes of contemporary French literature, and also of the later Romantic countermovement.

It was not until the nineteenth century that Russia, the late-comer in the family of European nations, produced an original literature of a quality and depth sufficient to place it among the world's great literatures. The nineteenth century was an era of creative explosion, the golden age of Russian literature. In the sixty years from 1820 to 1880—just two generations—Alexander Pushkin (1799-1837), Nikolai Gogol (1809-1852), Ivan Turgenev (1818-1883), Fyodor Dostoevsky (1821-1881), and Leo Tolstoy (1828-1910) wrote their masterworks, which also became the masterworks of Russian literature and contributed to the legacy of world literature. Dostoevsky asserted in a famous speech at Pushkin's grave in 1880 that the specifically Russian and the universally human were bound together in the great Russian writers, and that Pushkin, the great national poet of Russia, was the most universal of all the great European poets. Dostoevsky proclaimed Russia's peculiar mission to be the achievement of "the universal union of all mankind," through the works of the spirit, including literature and culture.

Although the contemporary world is divided on the claim of present-day Russia to universal moral and spiritual leadership, there can be no doubt that this late-comer to the world of literature has produced works of lasting and universal value. The works of the giants of Russian literature mentioned above—and particularly those of Tolstoy and Dostoevsky—are read and reread today all over the world. *War and Peace* and *The Brothers Karamazov* are almost as well known to readers in Chicago and Tokyo as they are in Moscow and Leningrad.

II

Leo Nikolayevich Tolstoy was born into a noble and rich family, of the class whose privileges and status he later sought to abolish. His youth was spent in a gay social life and desultory attendance at a university, interspersed by a vain attempt to manage the family estate and better the condition of his serfs. An enlistment in an artillery unit in the Caucasus introduced him to military life and was also the occasion for the beginning of his literary career. During the Crimean War he participated in active fighting against the Turks on the Danube and at the siege of Sevastopol. His *Sevastopol Sketches*, written during the fighting, made him famous in Russian social and literary circles. His army service also provided basic material for *The Cossacks* and *War and Peace*.

After he left the army, Tolstoy traveled in Western Europe. On the whole, he was unfavorably impressed by Western culture and institutions, but he found the German schools, and particularly Froebel's new kindergarten system, praiseworthy. Back home, he became a local magistrate, charged with arbitrating disputes between the landed gentry and their newly emancipated serfs. He also started a school for peasant children, directed toward fostering the growth of natural insight, rather than fitting them for the artificial culture of civilized society. Exhausted by these activities, and by the opposition they aroused, Tolstoy gave them up and retired to the steppes —"I threw it all overboard and drove out to the Kalmucks on the steppes to drink mares' milk and lead an animal life," he tells us in his *Confessions* (1879-1884).

After he returned from the steppes (1862), he married and entered into what he called "a correct, honorable family life." It was in this period of early marital happiness and tranquillity that he wrote his two greatest masterpieces, *War and Peace* (1865-1869) and *Anna Karenina* (1875-1877). Despite his literary creativity and fame and the satisfactions of family life, however, Tolstoy felt that his life was empty, frustrated, and meaningless. Looking backward, he saw the early stage of "innocent, joyous, poetic childhood," followed by a period of youth and young manhood "in the service of ambition, vanity, and above all, of lust." His marriage and family life he considered a third stage, which postponed but could not avert the inevitable spiritual crisis and his ascent to the fourth and final stage of religious life. This crisis occurred from about 1876 to 1879 and culminated in his conversion to the ethic of the Gospels and particularly to nonresistance (or nonviolent resistance) to evil.

He set forth his unorthodox views of the essence of Christianity in a series of books, tracts, and stories. One of his finest short stories, *The Death of Ivan Ilyitch* (1884), is an expression of his conversion experience. He also carried his views into actual life. He worked in the fields with the peasants, learned the trade of shoemaking, became a vegetarian, and lived the simple life. Feeling that private property was evil, he signed over his estate to his wife and children. He brought aid to the victims of the great famine of 1891-1892, and he helped the Dukhobors—a pacifist, communist Christian sect—to escape persecution by the government and emigate abroad. His last novel, *Resurrection* (1899-1900), which attacked the Orthodox Church, led to his excommunication in 1901.

A small Tolstoyan cult grew up in Russia in Tolstoy's lifetime, but it had little influence, and its members were often persecuted. Abroad, however, Tolstoy attained great fame for his religious and social views. His home became a center of pilgrimage for people from all over the world—from Asia as well as from Europe and America. He was regarded with a veneration comparable to that accorded Mahatma Gandhi and Albert Schweitzer in our day. In the period after his death, Tolstoy's social and religious views influenced in part the nonviolent resistance practiced in India and elsewhere, and the establishment of communal settlements such as those founded by the Zionists in Palestine. Tolstoy's educational theories—emphasizing freedom, experience, experimentation, and a pupil-centered approach—belong to the tradition of Rousseau, Pestalozzi, Montessori, and Dewey, and his ideas have been echoed in American programs of "progressive" education.

However important and characteristic all these activities were in Tolstoy's life and activity, his central gifts and creations were literary. It is more accurate to compare him with that other many-sided literary master, Goethe, than with Gandhi and Schweitzer. Tolstoy's greatness as a writer was recognized early in his career. It was Turgenev, himself considered as the consummate living Russian writer, who bestowed the accolade of "the great writer of Russia" on Tolstoy, his younger rival. Turgenev's verdict was shared by critics and readers both in Russia and abroad, and Tolstoy's stature as the Colossus of Russian literature continued long after his death.

Tolstoy himself—like Goethe, well aware of his great gifts—also shared Turgenev's opinion and extended it to his place in world literature. He compared himself with Homer, *War and Peace* with the *Iliad,* and saw Homeric qualities in his early trilogy, *Childhood, Boyhood, and Youth.* At a time when his great novels had not yet been completed, he wrote with supreme confidence in his diary that his works—finished, unfinished, or even unconceived—belonged with the greatest writings in world literature. Like Goethe, he regarded himself as a Titan or "Olympian" and, before his spiritual crisis at least, enjoyed this realization.

There is some point to Tolstoy's feeling of affinity with Homer, for one of the outstanding characteristics of his fiction is the capacity for the imaginative representation of objective reality—of human action and the natural world. This professed ascetic and hater of the flesh in later life demonstrated a remarkable power to evoke and render, in clear, luminous prose, the sensual aspect of things and the physical side of human nature and relations. His works contain vivid and unforgettable pictures of battle, the hunt, farm work, family life, and erotic love. These scenes, as well as landscapes and emotional turmoil, are presented in controlled, objective, deft prose, which often conveys much meaning in a few words. He never lost this literary power and deftness—usually associated with Classic or Neoclassic writers rather than with Russian novelists —even when he was writing the evangelical tracts and fiction of his later period.

In his old age Tolstoy reversed his early high opinions of his literary works, and dismissed them as sinful vanity and "artistic twaddle" which had earned "an unmerited significance." It was also in his old age that he wrote *What Is Art?* (1896), a systematic exposition of his views on art. This work sees art as the intentional communication of feeling from one human being to another through an objective form. The purely aesthetic value of a work of art is to be measured by the effectiveness with which the form conveys the feeling, by what Tolstoy calls its "infectiousness." But art is not to be evaluated by purely formal standards, for it has an effect on human life and society. It binds men together through their common response to works of art and unites them with the men of the past. It influences and shapes human feeling, imagination, emotion, and ideas and, hence, human conduct. Because of this decisive influence, a work of art must also be judged ethically by the criterion of whether the feelings it communicates are beneficial or injurious to human life.

Tolstoy did not say that the communication of "wholesome" and "positive" feelings by itself makes a work of art good. He insisted on the essential need of an adequate form to convey feeling and on the rare intuition and judgment required to construct such a form. He recognized that "unwholesome" and "negative" feelings may be conveyed in the most masterly and "infectious" manner. But it is for precisely this reason that he considered that formally perfect art may be the source of ethical and social evil. In Tolstoy's view, truly good art unites men with each other and with God. It conveys universally comprehensible feelings, which may be more accessible to a simple peasant or a child than to a highly educated person who has been uprooted from spontaneous feeling.

Tolstoy's examples of universal art are *Don Quixote*, Mollière's comedies, *David Copperfield*, *Pickwick Papers*, and the tales of Pushkin and Gogol. A truly Christian art, he said, must unite all men, not members of one nation or one church. He regarded *Les Misérables*, *A Tale of Two Cities*, *Uncle Tom's Cabin*, and Dostoevsky's *House of the Dead* as Christian art, but rejected Dante's *Divine Comedy* as exclusivist. He condemned Homer, Shakespeare, Goethe, Racine, and other great writers on moral or religious grounds. He included all his own literary works, except for two edifying short stories, in this condemnation.

What Is Art? is a landmark in modern aesthetic theory. The critics of Tolstoy's own day, committed to a purely formalistic approach to art, could not understand what he was talking about. But his little work proved to be the forerunner of similar theories in the twentieth century, which saw an intimate relation between art and life and judged art by its effects on human society, whether by Marxist, Christian, humanist, or other standards. The editors of mass-circulation magazines today, who call for an "affirmative" literature from American writers, are talking in the pattern set by Count Leo Tolstoy, the Russian nobleman and anarchist (who, however, would have considered affirmation of the American capitalist way of life as immoral and vicious).

For an example of Tolstoy's art criticism, see his hilarious description of the opera in *War and Peace,* pp. 318a-320b. Tolstoy himself has presented the essential information about his life and views concisely and eloquently in writings collected in three volumes of the Oxford World Classics: *A Confession and What I Believe, What is Art? and Essays on Art,* and *Childhood, Boyhood, and Youth.*

III

Anyone who has read *War and Peace* recognizes that it deals with the destinies of individuals and families—of three families over three generations, with the conflict between Russia and Napoleonic France, and with the causes of historical events. Any one of these subjects by itself would be enough for one book. The chapters on the writing of *War and Peace* in Ernest J. Simmons' biography *Leo Tolstoy* (Little, Brown, 1946) reveal the long and circuitous process that led to the complex finished work, and indicate something of the false starts, the zigs and the zags that generally mark the course of the creative writer on his voyage to his destination.

Tolstoy's original idea apparently had nothing to do with the novel that evolved. In 1856 he thought of writing a story about the return from Siberia of an exiled participant in the Decembrist revolt of 1825. When, in 1863, he felt ready to write a novel of epic proportions, he decided it would deal with this theme of the old Decembrist hero and would be set in the year 1856. After writing the first three chapters, he felt compelled to go further and further back into the life of his hero, to 1825, then 1812, and finally 1805. By that time his original hero and theme had practically disappeared and he found himself with a completely new story, dealing with the period 1805-1814. In his revised plan, this story was to be the first of three novels, and the other two were to deal with the years 1825 and 1856, respectively. As it turned out, only the first novel, *War and Peace,* was written.

This novel was originally intended to be a story of family life in a time of troubles, with the historical events as a mere setting for the development of the characters through various trials to final happiness and tranquillity. Hence, Tolstoy at first sought for his source material in personal memoirs, correspondence, and other documents of private life in the period with which he was concerned. He found living models for his fictional characters among his own family and friends. Natásha Rostóva was modeled on his young sister-in-law Tanya, down to the details of a caddish pursuer named Anatole (the model for Anatole Kurágin), her thrills-and-chills at attending the ball for the young Tsarevitch, and her engagement to Tolstoy's brother Sergei (the model for the relation between Natásha and Andrew). When Tolstoy read the first chapters to a gathering of relations and friends, they were delighted to recognize themselves or other persons present in Tolstoy's fiction—which they found remarkably "true to life." It seems quite certain that he himself was the source of his portraits of Andrew and Pierre.

Early in 1865, when the introductory chapters had been published in serial form, Tolstoy arrived at the idea of transforming his work into a war novel. At the end of 1865, with Book III ready to go to the printer, the basic theme had changed and grown far more complex. Apparently not fully aware of what had happened, Tolstoy looked forward to completing the novel by 1867 and intended to call it *All's Well that Ends Well.* Another factor further complicating the theme was Tolstoy's intense interest in the question of historical inevitability as opposed to individual freedom—a subject much discussed in the circles he frequented. This growing historical interest forced him to pay some attention to the role of the peasantry, as well as to that of the nobility and gentry, in the events he was depicting.

By March, 1867, Tolstoy had arrived at his definite plan for the novel and devised its final title—*War and Peace.* The work was published a book at a time, with the author driving the printer and proofreader mad with his constant corrections and recorrections. Tolstoy had many doubts about how his work would be received, fearing especially that his serious views on historical inevitability would be neglected for "the sentimental scenes with my young ladies, the laughter over Speránski, and such rubbish." In December, 1869, the sixth and final volume was published. Tolstoy's long task was at an end, and he had completed his Iliad of the Russian war against Napoleonic France.

The work was an instantaneous success. Tolstoy considered this opinion of N. N. Strakhov, a contemporary critic, as judicious and of permanent value: "A complete picture of human life. A complete picture of the Russia of that day. A complete picture of everything in which people find their happiness and greatness, their grief and humiliation. That is *War and Peace*." (Charles du Bos, a twentieth-century French critic, said similarly of this work: "If life could speak out, this is how it would express itself.")

The main criticisms of the novel were leveled at its philosophy of history and its neglect of the misery of the poor people in the period when the wellborn characters were enjoying such a full life. Tolstoy defended the novelist's right to present his vision of history, and protested that he had no intention of writing about social problems. Here is the defense of the writer who later considered *Uncle Tom's Cabin* greater literature than any of Shakespeare's dramas:

"The aims of art are incommeasurable (as they say in mathematics) with social aims. The aim of an artist is not to resolve a question irrefutably, but to compel one to love life in all its manifestations, and these are inexhaustible. If I were told that I could write a novel in which I could indisputably establish as true my point of view on all social questions, I would not dedicate two hours to such a work; but if I were told that what I wrote would be read twenty years from now by those who are children today, and that they would weep and laugh over it and fall in love with the life in it, then I would dedicate all my existence and all my powers to it."[1]

[1] Simmons, *op. cit.*, p. 276.

IV

War and Peace is by far the most voluminous literary work in the *Great Books of the Western World*. It deals with an estimated five hundred characters, follows the fortunes of several families over three generations, deals with the events of some of the most widespread campaigns in military history, and sets forth a theory of historical inevitability. Since it would be impossible to give a fully comprehensive outline of all these aspects of *War and Peace*, even within the generous proportions of this Reading Plan, we will limit ourselves to presenting the main lines of the family story, of the war story, and of the theory of history. For the sake of simplicity and clarification we will deal with each of these aspects separately, although in the work the family and war stories become inextricably involved, and the war story is often bound up with the theory of history.

The three main families in the story are the Bezúkhovs, the Rostóvs, and the Bolkónskis. Associated with them are the Kurágins and the Drubetskóys. The "Note on Russian Names," furnished by Simon and Schuster with their edition of this translation, should help us to avoid confusion about the names of the characters in this novel as well as in the next reading:

> The suffixes "ovich," "evich," "ich," and "ych" at the end of a Russian name mean "son of"; the suffixes "ovna," and "evna" mean "daughter of." Thus, Tolstoy's full name in Russian is Count Lev Nikolaievich Tolstoy. Nikolaievich is Tolstoy's patronymic. This indicates that Lev (or Leo) is the son of Nikolai (or Nicholas) Tolstoy.
> Frequently a character is referred to by his own first name, followed by his patronymic; sometimes by the patronymic alone.
> The Russians also add suffixes to first names to express endearment—as when they refer to Natasha as Natashenka.[2]

The main families and characters of the novel are members of the Russian aristocracy. Through their story we get a vivid picture of the upper level of Russian society at the time. Indeed, the main characters are introduced in Book I, mostly at social functions—Anna Schérer's soiree and Anatole Kurágin's

---

[2] "A Reader's Guide and Bookmark" for the Inner Sanctum Edition of *War and Peace* (New York: Simon and Schuster, 1942), p. 8 of "Guide."

party at St. Petersburg, and the Rostóvs' name-day party and dinner party in Moscow—with a glance at the Bolkónski estate near Smolensk. With an extraordinary vividness and clarity, more lifelike than life itself, Tolstoy presents the relations between the various characters, their reaction to the social and political events of their time, the clash between the older and younger generations, and the development of his main characters from impetuous and awkward youth to solid and settled middle age.

The major male characters are Pierre Bezúkhov and Andrew Bolkónski, who apparently expressed different aspects of Tolstoy's own character. Pierre at the beginning is a fat, clumsy fellow, lacking in the social graces, who dissipates his time and money, and can find no place for himself in society. At the death of his natural father, a wealthy count, he is legitimized, inherits his father's title and wealth, and suddenly becomes a welcome member of high society. This goodhearted and naïve young man, basking in his new-found friendships and popularity, is especially cultivated by Prince Kurágin,[3] who hopes to marry off his daughter, the beautiful Hélène—a selfish, amoral, and vapid young lady—to Pierre and his money. Hélène's statuesque and obvious charms draw Pierre to woo and wed her

[3] In old Russia, the nobility comprised princes, counts, and barons, in that order. Princes and princesses had some degree of blood relation to the royal dynasties of Russia. The counts were something like the landed gentry of England. But the order of precedence was not fixed by the law and custom, for administrative positions, possession of landed property, the number of serfs, and other factors often determined social rank. As generations and dynasties succeeded one another, there came to be many princes and princesses in Russia, and some of them were quite impoverished. In the present story, for instance, the Drubetskóys, of princely lineage, are very poor, and dependent on the good will of wealthy and socially prominent families such as the Rostóvs, who are counts and countesses. The appropriate title apparently was attributed to every member of the family. In the Kurágin and Bolkónski families, the fathers and the sons are both called "Prince" and the daughters "Princess." In the Rostóv family, the father and the sons are all called "Count" while the mother and daughters are all called "Countess." For the sake of simplicity, we have used titles very rarely in this Reading Plan.

and entangle him in a relationship which is a constant source of unhappiness to him. Empty and unsatisfied, he joins the Freemasons and studies their philosophy. He also carries out his inmost convictions and frees his serfs, attempting like Tolstoy to manage his estate himself. But Freemasonry offers him no final satisfaction, and he proves far too inefficient to manage an estate.

Pierre's good friend, Andrew Bolkónski, is a much different type of man. He is intellectually gifted, ambitious for fame and glory like the early Tolstoy, and corroded by a bitter and cynical attitude toward life. Although married to a fascinating and devoted woman, he finds marriage oppressive and joins the army, participating in the campaign of 1805. He is badly wounded at the battle of Austerlitz, and has a moment of peace and resignation as he lies stricken, looking up at the "remote, lofty, and everlasting sky." In comparison with that infinite realm, the conqueror Napoleon—previously his hero, his ideal of the great man—appears small and insignificant as he struts around, surveying the battlefield and the fallen soldiers. All Andrew's previous interests seem unimportant in the face of the "incomprehensible but all-important" greatness that he has encountered in the "lofty, equitable, and kindly sky," and he hopes to return to life with a new understanding and vision of its beauty and worth. (See pp. 156d, 162b-164c.)

In his absence, his wife has died giving birth to his son. Despite his new freedom and independence, and his decisive vision at Austerlitz, Andrew remains discontented and bitter. He refuses to return to military service when the conflict recommences in 1807, and he proclaims to Pierre his wish to live without doing harm to others, but also without trying to do good to them, as Pierre does. Pierre insists that life is meaningless without service to others and without faith in God and in a future life where harmony and good shall finally be achieved. "We must live, we must love, and we must believe that we live not only today on this scrap of earth, but have lived and shall live forever, there, in the Whole," he says, pointing to the sky. To which Andrew only replies, "Yes, if it were only so!" But he remembers the sky at Austerlitz; Pierre's appeal awakens a joyful vitality that has been slumbering in his soul, and life begins anew for him. (See pp. 214c-218b; see also pp. 235b-238a.)

His new will to live is expressed first by his attempt to participate in political and military reforms. This turns out to be a frustrating process, revealing the stupidity, vanity, and corruption in high places, including the idealistic reformers. More important in his return to life is his love for Natásha Rostóva, whose voice overheard at a window one night has been an essential element in his regeneration. (See p. 237a-c.) Natásha, as she appears in the earlier portions of the work, is the utter embodiment of the spirit of youth, of joy, tenderness, sweetness, high spirits—perhaps the most memorable portrayal of a young girl in fiction.

The love affair between the sixteen-year-old girl and the dashing widower proceeds with growing intensity, from the time he first holds her in his arms at the grand ball until they plight their troth. Because of her youth, her parents insist that the engagement be kept secret for a year, and Andrew is willing to give her that time to be sure of herself. But again Andrew's hopes are frustrated, for during his absence abroad Natásha succumbs to the attentions of Pierre's brother-in-law, Anatole Kurágin, and agrees to elope with him, not knowing he is already married. At the last moment the plot is discovered and the elopement is prevented. Natásha, ashamed and repentant, writes a letter to Andrew's sister Mary, breaking the engagement and leaving him free. Andrew's pride is so wounded that he decides never to have anything to do with her again. It is at this moment that Pierre Bezúkhov offers Natásha his friendship and devotion, and she becomes aware of the real goodness in this clumsy "buffoon."

This crucial moment in the private lives of Andrew and Natásha coincides with the advent of the portentous year 1812. With Napoleon's armies marching against Russia, the bitter and disillusioned Andrew is drawn into the military conflict. He is in the thick of the fighting and the retreat from Smolensk to Borodino, where he is severely wounded. In the hospital tent, where part of his thighbone is removed, he sees a man moaning with pain and sorrow at the amputation of a leg, and recognizes him as Anatole Kurágin, Natásha's seducer, whom he has hated so. But now he is full of pity and love for the poor fellow, and vividly recalls Natásha with tender love, regretfully, aware that it is too late. The final wisdom, he discovers, is universal compassion, for enemies as well as friends.

As the Rostóvs prepare to leave Moscow, before the advancing French army, they allow the carts bearing the wounded to accompany their caravan. Andrew is discovered among the wounded, he and Natásha are reconciled, and they have a final period of tender intimacy before his death. At the end he reaches an intimation of the eternal and binding force of love, and the realization that death is an awakening from life to eternity. "Love is God, and to die means that I, a particle of love, shall return to the general and eternal source." After his death, his saintly sister Mary and Natásha, bound by their common love and loss, become intimate friends.

Meanwhile, Pierre Bezúkhov has passed through crucial experiences and adventures, with many more to come. A tremendous striving and development takes place in this man who seemed such a buffon to conventional observers. At the time of Andrew and Natásha's engagement, life was utterly empty and meaningless to him—"the wealthy husband of an unfaithful wife, a retired gentleman-in-waiting, fond of eating and drinking and . . . of abusing the government a bit, a member of the Moscow English Club, and a universal favorite in Moscow society" (p. 304a). Questions ("What for? Why?") about the meaning of life constantly recurred to him but he found no answers. He could not assent to the conventional deceptions and hypocrisies—and he was convinced that in their hearts other people also saw them for what they were but would not admit it. "He had the unfortunate capacity many men, especially Russians, have of seeing and believing in the possibility of goodness and truth, but of seeing the evil and falsehood of life too clearly to be able to take a serious part in it" (p. 304d). He sought refuge in reading and drinking, determined to avoid the confrontation of the terrible question of the meaning of life—"What for?"

His friendship and growing love for Natásha after the breaking of her engagement to Andrew gave him the hope of "a realm of beauty and love which it was worth living for." But, realizing the growing love between them, which he was not free to fulfill, he stopped visiting the Rostóvs. Although he did not join the army, he, too, became involved in the campaign of 1812, coming under fire in hot fighting at Borodino and joining the retreat from that place. He envied the common soldier's capacity "to enter communal life completely," to endure God's will, death, and suffering in simplicity and silence.

"To endure war is the most difficult subordination of man's freedom to the law of God," the voice had said. "Simplicity is submission to the will of God; you cannot escape from Him. And *they* are simple. *They* do not talk, but act. The spoken word is silver but the unspoken is golden. Man can be master of nothing while he fears death, but he who does not fear it possesses all. If there were no suffering, man would not know his limitations, would not know himself. The hardest thing [Pierre went on thinking, or hearing, in his dream] is to be able in your soul to unite the meaning of all. To unite all?" he asked himself. "No, not to unite. Thoughts cannot be united, but to *harness* all these thoughts together is what we need! Yes, one *must harness* them, *must harness* them!" he repeated to himself with inward rapture, feeling that these words and they alone expressed what he wanted to say and solved the question that tormented him. (pp. 481d-482a)

Back in Moscow now, Pierre, suspected because of his connection with the Masons and the political reformers, is ordered to leave town. But, disguised in coachman's clothing, he remains to gather his confused thoughts together and to offer some resistance to the approaching invaders. He is there when the French army comes in, the popular tumults break out, and the great fire devastates the city. He becomes obsessed with the idea that he has been marked by destiny to assassinate Napoleon, recalling a cabalistic prophecy he had once worked out from a verse in the Book of Revelation. (See pp. 377d-378c, 514a-515a.) On the way to accomplish his deed, Pierre saves a child from the flames and defends a young woman from molestation by a French soldier. This results in his arrest for carrying a weapon—the dagger for killing Napoleon—and on suspicion of being an incendiary. After a farcical inquiry and a conversation with the French marshal Davout, Pierre is led away to the scene of execution. As it turns out, he is pardoned, but has to witness the execution of other prisoners, and this systematic murder of some men by others who do not wish to kill them makes the whole universe meaningless, insensate, empty for him.

From the moment Pierre had witnessed those terrible murders committed by men who did not wish to commit them, it was as if the mainspring of his life, on which everything depended and which made everything appear alive, had suddenly been wrenched out and everything had collapsed into a heap of meaningless rubbish. Though he did not acknowledge it to himself, his faith in the right ordering of the universe, in humanity, in his own soul, and in God, had been destroyed. He had experienced this before, but never so strongly as now. When similar doubts had assailed him before, they had been the result of his own wrongdoing, and at the bottom of his heart he had felt that relief from his despair and from those doubts was to be found within himself. But now he felt that the universe had crumbled before his eyes and only meaningless ruins remained, and this not by any fault of his own. He felt that it was not in his power to regain faith in the meaning of life. (pp. 551d-552a)

Pierre is saved from despair by the simple faith and wisdom of a fellow prisoner, Platón Karatáev, a peasant and "the personification of everything Russian." Karatáev loves everything and everyone he comes in contact with, particularly human beings, but without distinction and without grasping—he is able to love and let go. He cannot remember the words of his favorite song apart from the music, because nothing has meaning for him abstracted from its context.

Every word and action of his was the manifestation of an activity unknown to him, which was his life. But his life, as he regarded it, had no meaning as a separate thing. It had meaning only as part of a whole of which he was always conscious. His words and actions flowed from him as evenly, inevitably, and spontaneously as fragrance exhales from a flower. He could not understand the value or significance of any word or deed taken separately. (p. 555c)

The long hard march as a prisoner of war of the retreating, demoralized French army from Moscow to Smolensk is a decisive event in Pierre's moral development. The pampered wealthy nobleman, who has previously found so many occasions for unhappiness, now finds he can be happy if only the simple elemental wants of food and shelter can be met—"that all unhappiness arises not from privation but from superfluity." And he discovers that no human condition is too terrible to be borne, and that both suffering and freedom have limits. Karatáev's severe illness, the shooting of lagging prisoners, his own fate—none of these bothers him now.

Only now did Pierre realize the full strength of life in man and the saving power he has of transferring his attention from one thing to another, which is like the safety valve of a boiler that allows superfluous steam to blow off when the pressure exceeds a certain limit. . . . The harder his position became and the more terrible the future, the more independent of that position in which he found himself were the joyful and comforting thoughts, memories, and imaginings that came to him. (p. 605c-d)

The most holy and blessed thing is to love life—which is God—with all its sufferings. When Pierre realizes that Karatáev has been shot and killed, his mind shifts instantly to a summer evening with a beautiful lady at his country house in Kiev.

Pierre, along with other prisoners, is saved by a Cossack column. During his convalescence from the illness following his captivity, he is filled with a feeling of joyous freedom. He is no longer plagued by the question of the meaning of life, for now he has faith in the eternal God who is manifest in his fellow men, such as Karatáev. "All his life he had looked over the heads of the men around him, when he should have merely looked in front of him without straining his eyes" (p. 631b). He no longer tries to change other men's opinions, but allows all their individual views, as an expression of their own individuality. Now he listens with interest to other people and is full of concern and sympathy for them.

In Moscow on a visit to Andrew's sister, Princess Mary, he encounters Natásha. He immediately recognizes, to his confusion, that he is in love with her, and she too becomes aware that she returns his feeling. Since Hélène has died, he is once more, as Mary notes, "an eligible bachelor." Natásha has changed greatly. She is no longer the blooming, impulsive, joyous girl he has known, but a thin, pale, saddened woman.

And he too has changed, as she notes to Mary—"he has somehow grown so clean, smooth, and fresh—as if he had come out of a Russian bath . . . Out of a moral bath" (p. 639d). The two survivors of the maelstrom of events make tentative approaches toward one another, with Mary's blessing. Back in St. Petersburg, Pierre, waiting hopefully for the blessed consummation of his love, is seized by a "blissful insanity" in which the whole universe seems centered on his love. This period of joyful frenzy becomes in later life the model for Pierre in his attitude toward men and circumstances, because love and happiness give the insight and understanding needed to see the good in other people.

In the end, the Bolkónskis as well as the Bezúkhovs are united to the Rostóvs, for Natásha's brother Nicholas marries Andrew's sister Mary. Nicholas Rostóv, one of the most engaging characters in the book, is a kind of "natural man," a physically active person who goes through all the experiences of war mentally unscathed, and ends up as a bluff, successful country squire. One of the most memorable scenes in the book occurs at Nicholas' baptism of fire, when the ardent boyish hussar, with his horse shot from under him, watches with bewilderment as the enemy soldiers come toward him trying to kill him ("*Me* whom everyone is so fond of?"), and, full of fear for "his young and happy life," takes off for the bushes with the speed of a hare (pp. 103b-104a).

Mary is the most authentically Christian character in the book, kind and patient, imbued with the religious virtues, pointed toward the spiritual order. One of the most poignant and perceptive presentations of human relations in the book involves the relation between Mary and her father, the compulsively cruel old Prince Bolkónski. The old man loves his daughter more than any other human being, she is indispensable to his very existence, yet he maliciously inflicts the most brutal mental torment on her. "He knew that he was being cruel to her, but he knew he couldn't help it, and that she deserved it."

Like Pierre and Natásha, Mary finds peace and fulfillment

in married life. Written at the happiest period of Tolstoy's married life, *War and Peace* culminates in a celebration of the solid virtues and wholesome joys of family life. The young people we encountered at the beginning of the story are, in the First Epilogue, the parents of children themselves. Natásha, once the incarnation of girlish gaiety and youthful impulsiveness, is now a buxom housewife and mother with not a thought for social affairs, her personal appearance, or anything save the welfare of her husband and children. Mary, despite the usual man-woman misunderstandings between her and Nicholas and the discomfort of her many pregnancies, is happy, as she has never been before in her life—yet occasionally she thinks involuntarily of "another sort of happiness unattainable in this life." Pierre, still absent-minded and filled with idealistic plans to reform society, has also found contentment as a husband and father. And at the end of the story, the future of the families and the generations is indicated by the dreams and imaginings of little Nicholas, the orphan son of Andrew Bolkónski. As his adored father once did before him, little Nicholas looks forward to the day when he will do heroic deeds and all men shall know him and love him.

V

The development and shifting fortunes of individuals and families, which we have just followed above, take place against the gigantic backdrop of the Napoleonic Wars and particularly of the conflict between France and Russia. But the war is not merely a backdrop against which the real action takes place, for it intimately affects the lives of the individuals who figure prominently in the narrative, whether they participate directly in the fighting or not. We see a good deal of the war through the viewpoint and action on the main characters. And not only is the war presented as it involves the fictional characters, but it often takes the central attention of the narrator; and the historical events and characters are depicted independently, in their own right. Tolstoy spent years of solid research on this period and had immersed himself in the deeds and words of the historical characters of the time. Napoleon and Alexander, Bagration and Kutúzov, as well as Andrew, Pierre, and Nicholas, are central characters in his story.

Tolstoy begins his narration of the military events in Book II, with Kutúzov's inspection of the regiment at Braunau in October, 1805, and completes his account in Book XV, with the Russian entry into Vílna in November, 1812. He covers all the historical events listed in the table on page xvi and partially charted on the maps at the end of the volume. He re-creates the marshaling of forces, the discussion of grand strategy on the level of rulers and statesmen, the high staff discussions, the passive boredom and waiting of the common soldiers (the hurry-up-and-wait familiar to all armies), the approach to battle, the fear, horror, and elation of actual combat, and the grand confusion and chaos that predominate on the battlefield. Tolstoy's amazing capacity to handle the movement of masses and at the same time catch the involvement and response of individuals results in a picture of men in war that has made *War and Peace* the model for war novels. Any major novel about World War II, for instance, was inevitably compared with *War and Peace*.

But Tolstoy is concerned not only with the description, admittedly magnificent, of what goes on in combat, how men feel and act when thrown into the furnace of war, the sight and shape and sound of military events, and their effect on the noncombatants and the countryside. He is also deeply concerned with an interpretation of the meaning of the events, their causes and patterns, and their connection with the will of the human participants. At times this concern becomes central, and he devotes chapters, sections, and the whole of the Second Epilogue to a thoughtful discussion of this matter, apart from the thread of the story. But this concern is also expressed in his presentation of the thoughts, deeds, and words of both his historical and his fictional characters—through the story itself.

Quite early in the book, Prince Andrew, through his position as a staff officer, begins to get a picture of what goes on at the high directive levels of military operations. And his later experiences at high political levels, with the reformer Speránski and men close to the Tsar, add to his education in the non-effectiveness of the wills and plans of these self-important men upon historical events and the destiny of nations. The "realization" scenes as he lies fallen on the battlefield, at Austerlitz and Borodino, are prepared for by a series of experiences he and other characters have. Nicholas Rostóv, for instance, witnesses the brilliant and brave General Bagration save the day at Austerlitz simply by being present, by the upsurge of morale caused by his mere appearance—not by the careful deliberation, intelligently planned operations, and military skill that historians will attribute to him later after the event.

Tolstoy was convinced that military theory and historical explanation are completely irrelevant to what actually goes on in war. He reserves his most sarcastic passages for the German military theoreticians, Pfuel and Bennigsen, who talk utterly irrelevant, academic nonsense at the Russian staff meetings. He arrived at a sort of "proletarian" interpretation of military events: that war is conducted and affected by the ordinary anonymous soldiers who do the shooting and the dying, by "G.I. Joe"—not by the "managers" who fatuously presume to be the directors of events, not by the high "brass." And this is true also of the larger social context, of the people as a whole, for the comeback of the Russians after the fall and burning of Moscow was, in Tolstoy's view, not due to the heroic sacrifices and deeds of individuals consciously striving for the common good, but due to ordinary little persons attending to their own personal affairs. (See p. 537b-d.)

In this view, which pervades Tolstoy's whole presentation of the war between France and Russia, the military genius Napoleon is a fool, a phony, a self-deluded and deluding charlatan, while the plain and unassuming Russian General Kutúzov, who proceeds by a kind of vague intuition and does not presume to direct events, is the model of the military commander—the hero among the generals in this book. Just as Tolstoy, looking back at what took place, realized the enormous number of events and individual acts which affected the final outcome, so Kutúzov, looking forward at the shape of things to come, realizes the enormous number of contingencies, the thousands of "ifs" and "maybes" unknowable to any one mind, which will affect the course of battle. It is this deep, unbrilliant, solid wisdom, derived from much experience and intuitive judgment, that makes Kutúzov sounder and greater than the German theoreticians, than his intelligent, articulate young staff officers, and, above all, than that brilliant luminary of the era, the Emperor and great Generalissimo Napoleon Bonaparte.

The attack on the "great man" theory of history in the two Epilogues is prepared for in the presentations of Napoleon throughout the narrative. Tolstoy constantly seizes every opportunity to take him down a peg, to show his pettiness, vanity, ordinary human weaknesses and failings, to see him in his bath, to see the "great man" with his pants down. On the basis of the Napoleon presented in the story, the reader is ready to approve Tolstoy's sarcastic rejection of the theory that the "great genius"—who earned his reputation by his skill in mass murder, first of Africans and then of Europeans—had a decisive role in determining the history of Europe in the first fifteen years of the nineteenth century. Tolstoy's rejection is universal, applying not only to Napoleon the "invader" of Russia, but to Tsar Alexander the "defender" of Russia. To rest the movement of these masses of men, and the course of events over vast spaces of the European continent, on such individuals is, for Tolstoy, like trying to support the universe on a pinhead. (See First Epilogue, Ch. 1-4.)

As he sees it, the only personal will that could direct this "whole series of events occurring over a period of years or centuries" is Divine Providence. To explain the course of history by an individual human will is ridiculous. For instance, to say that the French invaded Russia because Napoleon commanded it explains nothing at all. In the first place, this theory ignores the whole complicated background of events and contingencies which led to Napoleon's order. In the second place, it naïvely assumes that the issuance of an order, on paper or by word of mouth, leads to certain results in historical actuality. A careful inquiry into the way in which wars are fought and armies are constituted leads to quite a different conclusion, for the men who command have the least effect on the course of operations, and the common soldiers, the furthest away from positions of command, have the most effect through their direct participation in the action. It is the collective action of many men, without conscious purpose and planning, that determines the course of events.

As far as historical events are concerned, that is, vast social movements, involving thousands and even millions of men, they happen "inevitably"; they could not have happened otherwise just because some ruler or general arbitrarily might have decided other than he did. "Freedom of the will" is of no effect in this sphere, and "chance" is just an expression of our inadequate understanding of events. Tolstoy compares the "great man" to the bellwether ram—the ram gets special feeding and attention, but his role is not due to his "genius" or his free will, but to a purpose that far transcends his sheepish aims and ken and that of the fattened rams who follow him. Similarly, men being led to the slaughterhouse of war should recognize that neither they nor their leaders understand the purpose and meaning of the conflict. Men like Napoleon and Alexander are passive vehicles or instruments serving rather than directing the historical process. They are raised—or dashed—by the tide of history which rolls on inevitably. Or, to change the metaphor, they have star billing in the drama, and they get the spotlight and the acclaim, but they are not the authors or the directors of the play. And after the play has had its run, they, along with their tinsel trappings, are thrown, in Leon Trotsky's phrase, into the ash can of history.

Que sera, sera, "What will be, will be"—that is Tolstoy's message. And the human mind cannot know the determining causes either before or after the event (although the further away we are from the event, the more inevitable it appears). No moral meaning can be assigned to the course of events—they just happen that way. The first causes of historical events and social movements come from a sphere that transcends human understanding and moral judgment. Wisdom and peace of mind require us "to renounce a freedom that does not exist, and to recognize a dependence of which we are not conscious." With these words Tolstoy ends his work on war and peace. (See the Second Epilogue.)

For an informative and stimulating present-day interpretation of Tolstoy's theory of history in *War and Peace,* see Isaiah Berlin's *The Hedgehog and the Fox* (Mentor Books).

VI

If Tolstoy's theory of art were the measure, how would you judge this novel as a work of art?

Does this work communicate human experience, feeling, and emotion "infectiously"? Many critics and readers have said that no other writer excels Tolstoy in his ability to re-create concrete human experience in all its vividness and uniqueness. Do you agree? Does Tolstoy express the quality and texture of common human experience as you have known it?

What is the moral lesson, if any, of *War and Peace?* Does Tolstoy put it across effectively? If so, does he do so through his story and characters, through his nonfictional passages, or through both?

Does Tolstoy's theory of art do justice to this book? If you don't think so, in what respect do you find this theory inadequate? Why did Tolstoy, in accordance with his theory, reject this work, which he once regarded as a masterpiece?

Is this book a unified whole?

The British critic Percy Lubbock complains in *The Craft of Fiction* that Tolstoy wrote two novels—one of family life and one of war—and mixed the two together so confusedly that we cannot discern a single subject, a fixed theme. Tolstoy, according to Lubbock, jumps around from the absorbing story of personal lives and destinies to the saga of Russia's struggle with the invaders from the West, pushing the individual Bolkónskis, Rostóvs, and Bezúkhovs into the background or dropping them completely to concentrate on Napoleon and Alexander, Kutúzov and Murat. There are two good stories, says Lubbock, but one too many to be worked out in a single novel since the completed work is left without a center, without a fixed point of view.

Does the account of the process of composition of this book given above (pp. 179-180) offer any support to Lubbock's suspicion that Tolstoy started with one story and suddenly got interested in quite another story? Without taking into account the way in which this book came to be written—the false starts, the changes of direction, and all the rest—what about the finished product? Do you now find two separate stories, cutting across one another in disconnected fragments, not held together by a synoptic vision? Or do you accept Tolstoy's panoramic presentation, switching from private to public events, from one scene and viewpoint to another?

Does the story of family and personal life complement and counterpoint the story of historical events? Is the representation of reality fuller and more believable through the juxtaposition and fusion of the two stories? Or would the war story and the impotence of directors of affairs be more readily grasped if Tolstoy had eliminated Natásha, Andrew, Pierre, and other fictional characters in order to concentrate on Napoleon, Alexander, Speránski, Talleyrand, etc.? And would the story of the families and individuals be much clearer and fuller if the historical events and figures had been kept in the background and the writer had concentrated on the personal destinies?

If you think that *War and Peace* is a unity, that Tolstoy has created a cosmos rather than a chaos, what do you see as its unifying principle or vision? Lubbock says the unifying theme of a book can be expressed in ten words. Can you express the theme of *War and Peace* in ten words?

Is a philosophical discussion of historical inevitability and freedom of the will out of place in works of fiction?

Ever since the work first appeared, readers and critics have objected to Tolstoy's inclusion of a philosophy of history in *War and Peace*. Turgenev used such harsh words as "charlatanism," "farcical," and "trickery" to describe Tolstoy's discussion of history. Flaubert, a great admirer of the fictional portions of the work, complained of the historical discussion, "he repeats himself, he philosophizes." Lubbock, writing in our own time, says: "He, whose power of making a story *tell itself* is unsurpassed, is capable of thrusting into his book interminable chapters of comment and explanation, chapters in the manner of a controversial pamphlet, lest the argument of his drama should be missed." The wise reader, says Lubbock, skips "these maddening interruptions" and rejoins the author when he remembers "that he is writing a novel." And Ortega y Gasset, writing about the novel in general, says that "every novel is still-born that is laden with transcendental intentions, be they political ideological, symbolical, or satirical," for it shatters the illusion of the fictional world the author has created by bringing in problems from the actual world.

Do you agree that the particular criticisms of Turgenev, Flaubert, and Lubbock are justified and that the general criticism of Ortega applies to *War and Peace?* Are the discursive passages annoying to you? Do they spoil your enjoyment of the story or shatter the illusion of Tolstoy's fictional world and characters? Did you skip the historical discussions or have the temptation to do so? Would the book be just as good or even better if the philosophy of history were taken out and published separately?

Or did Tolstoy's commentary, like the chorus in a Greek tragedy, add depth and understanding to your reading of the work? Does the abstract, theoretical discussion add another dimension to the imaginative, concrete presentation, another "string" to Tolstoy's "lyre"? Or does it just result in harsh discord? Leaving aside the general question of the appropriateness of a philosophical discussion in a work of fiction, does Tolstoy's theory of history harmonize with his fictional presentation of historical events and forces? Is it in accord with the development and final situation of the main fictional characters, or completely irrelevant to their story?

Ortega, in the essay mentioned, gives us this measuring rod for the admittance of "alien" elements in the novel. He says

that the novel lends itself more easily than any other literary form to absorbing elements alien to art. *Within* the novel almost anything fits: science, religion, sociology, aesthetic criticism—if only it is ultimately derealized and confined within the inner world of the novel; i.e., if it remains without actual and effective validity . . . The dose of alien elements a book can bear, lastly, depends on the author's capability of dissolving them in the atmosphere of the novel as such.[4]

How would Tolstoy's work be judged, according to this criterion? Does Tolstoy intend his philosophy of history to be valid in the actual world outside the novel? Is Ortega's criterion generally valid? What is the relation between the imaginary world and the actual world? Are the two completely separated? Can fiction reveal anything about reality? If so, may what is revealed be presented discursively as well as fictionally in a novel?

Is the historical novel a "bastard" art form?

Critics like Ortega complain that historical novels are like centaurs or other mythological creatures, half one thing and half another, forcing the author and the reader to jump constantly from the realm of actual fact to the realm of fictional events. As you read the novel, did you feel that Tolstoy was presenting historical events and personages as they actually were, or did you accept these also as part of Tolstoy's new-made fictional world? Would it impair your enjoyment of the novel to learn that Tolstoy had deliberately ignored or distorted historical facts to fit in with his philosophical thesis? Does it matter that the actual Kutúzov was, in Isaiah Berlin's words, a "sly, elderly, feeble voluptuary," a "corrupt, and somewhat sycophantic courtier," transformed in the later drafts of *War and Peace* into a paragon of Russian "simplicity and intuitive wisdom"? Similarly, Tolstoy's portrait of Napoleon has been found to be inaccurate. Is Tolstoy a deliberate liar, or is the question of truth in the actual world out of place here, or is a different mode or level of truth involved?

You may remember that Aristotle in the *Poetics* distinguished between history as the realm of actual particulars and poetry as the realm of universal possibilities. (See Vol. 9, p. 686a-c.) But how does this solve the problem of the historical novelist, when he deals with actual historical events and personages?

---

[4] Ortega y Gasset, *The Dehumanization of Art and Notes on the Novel* (Princeton, N.J.: Princeton University Press, 1948), p. 103.

Tolstoy is not merely expressing some of the universal possibilities of the human experience of war through his fictional
events and characters, but he is portraying actual men and
events, what happened in history.

We might solve the problem of Tolstoy's treatment of historical facts by the classical plea of "poetic license," that is, that
the writer of fiction may treat his factual material as he pleases,
to suit his artistic purposes. How, then, would it affect Tolstoy's
story, as a story, if Napoleon and Kutúzov were presented in a
more historically authentic fashion? How would it affect Tolstoy's thesis about historical inevitability? Would it be less
cogent if Napoleon were shown as greater and Kutúzov as less
wise? What truth, if any, is Tolstoy trying to communicate
through his historical distortions and inaccuracies? Can truth
on one level be expressed through what is a lie on another
level?

Would this novel have been better both as fiction and as history if it had left the question of historical inevitability and
human freedom open, been more ambiguous and more am-
bivalent in its final impression?

In what respects does a historian resemble a novelist like
Tolstoy? Does he also make "constructions" through his imagination and intuition to represent what actually happened? Or
does he arrive at historical truth solely through logical conclu-
sions from material evidence and documents? Must history
take the narrative form? What is the essential difference between the historian and the historical novelist?

What is the ultimate message of this book about war and peace?

The early Greek philosopher Heraclitus said that war, that
is, the conflict of opposites, is the basic principle through
which harmony and order are achieved in the universe. Do we
get any such metaphysical proclamation about the value and
purpose of war from Tolstoy in this book? Does war have any
meaning for the fictional characters in this book besides being
a brute, unavoidable fact that must be endured? What is the
nature of the "peace" that characters such as Pierre and

Natásha find at the end of the story? What is the relation of that peace to the war that has shaken and shifted their lives? What is "war" in this book? What is "peace"?

Is this work an "epic"?

Comparison is inevitable between *War and Peace* and the *Iliad* and the *Aeneid*. Tolstoy himself welcomed such comparisons. The ancient epics celebrate heroic actions in the historical or legendary past of a people. In what sense does *War and Peace* do this, and who are the heroes whose exploits are celebrated? Tolstoy's work is certainly "epic" in scope, dealing with the movements and struggles of peoples in the greatest war in history up to that time. But who is the hero or who are the heroes who perform the epic deeds? Are Andrew and Pierre epic heroes? What do they do to decide the action? Are Napoleon and Alexander epic heroes? Can they be, in view of Tolstoy's theory of history? Can anyone be an epic hero for Tolstoy? Is Kutúzov the closest thing to a hero in this book? If so, what kind of hero is he—a hero of watchful waiting and non-doing? Do we have a new kind of epic here, an epic of events instead of one of decisive deeds? Is the Russian people —"this original, peculiar, and unique people"—the hero of *War and Peace*? Is it man, who suffers, endures, and arrives at submission and balance? Or is it the historical process or the ultimate power behind it?

The following questions are designed to help you test the thoroughness of your reading. Each question is to be answered by giving a page or pages of the reading assignment. Answers will be found on page 248 of this Reading Plan.

1 Who was regarded as "the most fascinating woman in Petersburg" in 1805?

2 To which character is this Gospel verse applied: "To him that hath shall be given, and from him that hath not shall be taken away"?

3 Why does Pierre challenge Dólokhov to a duel?

4 Who is Joseph Alexéevich Bazdéev?

5 What ancient curse and sense of guilt does military service abolish?

6 What feminine character receives the accolade of "a superb animal" from Napoleon?

7 What two factors does Kutúzov consider as his main aid in winning the war?

8 Why does Hélène become converted to Roman Catholicism?

9 What is the unknown factor in the strength of armies?

10 What method, borrowed from mathematics, must be used to understand historical events?

DOSTOEVSKY

The Brothers Karamazov

Vol. 52

In our time the novel has supplanted dramatic and epic poetry as the dominant form of literary expression. Through the novel, writers express not only the comic and prosaic aspects, but also the most tragic and serious levels of human existence. The contemporary emulator of Homer, Dante, and Shakespeare usually turns to the prose novel to mirror and interpret the tragic and heroic—or pathetic—life of man.

Fyodor Mikhailovich Dostoevsky is the prime example of the modern poet in prose, the Dante and Shakespeare of modern society. This Russian genius created an extraordinary number of unique, living characters, absorbing plots about the maelstrom of incidents and passions in which these characters are caught up, and marvelous conversations which carry the action forward and comment on it. His works present the depths and heights of human existence, the most seamy and sordid side of life together with an irradiating spiritual vision and concern. His compassion, his tragic insight, and his religious attitude are as important in his novels as his literary craftsmanship and his psychological astuteness.

The Brothers Karamazov, generally regarded as Dostoevsky's greatest work, is the story of a remarkable family and a sordid and shocking murder—a parricide. It is a fascinating and absorbing tale, which presents the struggle in the human heart between good and evil, faith and doubt, freedom and bondage. Gross sensuality and spiritual impulses—"Sodom" and "the Madonna"—accompany one another, often in the same person. A simple goodness of heart and profound spiritual potentialities are revealed in the roisterer and brawler. And the complete devotion and self-sacrificial love of the noble and good young lady express a spiteful revenge and self-laceration.

This novel, written by a man who had to live most of his life as a hack writer struggling to meet deadlines, is one of the great spiritual documents of the modern age. It is a source of illuminating insights for present-day philosophers, theologians, and psychologists, and an instructive example for the contemporary writer of existentialist, psychological, and religious novels. Above all, it is a moving and enlightening experience for the reader of today, one which is repeated and enriched with each rereading.

Seventh Reading

I

The biographical note in Vol. 52 on pp. v-vi gives the essential details of Dostoevsky's remarkable life. An epileptic, with an irresponsible father who was murdered by his serfs, he achieved immediate literary success by writing touching stories of the humiliated and the injured. Then followed a period of literary failure and hard times, climaxed by his imprisonment for belonging to a socialist study group and the horrible experience of his near execution (coffins ready, bound to the stake, the last rites offered, and then the sudden reprieve), an experience which permanently affected Dostoevsky. Also of permanent affect was the prison sentence which followed—the four years of hard labor in Siberia which he considered being buried alive. His experiences intensified his epilepsy, but also opened his heart and mind to religious attitudes, especially that of universal compassion and pity for human suffering.

When he returned to normal life, ten years after the mock execution, he and his brother began a journal dedicated to a Christian nationalism which regarded the Russian peasantry as the peculiar repository of Russian spiritual values. His novels, including *The House of the Dead* (about the Siberian penal colony) and *The Insulted and the Injured,* were published in this new journal in serial form. It was a financial success, but the government, misunderstanding its purpose, suppressed it. Again Dostoevsky was in a bad way financially; he tried to recoup his fortunes at the gambling tables, but only added to his losses. He was forced to turn out stories at enormous speed in order to obtain the money to keep his head above water. Some of his best works, such as *Crime and Punishment,* were produced in these circumstances. Though he was plagued by epilepsy, poverty, and the gambling mania, the later period of his life was richly creative—*The Idiot, The Possessed,* and *The Brothers Karamazov* were all written in the last twelve years of his life. His literary success finally brought him financial solvency and comparatively easy circumstances.

By the end of his life he had attained public acclaim as one of the greatest of Russian writers. His magnificent speech on the mission of Russia and of the Russian writer—delivered before the Society of Lovers of Russian Literature at the unveiling of the Pushkin monument in 1880—made a tremendous impression. When he died his funeral procession was attended by tens of thousands of people, paying homage to Russia's spiritual hero and literary saint.

Outside of Russia, Dostoevsky had a very slow rise to fame. Compared with Gogol, Turgenev, and Tolstoy, he was a rather obscure figure who was not regarded as very important. But as the twentieth century progressed, and the spiritual and historical crises of the West intensified, Dostoevsky's writings became one of the chief sources of illumination of the spiritual condition of modern man. Philosophers and theologians, as well as literary critics and the common reader, sought depth of understanding in the writings of this story writer, who had often worked as a hack, at top speed, to pay off his debts and meet newspaper deadlines. Serious thinkers regarded *Notes from Underground, Crime and Punishment, The Idiot, The Possessed,* and *The Brothers Karamazov* as documents of the human soul in the modern age.

Dostoevsky's novels have a unique effect on the reader. He had learned from the great prose writers of his time—from Gogol, Balzac, George Sand, and Dickens. His wide range of characters and his concern with the lower depths of human existence led many people to compare him to Dickens. But there is something different about Dostoevsky. His characters, no matter how hypocritical or comical, are never caricatures or types; they are full human beings, more alive than life itself and understood in their full reality. We understand them from the inside. He makes us see their souls, the characteristic marks, direction, and distortion of their spirits, rather than their external physiognomy, figure, or appearance. Nothing could be more real to the reader, once he begins one of Dostoevsky's great novels, than the fictional life and world that the writer has created with his literary imagination. We are plunged into the passions, conflicts, amazing conversations, aspirations, and degradations of the many characters. Dostoevsky's novels are characterized by a remarkable vitality and spirituality. In his greatest works a kind of radiance suffuses the portrayal of the most noisome and degrading aspects of human existence. He has remained an inspiration and a model to serious writers of fiction in Europe and America throughout the twentieth century.

II

The Brothers Karamazov was the fulfillment of Dostoevsky's long-held ambition to write a major work that would express all he had to say on the "eternal questions" of human existence. In a letter in December, 1870, he spoke longingly of finding the time to write this work, unhampered by deadlines and the other necessities of hack journalism. In the December, 1877, issue of his monthly journal, *A Writer's Diary*, he informed his readers that he was suspending publication "to engage in belletristic work which imperceptibly and involuntarily moulded itself during the last two years." The book, which he started work on in 1878, was to be part of a cycle of five novels, entitled *The Life of a Great Sinner*. It was to deal with sin and suffering and the existence of God—"the problem that has consciously and unconsciously tormented me all my life." It was, like *War and Peace*, to tell the story of many generations. But when he began work, he decided to scale down his original plan to two novels, of which *The Brothers Karamazov* is the first.

Thus the novel we have before us is only the first half of the author's intended work, for Dostoevsky died shortly after completing it. But its unfinished state is no longer noticed, and critics and readers alike take it as it is and generally acclaim it as the greatest of Dostoevsky's novels. It is certainly the most ambitious, the widest in scope, encompassing a whole universe of human thought and experience.

It is, first of all, the story of a family—and what a family! The father, Fyodor Pavlovitch Karamazov, is a selfish sensualist, interested only in his own power and pleasure. He has three legitimate sons, who embody three distinct types of character, and perhaps represent the different aspects of the Russian soul. The eldest son, Dmitri (also called Mitya), is a military man, who is passionate, reckless, and sensual. The second son, Ivan (also called Vanya), is an intellectual, educated in the thought and literature of the past, and receptive to the philosophic currents of his own day, particularly nihilism (a Russian form of anarchism, which aimed at the abolition of the traditional social and moral order and its replacement by complete individual freedom). The youngest son, Alexey (also called Alyosha), is a gentle, spiritual, compassionate, loving person, a novice at the local monastery. Fyodor also has a fourth son, Smerdyakov, the illegitimate offspring of an idiot girl. Smerdyakov, an epileptic, acts as a servant to Fyodor and plays an enigmatic but important role in the novel.

The Brothers Karamazov consists of four parts and an epilogue. Each of the four parts has three books, which are numbered in sequence from I to XII. Each of the books, as well as the epilogue, is divided into chapters.

Book I, "The History of a Family," gives us the historical and biographical background of this remarkable family. Book II, "An Unfortunate Gathering," begins the essential action of the book and signals to us some of the basic tones and themes of the work. Dmitri, who has clashed with his father frequently, has come to collect an inheritance left by his mother; he claims Fyodor is holding it back from him. The whole family meets in the cell of the famous holy man Father Zossima at the monastery to get his aid in settling the dispute.

It is the skeptical, intellectual Ivan who paradoxically introduces the religious theme of the book in this "gathering." He propounds the startling thesis that where men have ceased to believe in God and immortality, nothing is immoral and everything lawful, even cannibalism. Love of neighbor depends on these beliefs, not on any natural moral law. Hence, doing harm to one's fellow-men and committing crimes is the inevitable and rational consequence, once these beliefs are gone. Dmitri, hearing this provocative thesis, says, "I'll remember it."

Fyodor embarrassingly plays the buffoon, admitting to Zossima that he does so habitually and compulsively. A bitter and ugly clash between Fyodor and Dmitri discloses that they are both interested in the same girl, Grushenka—who is now being kept by an old merchant in town—and the old man says Dmitri wants the money just to win the girl's favors. Dmitri retorts with some choice words about his father's vicious sensuality and cries, "Why is such a man alive? . . . Tell me, can he be allowed to go on defiling the earth?" (p. 36b) At this point Zossima kneels down before Dmitri, touching the floor with his forehead, then arises and begs his guests' forgiveness. The astounded Dmitri hides his face in his hands and rushes out of the room, the guests following after him.

When the holy man and Alyosha are alone, Zossima tells the youth to leave the monastery and go out in the world when Zossima dies. Alyosha's place is not in the monastic life at this time. He must first serve in the world and experience great sorrow, but thereby he shall find great happiness—"in sorrow seek happiness." He does not reveal the meaning of his bowing down before Dmitri which is fraught with a "Mysterious, and perhaps awful" significance for Alyosha.

Book III, "The Sensualists," reveals the various erotic relations and conflicts among the Karamazovs. After his talk with Zossima, Alyosha is on his way to visit Katerina Ivanovna, the respectable young lady to whom Dmitri is engaged. Alyosha is somehow afraid of the "beautiful, proud, imperious girl," with the lofty sentiments, who is generously trying to save his brother. He meets Dmitri, who pours out "The Confession of a Passionate Heart," revealing the origin of his relation to the young lady, the present state of his love life, and the nature of Karamazov sensuality. This roistering, hard-drinking, profligate young man utters verses from Schiller's "Hymn to Joy," praises nature, and laments his own degradation.

". . . And in the very depths of that degradation I begin a hymn of praise. Let me be accursed. Let me be vile and base, only let me kiss the hem of the veil in which my God is shrouded. Though I may be following the devil, I am thy son, O Lord, and I love Thee, and I feel the joy without which the world cannot stand . . ." (p. 53d)

He comments on the "sensual lust" that Schiller attributes to insects, as opposed to the "vision of God's throne" that he attributes to angels.

". . . I am that insect, brother, and it is said of me specially. All we Karamazovs are such insects, and, angel as you are, that insect lives in you, too, and will stir up a tempest in your blood. . . . I can't endure the thought that a man of lofty mind and heart begins with the ideal of the Madonna and ends with the ideal of Sodom. What's still more awful is that a man with the ideal of Sodom in his soul does not renounce the ideal of the Madonna, and his heart may be on fire with that ideal, genuinely on fire, just as in his days of youth and innocence. Yes, man is broad, too broad, indeed. I'd have him narrower. The devil only knows what to make of it! What to the mind is shameful is beauty and nothing else to the heart. Is there beauty in Sodom? Believe me, that for the immense mass of mankind beauty is found in Sodom. Did you know that secret? The awful thing is that beauty is mysterious as well as terrible. God and the devil are fighting there and the battlefield is the heart of man . . ." (p. 54a-b)

Then he confesses to Alyosha what a "bug," a "noxious insect," he has been in his relations with women, a lover of "side-paths, little dark back-alleys"—in the moral, not the literal sense—"I loved vice, I loved the ignominy of vice. I loved cruelty. . ." Alyosha blushes at the tale of Dmitri's adventures but confesses, "I blushed because I am the same as you are." He compares sensuality to a ladder, in which he is on the bottom step, but bound to go to the top one. Dmitri then goes on to tell of the "tragedy" of his relation with Katerina Ivanovna.

Katerina was the beautiful young daughter of the colonel commanding Dmitri's regiment. Dmitri, irked at not getting the attention and admiration from the young lady that he thought he deserved, resolved to "revenge" himself on her. Finding that the colonel was short 4,500 roubles in the regimental accounts, he sent word to Katerina that he would give her father the money and save him from disgrace if she would come to him secretly to collect the money. One evening she walked into his apartment and said she had come for the money. She was more beautiful than ever in that moment of ultimate generosity and self-sacrifice. Dmitri had the "venomous thought" ("I felt a centipede biting at my heart then") to take the beautiful young woman—completely at his mercy—at once. But, being an honorable man in spite of his propensities, he knew he would ask her to marry him the next day—and probably be contemptuously refused by this proud young lady. So, in a spirit of spiteful revenge, filled with a "fearful hatred," he handed her a five-thousand rouble bank note (practically his whole fortune), bowed respectfully, and opened the door into the passage. She shuddered, turned white, then bowed down at his feet in the Russian fashion, "with her forehead to the floor." He was filled with boundless delight at her humiliation.

Later on, when she came into a handsome inheritance, she wrote him, declaring her passionate love, and offering to become his wife, indeed his chattel, the carpet under his feet, ending "I want to save you from yourself." Disturbed, he sent Ivan to talk to her for him, and Ivan fell in love with her. Dmitri tells Alyosha that he does not want the girl "to sacrifice her life and destiny out of gratitude." Besides, he observes, "She loves her own *virtue*, not me." Despite the formal and solemn engagement between him and Katerina, he would like things arranged so that she would get Ivan and he would return to his "back-alley"—in this case, Grushenka.

He had originally visited Grushenka to beat her, because she held an I.O.U. of his that Fyodor had passed on to her. But he had fallen completely and irrevocably in love with her, and taken her at once on a wild spree, in which, says Dmitri, he spent three thousand roubles he happened to have on him. He is willing to be her valet, or her husband—even a willing cuckold—if only she will let him stay with her. But the "tragedy" lies in the fact that the three thousand roubles he spent on Grushenka were entrusted to him by Katerina to be mailed to her sister.

Unwilling to become "a thief and a pickpocket," as well as a scoundrel, he begs Alyosha to get three thousand roubles for

him from their father. Indeed, he has certain knowledge that
Fyodor, worried about Dmitri's courting of Grushenka, has
three thousand roubles in an envelope, which is inscribed "To
my angel, Grushenka, when she will come to me." Dmitri cannot bear the idea of Grushenka going to the old man, and he
needs the money to redeem his honor. Dmitri believes that
Fyodor will miraculously accede to his request, for God surely
"won't let something awful happen." If Grushenka does go to
Fyodor, the result will probably be murder, for he will murder
his father, for whom he feels the utmost repulsion.

Alyosha is commissioned to ask Fyodor for the money and
to deliver Dmitri's message to Katerina Ivanovna, "He sends
his compliments to you," with or without the money. Alyosha,
trusting "that God will order things for the best, that nothing
awful may happen," departs on his impossible errand. Going to
his father's house, he finds Fyodor, Ivan, Smerdyakov, and
Grigory, the old family servant, engaged in a theological discussion (whether it is a sin to renounce the Christian faith
under threat of death).

Under Fyodor's questioning, Ivan says there is no God or
immortality, and Alyosha says there is. But Ivan points out:
"There would have been no civilisation if they hadn't invented
God." The incorrigible old father shifts the discussion from
theological problems to sensual delights, which for him are
connected with sadism and masochism.

He dwells on the Russian propensity for flogging, and notes
that the lads who carry out the orders to whip the peasant girls
propose marriage to them the next day. His principle is that
"there are no ugly women," that there is "something devilishly
interesting in every woman." Ugly girls are grateful for a man's
attention, and the master-slave relation is a wonderful thing
between a man and a woman. He even tells intimate details of
his relation to the mother of Ivan and Alyosha and how he
drove her mad. Alyosha breaks out in a fit of hysterical weeping.

At that moment Dmitri bursts into the room, hunting for
Grushenka, whom he believes to be in the house. He beats
Fyodor and threatens to kill him the next time. After he leaves,

Ivan says to Alyosha, "One reptile will devour the other. And serve them both right, too" (p. 72a). Alyosha asks Ivan, ". . . has any man a right to look at other men and decide which is worthy to live?" Ivan replies that it is not a matter of worth, but of natural necessities and needs. Besides, "who has not the right to wish?" As far as killing his own father is concerned, Ivan says, "in my wishes I reserve myself full latitude. . . ." (p. 73a).

From his father's house Alyosha goes to Katerina Ivanovna's. At first he is impressed by the surprisingly "spontaneous good-natured kindliness, and direct warm-hearted sincerity" of this girl, whom he has always regarded as haughty, proud, and self-confident. In spite of "the tragedy of her position" in her relation to Dmitri, she is full of "faith in the future." She has known all the time about her missing three thousand roubles, and only wants Dmitri to confide in her, to understand that she is his true friend, who will bear anything. As for Grushenka, says Katerina, she will not marry Dmitri, for she is an angelic creature. Indeed, the "angel" is right behind the portiere.

As she emerges, Alyosha is surprised to find that the person he has thought of as a shameless hussy is a simple, ordinary, good-natured woman, beautiful in the Russian way.

She had a full figure, with soft, as it were, noiseless, movements, softened to a peculiar over-sweetness, like her voice. She moved, not like Katerina Ivanovna, with a vigorous, bold step, but noiselessly. Her feet made absolutely no sound on the floor. She sank softly into a low chair, softly rustling her sumptuous black silk dress, and delicately nestling her milk-white neck and broad shoulders in a costly cashmere shawl . . . What struck Alyosha most in that face was its expression of childlike good nature. There was a childlike look in her eyes, a look of childish delight. She came up to the table, beaming with delight and seeming to expect something with childish, impatient, and confiding curiosity. The light in her eyes gladdened the soul—Alyosha felt that. There was something else in her which he could not understand, or would not have been able to define, and which yet perhaps unconsciously affected him. It was that softness, that voluptuousness of her bodily movements, that catlike noiselessness. (p. 76a-b)

Katerina is full of the news that Grushenka plans to return

to her first love, the man who had seduced and abandoned her five years before to marry another and reduced her to the situation where she had to accept the protection of the old merchant who is now keeping her. The ex-lover, now a widower, has written to her that he is coming for her, and she will give up Dmitri. But Grushenka protests that that is Katerina's idea, not hers—maybe she'll give up Dmitri and maybe she won't. Katerina, who has been kissing Grushenka's hand, begins to kiss it all over again, showering sweet compliments on her. Whereupon Grushenka proposes that now she kiss Katerina's hand in return, holds it for several minutes, then says, "Do you know, angel lady . . . after all, I think I won't kiss your hand? . . . So that you may be left to remember that you kissed my hand, but I didn't kiss yours" (pp. 77d-78a). She says Dmitri will laugh when she tells him about it. An ugly exchange follows between the two young women, who have just been exchanging endearments—with "Insolent creature!" "Vile slut!" and "a creature for sale!" from Katerina, and the charge from Grushenka that "You used to visit gentlemen in the dusk for money once; you brought your beauty for sale." Grushenka leaves, telling Alyosha she put on the scene for his benefit, while Katerina voices her deep humiliation that Dmitri has revealed their secret to Grushenka. "Your brother's a scoundrel," she tells Alyosha.

On the road back to the monastery, Alyosha meets Dmitri, to whom he tells the whole story of what has passed. Dmitri does roar with laughter, as Grushenka predicted. He seems to be glad that Katerina was humiliated. He sees Katerina as a bold, proud, utterly confident person, set on having her own way in everything. He admits her charge that he is a scoundrel, but now he hints at something worse, in a speech that is of great importance in what follows.

"Stay, Alexey, one more confession to you alone!" cried Dmitri, suddenly turning back. "Look at me. Look at me well. You see here, here—there's terrible disgrace in store for me." (As he said "here," Dmitri struck his chest with his fist with a strange air, as though the dishonour lay precisely on his chest, in some spot, in a pocket, perhaps, or hanging round his neck.) "You know me now, a scoundrel, an avowed scoundrel, but let me tell you that I've never done anything before and never shall again, anything that can compare in baseness with the dishonour which I bear now at this very minute on my breast, here, here, which will come to pass, though I'm perfectly free to stop it. I can stop it or carry it through, note that. Well, let me tell you, I shall carry it through. I shan't stop it. I told you everything just now, but I didn't tell you this, because even I had not brass enough for it. I can still pull up; if I do, I can give back the full half of my lost honour tomorrow. But I shan't pull up. I shall carry out my base plan, and you can bear witness that I told you so beforehand. Darkness and destruction! No need to explain. You'll find out in due time. The filthy back-alley and the she-devil. Good-bye. Don't pray for me, I'm not worth it. And there's no need, no need at all . . . I don't need it! Away!" (p. 80b-c)

At the monastery Alyosha finds that Zossima has been getting weaker. In his room he reads a note from Lise, the young crippled daughter of Madame Hohlakov, a local society lady. Lise tells of her love since childhood for Alyosha and proposes that he marry her: "My heart has chosen you, to unite our lives, and pass them together till our old age." She voices her embarrassment at revealing her feelings and "ruining" her reputation and her apprehension of their next meeting, "our *awful* meeting." But her P.S. says, "Alyosha! You must, must, must come!" Alyosha is startled at first, but then he laughs "a soft, sweet laugh," and happiness quiets the agitation in his heart. He utters this prayer before falling asleep:

"God, have mercy upon all of them, have all these unhappy and turbulent souls in Thy keeping, and set them in the right path. All ways are Thine. Save them according to Thy wisdom. Thou art love. Thou wilt send joy to all!" (p. 82d)

This marks the end of Part I.

III

Part II opens with Book IV, "Lacerations," which deals with the self-inflicted sufferings of the characters, particularly Katerina. As the book opens, Alyosha listens to Father Zossima telling the monks that they are worse rather than better than other men, are responsible for all men and their sins, and must love all men, particularly the skeptics and materialists who oppose their faith. There is a general expectancy among the monks of a remarkable miracle that will mark the approaching death of Zossima. Only the rigorous and fanatic Father Ferapont, who claims to see devils and converse with the Holy Ghost, opposes the notion that Father Zossima is a saint. At Zossima's bidding, Alyosha goes forth again to meet his family, listening before he departs to the warning words of Zossima's aide, Father Païssy, against the secular science which attempts to destroy the Christian faith in the modern world. Alyosha surmises that Zossima has "bequeathed" him to Father Païssy, who will be his new spiritual father after Zossima dies.

When he arrives at his father's house, Fyodor tells him that he will not give Dmitri or Ivan a penny, for he intends to keep all his money for himself, so he can have all the girls he wants, no matter how old and ugly he gets—he'll squash his elder sons like beetles, he mutters. Alyosha kisses the old man's shoulder before he leaves, and Fyodor, surprised, says "What's that for? . . . We shall see each other again, or do you think we shan't?"

On the way to visit Madame Hohlakov and Lise, Alyosha runs across a skinny little schoolboy who throws stones at him and then bites his finger almost to the bone. Despite his pain, Alyosha looks at the boy gently and asks him why he hates him so, but the boy just sobs and runs away. At the Hohlakovs, Alyosha encounters Katerina Ivanovna, engaged in conversation with Ivan Karamazov. Ivan has been in love with her for some time, and Alyosha is apprehensive about the trouble this might cause between Ivan and Dmitri, both of whom he loves. The key word in this scene (Book IV, Ch. 5) is "lacerations." Madame Hohlakov asserts

. . . that Katerina Ivanovna was in love with Ivan, and only deceived herself through some sort of pose, from "self-laceration," and tortured herself by her pretended love for Dmitri from some fancied duty of gratitude. (p. 95c)

The motivations of this remarkable young lady—especially her revengeful pride—become clear through her own words, cloaked with conventional moral pretenses though they are.

". . . I've already decided, even if he marries that—creature," she began solemnly, "whom I never, never can forgive, *even then I will not abandon him.* Henceforward I will never, never abandon him!" she cried, breaking into a sort of pale, hysterical ecstasy. "Not that I would run after him continually, get in his way and worry him. Oh, no! I will go away to another town—where you like—but I will watch over him all my life—I will watch over him all my life unceasingly. When he becomes unhappy with that woman, and that is bound to happen quite soon, let him come to me and he will find a friend, a sister. . . . Only a sister, of course, and so for ever; but he will learn at least that that sister is really his sister, who loves him and has sacrificed all her life to him. I will gain my point. I will insist on his knowing me and confiding entirely in me, without reserve," she cried, in a sort of frenzy. "I will be a god to whom he can pray—and that, at least, he owes me for his treachery and for what I suffered yesterday through him. And let him see that all my life I will be true to him and the promise I gave him, in spite of his being untrue and betraying me. I will—I will become nothing but a means for his happiness, or—how shall I say?—an instrument, a machine for his happiness, and that for my whole life, my whole life, and that he may see that all his life! That's my decision . . ." (pp. 96d-97a)

Alyosha calls her to task for her play-acting and insists on telling her the truth—that she does not really love Dmitri but loves Ivan, whom she is torturing through her "self-laceration." Katerina, furious, calls Alyosha "a little religious idiot," while Ivan insists that she does not love him, for she is too proud to need a friend—she has just used him as a tool to revenge herself on Dmitri for his insults; indeed she loves Dmitri for insulting her.

". . . Katerina Ivanovna, you really love him. And the more he insults you, the more you love him—that's your 'laceration.' You love him just as he is; you love him for insulting you. If he reformed, you'd give him up at once and cease to love him. But you need him so as to contemplate continually your heroic fidelity and to reproach him for infidelity. And it all comes from your pride . . ." (p. 98c-d)

He bids her good-by forever, protesting, "I don't want to sit beside a 'laceration.'"

After Ivan leaves, Katerina gives Alyosha some money to give to a discharged army officer, Captain Snegiryov, whom Dmitri had cruelly insulted, while the captain's son begged him to quit and a jeering crowd looked on. As Alyosha surmises, this is the little schoolboy who bit his hand, and the boy's father

tells how deeply crushed Ilusha, the son, was by the humiliation and injustice of the incident and how he had piteously
begged Dmitri to let his father go. Snegiryov is overwhelmed
by the gift of money from Katerina, and goes into ecstatic
dreams of what he will do with the money for the various
needy members of his family, when suddenly he turns and
crumples up the bills, tramples them in the sand, and proudly
protests that he will not sell his honor for money. "What
should I say to my boy if I took the money from you for our
shame?" he cries. He kisses Alyosha's hand and runs away.

As Book V, "Pro and Contra," begins, Alyosha discusses what
has happened with Lise Hohlakov. He understands Snegiryov
as a sensitive man who was ashamed at having shown his joy
at the offer of the money, and in his humiliation hated Alyosha
for offering even more help, should he need it, for "it's awfully
hard for a man who has been injured, when other people look
at him as though they were his benefactors.'" But it is all for
the best, for he still needs the money badly, and he has vin-
dicated his honor by spurning it. Now he can receive it with
pride, if Alyosha begs him to, asking forgiveness, and putting
Snegiryov on a higher, not a lower, footing than the donors.
Lise asks acutely if all this analysis of Snegiryov's soul is not a
form of contempt from above, but Alyosha says this is not so,
for "we are all like him." Indeed Alyosha feels that he himself
may be much worse.

> "My brothers are destroying themselves," he went on, "my father,
> too. And they are destroying others with them. It's 'the primitive force
> of the Karamazovs,' as Father Païssy said the other day, a crude, un-
> bridled, earthly force. Does the spirit of God move above that force?
> Even that I don't know. I only know that I, too, am a Karamazov. . . .
> Me a monk, a monk! Am I a monk, Lise? You said just now that I
> was."
> "Yes, I did."
> "And perhaps I don't even believe in God." (p. 113c)

As this scene ends Alyosha and Lise plight their troth, to the
consternation of Madame Hohlakov who has been eaves-
dropping on their interview.

A further revelation of the Karamazov soul occurs when
Alyosha meets his brother Ivan at a restaurant. Ivan announces

that his main characteristic is the love of life, in spite of all disbelief and disillusionment, and that this thirst for life is the main Karamazov characteristic.

". . . Though I may not believe in the order of the universe, yet I love the sticky little leaves as they open in spring. I love the blue sky, I love some people, whom one loves you know sometimes without knowing why . . . It's not a matter of intellect or logic, it's loving with one's inside, with one's stomach. One loves the first strength of one's youth . . ." (p. 118c-d)

He and Alyosha go on to discuss "the eternal questions" which young Russians always discuss, even in a "stinking tavern" such as this. Russian youths talk about the existence of God and immortality,

". . . And those who do not believe in God talk of socialism or anarchism, of the transformation of all humanity on a new pattern, so that it all comes to the same, they're the same questions turned inside out . . ." (p. 120c)

Ivan understands that Alyosha does not want an abstract discussion from him, but a statement of what he, Ivan, really believes in, what there is in his heart. He says that he accepts God and his wisdom and purpose and the ultimate salvation which He will establish, but he will not accept God's creation, this world of evil and suffering.

In the first place, Ivan regards man as "a savage, vicious beast" who it is ludicrous to imagine is made in the image of any believable God. Men inflict unspeakable suffering on innocent, helpless children, and all kinds of fiendish atrocities and cruelty on one another. The Russians, in particular, are fond of flogging—beasts, children, women, men—to the point of death.

". . . In every man, of course, a demon lies hidden—the demon of rage, the demon of lustful heat at the screams of the tortured victim, the demon of lawlessness let off the chain, the demon of diseases that follow on vice, gout, kidney disease, and so on." (p. 124d)

Ivan curses the knowledge of good and evil that is given as an explanation for the horrible cruelties of adults toward children. "Why, the whole world of knowledge is not worth that child's prayer of 'dear, kind God'!" Ivan refuses to be solaced by the assurance that all such suffering will be made good ultimately in some transcendent harmony. He refuses to accept a harmony that is bought with the sufferings of helpless children. Their tears must be atoned for, but not by vengeance, not by hell, which will not annul the children's suffering, and only add to the total of suffering.

". . . I don't want harmony. From love for humanity I don't want it. I would rather be left with the unavenged suffering. I would rather remain with my unavenged suffering and unsatisfied indignation, *even if I were wrong*. Besides, too high a price is asked for harmony; it's beyond our means to pay so much to enter on it. And so I hasten to give back my entrance ticket, and if I am an honest man I am bound to give it back as soon as possible. And that I am doing. It's not God that I don't accept, Alyosha, only I most respectfully return Him the ticket." (p. 126d)

To Alyosha's charge that this is "rebellion," Ivan responds by putting before him the possibility that the whole world could be made a paradise if one little baby is tortured to death. Would Alyosha accept a harmony purchased at such a price? No, says Alyosha. But he brings up Christ as the one being who would have the right to forgive the cruelties inflicted on helpless children. Ivan responds with his "poem" entitled "The Grand Inquisitor."

This story within a story is probably the best known section of *The Brothers Karamazov*. It is often published separately in anthologies of Russian or world literature. It is a vivid presentation of the conflict between spiritual freedom and material necessities, dramatized in the discussion between the Grand Inquisitor and Christ returned to earth—in Seville, at the moment when heretics are being burned in the square. The Grand Inquisitor (the cardinal directing the procedure) prevents a public disturbance by having Christ arrested and placed in one of the dungeons. The Inquisitor argues that Christ does not really love mankind, because He has refused to conquer them with miracles, a descent from the cross, or the bestowal of earthly bread. Christ's call is to an elite, a remnant who can follow the heroic way of freedom, but the mass of mankind cannot endure the suffering that accompanies freedom. The way of conscience and spiritual inwardness is too hard. Better the way of the Inquisitor, with its safe and sure system of rewards and punishments, tangible and available, appealing to the human, all too human, fears and desires. He portrays the earthly paradise of the future, where all men's earthly needs will be satisfied, and they will be allowed to sin, if only they are obedient to the authorities, who will bear the burden of all their sins. Christ in returning threatens that happiness, hence He must die at the stake, and the people who have hailed Him today will help to burn Him tomorrow. Christ, who has listened silently to the Inquisitor's discourse, replies by kissing the old cardinal on "his bloodless aged lips." The Inquisitor opens the door and says to Christ, "Go and come no more . . . come not at all, never, never!" And so Christ goes away, and the kiss glows in the old man's heart, while he continues to adhere to his idea.

Alyosha is vexed with Ivan for this story, says it is fantastical nonsense, having nothing to do with the Orthodox Church, and only with the worst elements of the Roman Catholic Church. When he asks Ivan how he hopes to carry on and love life with such a hell in his heart and head, Ivan replies that he has one mainstay—"The strength of the Karamazovs—the strength of the Karamazov baseness." He will follow the way of debauchery and corruption, and his announced principle that "Everything is lawful." Alyosha, like the Christ of Ivan's story, kisses him on the lips. Ivan assures him that he will love life as long as he knows there is an Alyosha in the world.

At this point the center of the narrative shifts from Alyosha to Ivan, and we follow him after he leaves Alyosha. Ivan is all set to start a new life, to leave his father's house and return to Moscow. But he is vaguely disturbed and depressed, and a conversation he has with Smerdyakov makes him feel still lower. Ivan has an intense loathing for his half-brother, who has presumed to be on familiar terms with him, perhaps, because of the philosophical discussions they have had together. A curious conversation takes place now, one that is crucial for the development of the story.

Smerdyakov suggests that Ivan go to Tchermashnya, a nearby town where old Karamazov has some forest land. He is not explicit on why he wants Ivan to go there, but launches on a description of his difficult situation—under orders by Fyodor to signal him when Grushenka comes and to warn him if Dmitri shows up, and at the same time under the threat of death by Dmitri if he does not warn him when Grushenka is in the house. Indeed, he has a presentiment that he is going to have one of his long epileptic fits, perhaps occasioned by a fall down the cellar steps. He does not deny that he may be seeking this illness as an excuse to get out of his difficulties, and in order not to be involved in what may happen—perhaps Dmitri will murder his father if Grushenka shows up, or simply in order to take the three thousand roubles that Fyodor has put in the envelope for Grushenka. Ivan suggests to Smerdyakov that he is advising him to go to Tchermashnya so that he will be out of the way when whatever is going to happen takes place, and to go to Tchermashnya instead of Moscow, so as to be nearby when he will be needed. To which Smerdyakov answers, "Precisely so."

Ivan is in "a nervous frenzy" after this strange conversation. He is prey to intense excitement, an "inexplicable humiliating terror," and feelings of hatred and vengefulness. He even gets up to spy on his father's actions that night, which he regards in later days as "infamous," the basest thing he has ever done. But after a good night's sleep he is in a good mood, and happily packs his trunks to take off for Moscow, and leave the Karamazov house for good. However, his father insists that he stop over at Tchermashnya and settle some business about the forest land, and he finally gives in. "You see . . . I am going to Tchermashnya," he says with a nervous laugh to Smerdyakov. "It's always worth while speaking to a clever man," replies Smerdyakov with a meaningful look.

Ivan is in a happy mood as he leaves, but he soon begins to wonder about this last remark of Smerdyakov's. Suddenly he changes his mind and decides to go directly to Moscow. "Away with the past. I've done with the old world for ever, and may I have no news, no echo from it. To a new life, new places, and no looking back!" (p. 145d). But he is filled with gloom and dread, with utter, deep, dark anguish. As the train nears Moscow he whispers to himself, "I am a scoundrel."

Meanwhile, back home, Smerdyakov causes a disturbance and inconvenience by falling down the cellar steps and having an epileptic fit. Fortunately no bones are broken, but he remains unconscious and has a series of convulsions. The local doctor concludes that he is suffering from a very violent and serious fit. Fyodor is displeased and disturbed by this hitch in his plans, but he keeps looking expectantly for Grushenka, with high voluptuous hopes, also keeping a wary eye cocked for the threatening Dmitri.

Book VI, "The Russian Monk," consists of Father Zossima's story of his life, and his vision of the role of the Russian monk in modern society. Zossima was, like Dmitri, a profligate young officer with a vicious streak in him. He tells the moving and convincing story of how, unconsciously inspired by the memory of a dead brother who was much like Alyosha, he rose from egocentric pride to the way of love, humility, and service. Like Ivan, he sounds the theme of joy in the world, putting it in the context of the religious life. Zossima's story and commentary are presented in the form of biographical notes by Alyosha, based on Zossima's own words; this is another story within the story, paralleling Ivan's "Grand Inquisitor." (Book VI is discussed in its entirety in the Fourteenth Reading of *Religion and Theology*.)

Father Zossima dies shortly after uttering these confessions, with a smile for his disciples, kissing the ground in joy. His death marks the end of Part II.

IV

Part III begins with Book VII, "Alyosha," which deals with the decisive response of Alyosha to Father Zossima's example and teaching. He begins with an agonizing disillusionment, caused by the quick corruption of the elder's corpse. It begins to stink soon after his death, "in excess of nature," instead of remaining fresh and fragrant or being the occasion of miracles, as had been expected. This phenomenon is regarded by many

—especially by the fanatic Father Ferapont, as a judgment of heaven against Father Zossima for his unorthodox religious opinions and practices and for letting people take him for a saint. Alyosha is struck at the very heart of his faith and love, which for years have been centered in the elder. His sense of justice—of "the higher justice"—is outraged that this saintly man whom he had revered as his spiritual father has been degraded and dishonored. Ivan's words in their memorable conversation begin to tempt him to rebel against God, or, rather, against His creation.

A fellow novice, Rakitin, a skeptical youth, senses this. "So now you are in a temper with your God, you are rebelling against Him; He hasn't given promotion. He hasn't bestowed the order of merit!" To which Alyosha replies with Ivan's words, "I am not rebelling against my God; I simply 'don't accept His world'" (p. 179a). Rakitin ends the argument with the suggestion that they go visit Grushenka. "Let's go," replies Alvosha. Rakitin looks forward to seeing "the downfall of the righteous" and Alyosha's fall "from the saints to the sinners," as well as to collecting a generous tip that Grushenka has promised him for bringing Alyosha to her.

But things do not turn out as Rakitin had expected. Grushenka sits on Alyosha's knee, nestling in his lap and clasping him affectionately, but Alyosha, in his deep grief, is neither lustful nor afraid, as he has always been, of the erotic appeal of woman. Grushenka confesses to him that he has been like a conscience for her, someone compared with whom she is unclean, before whom she is ashamed of being what she is. But since he has always avoided her gaze, seeming to despise her, she has wanted to get him in her clutches, seduce him, and then scoff at him. She claims to be a violent, spiteful, and resentful creature. "I wanted to ruin you, Alyosha," she says, "that's the holy truth."

But Alyosha confesses in turn that in coming here, in his grieving disillusionment, he intended to soak himself in evil, seeing Grushenka as the embodiment of wickedness. "I came here seeking my ruin." But now he has found instead "a true sister . . . a loving heart," and one of more enduring holiness than himself. For she is waiting for the word from the man who seduced and abandoned her five years ago, the man on whom she had long vowed revenge, but now forgives and is ready to run to with "an abject heart." Alyosha acknowledges Grushenka's greater worthiness in love and forgiveness, while she hails him as the first person to pity her, the first man to offer forgiving love to her, as she is—"nasty as I am."

Alyosha and Rakitin leave her as she prepares to go to her first lover. Rakitin is angry at the spiritual crises he has witnessed but cannot share in, and he is also peeved because Alyosha has seen Grushenka paying him off for bringing Alyosha to her. He mocks Alyosha for fancying he has miraculously turned a Magdalene away from sin or that he is the Christ whom Rakitin has sold to Grushenka for twenty-five roubles. "I don't want to know you from this time forward," he shouts. "Go alone, there's your road!" And he turns off, "leaving Alyosha alone in the dark." The latter makes his solitary way back to the monastery.

There, before the coffin of Father Zossima, he has the saving experience of "joy, joy . . . glowing in his mind and in his heart . . . a sense of the wholeness of things." He hears Father Païssy reading the story of the wedding at Cana, of Christ's first miracle, addressed not to men's grief, but to their joy. He remembers that Dmitri has said, "There's no living without joy." Christ knew that too and opened His heart "to the simple, artless merrymaking of some obscure and unlearned people," providing wine for "their poor wedding." At this point Alyosha falls asleep and dreams that Father Zossima arises from the coffin, proclaims rejoicing, the drinking of "the wine of new, great gladness," and begs Alyosha, "Begin your work, dear one, begin it, gentle one!"

Alyosha awakes in ecstasy, yearning "for freedom, space, openness." He goes out in the night, reverencing the mystery of the earth and of the stars. He throws himself down on the earth, embraces it passionately, kisses it, and vows to love it forever. He is filled with universal love and compassion.

But with every instant he felt clearly and, as it were, tangibly, that something firm and unshakable as that vault of heaven had entered into his soul. It was as though some idea had seized the sovereignty of his mind—and it was for all his life and for ever and ever. He had fallen on the earth a weak boy, but he rose up a resolute champion, and he knew and felt it suddenly at the very moment of his ecstasy. And never, never, all his life long, could Alyosha forget that minute. (p. 191c)

Three days later he leaves the monastery to begin his "sojourn in the world." Alyosha's decisive experience is entitled "Cana of Galilee." (See p. 189a.)

Book VIII, "Mitya," centers on Dmitri Karamazov, and presents the climactic events of the novel. Dmitri is in a state of wild enthusiasm as he looks forward to starting a new and virtuous life with Grushenka, whom he deeply and truly loves. But he needs money desperately, to pay his debt of honor to Katerina and support Grushenka in their new life. He engages in pathetic and comical attempts to get the money. When he approaches Grushenka's protector, the old merchant, with a harebrained proposition, the latter, in mere spite and malevolence, sends him out in the country on a wild-goose chase. Then the desperate and frustrated Dmitri begs Madame Hohlakov for a loan of three thousand roubles. But that wealthy lady, offering free advice but no money, only wants to send him out to some unspecified "gold mines" to make his fortune.

Dmitri then begins chasing after Grushenka, who has already gone off to her rendezvous with her first lover. He seeks her first at the Karamazov house, but soon ascertains that she is not there. Hiding in the bushes, however, he sees his father at the window, is filled with utter loathing, the impulse to kill him, and grasps a brass pestle that he has taken from a mortar in Grushenka's house. There is a gap in the narrative, and in the next scene the old servant Grigory runs after a fleeing figure, catches him by the leg as he tries to get over the fence, and recognizes it is Dmitri. Grigory shouts "Parricide!" and then is felled by a blow of the pestle. Dmitri, deeply concerned, examines the fallen man, getting blood over his hands and clothes. He leaves, uncertain of whether he has killed him or not.

When Dmitri finds out where Grushenka has gone—to Mokroe, where they had had their grand spree—he proceeds to make arrangements to join her, just to see her once more and to wish her happiness. He flashes a big role of bank notes, with which he purchases provisions for a great party, like the one he had had before on the money borrowed from Katerina. His acquaintances and others begin to speculate that he must have got the suddenly acquired money by robbing his father—and perhaps worse. Dmitri, with his load of provisions, rides to the tavern at Mokroe, where Grushenka is meeting her ex-lover. A typical Dostoevskean scene, combining the poignant with the comic, ensues.

Grushenka's ex-lover, a Pole, turns out to be a vain, fatuous, middle-aged, commonplace fellow—nothing at all like the young man whom she remembered and had longed for during five long years. She tells Dmitri how she drove to the inn with quivering expectancy.

". . . My soul was faint, and all of a sudden it was just as though he had emptied a pail of dirty water over me. He talked to me like a school-master, all so grave and learned; he met me so solemnly that I was struck dumb. I couldn't get a word in . . ." (p. 232b)

She is ashamed now for her whole life and the five lost years, which are perhaps as much the expression of anger as of yearning. She ends by confessing her love for Dmitri.

In the sometimes ludicrous scene between Dmitri and the Pole, Dmitri progresses from gentle friendliness to furious out-rage, ending by locking up the ex-lover. Thus the "terrible phantom" he had feared—the man who had emerged out of the past to take Grushenka away from him—turns out to be a comical figure he has picked up and locked in a bedroom. But he is oppressed by another incubus—the near certainty that he has killed the old servant and must pay for it.

After the Pole is locked away, a wild party follows in which Dmitri wines and dines the whole countryside—an "absurd chaotic confusion" in which Dmitri revels. But as he is in Grushenka's embrace, the curtains of their room are parted and Dmitri confronts the police. "The old man and his blood!" he cries, "I understand." The police captain replies, "Monster and parricide! Your father's blood cries out against you!" The "investigating lawyer" for the state, who is present with the deputy prosecutor, thereupon announces:

"Ex-Lieutenant Karamazov, it is my duty to inform you that you are charged with the murder of your father, Fyodor Pavlovitch Karamazov, perpetrated this night . . ." (p. 235c-d)

Dmitri, silent and not understanding, just stares at the officials "with wild eyes."

Book IX, "The Preliminary Investigation," begins with the background that has led to Dmitri's arrest. Fyodor has been found dead, his skull crushed, presumably by the same weapon that knocked out old Grigory, who has recovered from Dmitri's blow. The envelope with the three thousand roubles, addressed to Grushenka, has been opened and the money is gone. Dmitri's activities that night—his sudden acquisition of money, the blood, the pestle—everything points to him as the murderer. But he protests:

"I'm not guilty! I'm not guilty of that blood! I'm not guilty of my father's blood. . . . I meant to kill him. But I'm not guilty. Not I." (p. 242b)

He does admit guilt for having killed Grigory, for *that* old man, but not for his father. Overjoyed to find that Grigory is alive and recovering, he feels cleansed of bloodguilt in the sight of God.

There follows the "preliminary investigation," which was part of the Russian legal system, addressed to the ascertaining of facts about the crime from all the parties involved. Dostoevsky entitles the questioning of Dmitri "The Sufferings of a Soul," and divides it into three "ordeals." (See Book IX, Ch. 3-5.) In "The First Ordeal,'" Dmitri admits that he was on bad terms with his father and often wanted to kill him, indeed that he had threatened to do so. He admits that he considered the three thousand roubles in the envelope his own property. He explains that, out of his own sense of honor he loathed his father as being the opposite of all that was noble and good.

In the second phase or "ordeal," Dmitri becomes annoyed at what he considers the pettiness and obtuseness of the questioning. He will not tell the investigating lawyer why he needed exactly three thousand roubles, except to say it is a debt of honor, a strictly personal matter. He cannot say why he picked up the pestle at Grushenka's place, for he had no conscious object or purpose at the time. He proclaims that the investigators are hunting him down, as if he were a wolf, as in a nightmare which he frequently has.

As the interrogation goes into its third phase, Dmitri gives a clearly detailed account of his movements that night up to the point where he pulled out the pestle. Through some heavenly intervention, he says, the devil in his heart was conquered and he ran away, but his father saw him and shouted, then sprang back from the window. What happened after that he does not know. He is sure that the house door into the garden was closed at the time, and is surprised to hear that it was open and that the murder was committed from inside the room where old Karamazov was found. When he informs the investigator about the signals known only to Fyodor, Smerdyakov, and himself, the question arises as to whether Smerdyakov did it. But Dmitri refuses to accuse Smerdyakov, for he considers him too timid and lacking in motive. Informed that Smerdyakov has been the victim of a probably mortal epileptic fit, definitely, eliminating him as the murderer, Dmitri says, "Well, if that's so, the devil must have killed him."

Dmitri refuses, as a point of personal honor, to tell where he got the money he has flashed around that night. Finding only part of the money on him, they force him to strip to the skin while they search his clothes for the remainder. He is ashamed to be naked while everyone else is clothed. It is a crowning indignity, like a bad dream. And to top it off, they keep his clothes as exhibits, giving him someone' else's illfitting clothes. He is filled with such loathing for the investigating officials—"blind moles and scoffers," who will not believe the truth he has been telling them—that he refuses to answer any more questions. But when he is shown the opened and empty envelope inscribed to Grushenka, he is sure that Smerdyakov alone could have killed the old man. The amazing statement previously made by Grigory to the police that the door to the garden was open forces him in self-defense to tell where he got the money he has been spending so freely.

He says that the money was his own, or, rather, the remainder of the money entrusted to him by Katerina Ivanovna.
He only spent half of it on the first spree at Mokroe, and has
carried the rest in a rag worn around his neck for over a month.
He reveals that he had purposely kept this secret nest egg in
order to have money to begin a new life with Grushenka, in
case he did not get the inheritance money from his father. He
tries to explain to the investigator why he felt this fact was
too shameful to confess to them. The shame, for him, lies in
the calculated, scoundrelly action of secretly holding back half
of Katerina's money, and pretending he had squandered it all
on the first spree. He had long wavered and even thought of
giving the money back to Katerina—or even venturing the
further infamy of asking her to lend it to him—but when he
discovered that Grushenka was returning to her first lover, he
decided to spend it all and kill himself, since shame meant
nothing to him anymore. But he has learned this night that "it's
not only impossible to live a scoundrel, but impossible to die a
scoundrel."

The investigator, however, does not believe him, for Dmitri
himself has boasted that he spent all of the original three
thousand roubles on the first spree, and the other witnesses all
confirm that he did so, including Grushenka (who assures
Dmitri of her love, her belief that he is innocent, and her will
to share his destiny). Before Dmitri signs the protocol, recording the testimony of the original investigation, he naps and
has a portentous dream about a weeping babe and starving,
hungry people. In the dream, he has an impulse to remove the
misery and the weeping and to replace them with joy, a longing "to live, to live, to go on and on, towards the new, beckon-
ing light, and to hasten, hasten, now, at once!" (p. 269d).

After Dmitri signs the protocol, he makes this statement to
the officials:

"Gentlemen, we're all cruel, we're all monsters, we all make men
weep, and mothers, and babes at the breast, but of all, let it be settled
here, now, of all I am the lowest reptile! I've sworn to amend, and every
day I've done the same filthy things. I understand now that such men
as I need a blow, a blow of destiny to catch them as with a noose, and
bind them by a force from without. Never, never should I have risen

of myself! But the thunderbolt has fallen. I accept the torture of accusa-
tion, and my public shame; I want to suffer and by suffering I shall
be purified. Perhaps I shall be purified, gentlemen? But listen, for the
last time, I am not guilty of my father's blood. I accept my punishment,
not because I killed him, but because I meant to kill him, and perhaps
I really might have killed him . . ." (p. 270b-c)

But now that Dmitri is an accused criminal, no one is anxious
to shake his hand. Men he has known and even favored with-
draw from him or act surly toward him. One friend runs out
to clasp his hand as he is taken away, and that friend is miserable with grief, believing that Dmitri is guilty. His faith in
men is shattered, and he wonders if it is worthwhile to go
on living.

V

Part IV presents—in most dramatic fashion—the final un-
raveling of the action and the ideas of the novel. It begins with
Book X, "The Boys," which picks up again the story of little
Ilusha and the other boys, which runs as a subtheme through
the novel, and is returned to again in the final chapter of the
Epilogue. Book XI, "Ivan," reveals fully the underlying motives, ideas, and events that have brought about the murder
of Fyodor Karamazov.

Chapter 3, "A Little Demon," dealing with a conversation
between Alyosha and Lise, returns to the theme of "lacerations"
and provides a foretaste of things to come. Lise claims she is
rejecting Alyosha. She wants someone to marry her, torture
her, and make her unhappy. She has impulses to hurt and
destroy, such as setting fire to the house. "I want to do evil,"
she says, and adds that she wants to do it on the sly and then
enjoy being discovered. Alyosha replies that she is passing
through a crisis where she takes evil for good, craves to destroy
the real good. "There are moments when people love crime," he
observes.

Lise counters that people secretly love crime and evil-doing
all the time, that they really love his brother for killing his
father; indeed, she herself loves it. She has a dream where she
alternately attracts and repels the devil, first reviling God and
then crossing herself—"It's awful fun." She tells also of her
craving to witness a tortured and crucified child die slowly,

while she eats pineapple compote. She reveals that she has told "a certain person" (Ivan) about her strange craving, but he merely laughed and went away. Alyosha remarks that "perhaps he believes in the pineapple compote himself." Lise feels that Ivan despises her and she enjoys being despised. She finally begs Alyosha to save her, for she loathes everything, and wants to kill herself. She can only be saved by his utterly unselfish love and tears. She hates everyone else, including Ivan.

She pushes Alyosha out the door, entrusting him with a tiny letter addressed to Ivan. After he is gone, Lise opens the door, puts her finger in the crack, and slams the door on it as hard as she can. She looks at her blackened finger, with the blood oozing out, and whispers to herself, "I am a wretch, wretch, wretch, wretch!"

Alyosha goes first to the jail to visit Dmitri, who is awaiting trial. Dmitri has been passionately interested in moral ideas, and looks forward enthusiastically to his coming ordeal. He dismisses all theories that human acts—murder, for instance— may be explained by physiological or sociological factors. He announces to Alyosha that "a new man" has arisen in his heart, a hidden, suppressed man who would never have become known to him, if not for this "blow from heaven." He does not care now if he has to work for twenty years in the mines in Siberia, for there "underground" he may live and love and raise another human creature from the dark depths. The meaning of his strange dream at the interrogation is that

". . . we are all responsible for all. For all the 'babes,' for there are big children as well as little children. All are 'babes.' I go for all, because someone must go for all. I didn't kill father, but I've got to go. I accept it. It's all come to me here, here, within these peeling walls. There are numbers of them there, hundreds of them underground, with hammers in their hands. Oh, yes, we shall be in chains and there will be no freedom, but then, in our great sorrow, we shall rise again to joy, without which man cannot live nor God exist, for God gives joy: it's His privilege—a grand one. Ah, man should be dissolved in prayer! What should I be underground there without God? Rakitin's laughing! If they drive God from the earth, we shall shelter Him underground. One cannot exist in prison without God; it's even more impossible than out of prison. And then we men underground will sing from the bowels of the earth a glorious hymn to God, with Whom is joy. Hail to God and His joy! I love Him! ..."

". . . What if He doesn't exist? What if Rakitin's right—that it's an idea made up by men? Then if He doesn't exist, man is the chief of the earth, of the universe. Magnificent! Only how is he going to be good without God? That's the question. I always come back to that. For whom is man going to love then? To whom will he be thankful? To whom will he sing the hymn? ..." (pp. 313d-314c)

In addition to his hymn, Dmitri has a secret, Ivan's plan to have Dmitri escape from prison and go to America. But this raises "a question of conscience, question of the higher conscience," for does he have the right to flee from suffering, to turn his back on "the sign" of his dream, to reject the way of salvation? Ivan is insistent, however, that he escape.

When Alyosha encounters Ivan later, the latter speaks of Dmitri as "the murderer" and "that monster." Alyosha pulls him up short by telling him that Dmitri is not the murderer.

Ivan suddenly stopped.

"Who is the murderer then, according to you?" he asked, with apparent coldness. There was even a supercilious note in his voice.

"You know who," Alyosha pronounced in a low, penetrating voice.

"Who? You mean the myth about that crazy idiot, the epileptic, Smerdyakov?"

Alyosha suddenly felt himself trembling all over.

"You know who," broke helplessly from him. He could scarcely breathe.

"Who? Who?" Ivan cried almost fiercely. All his restraint suddenly vanished.

"I only know one thing," Alyosha went on, still almost in a whisper, "*it wasn't you* killed father."

"'Not you'! What do you mean by 'not you'?" Ivan was thunderstruck.

"It was not you killed father, not you!" Alyosha repeated firmly.

The silence lasted for half a minute.

"I know I didn't. Are you raving?" said Ivan, with a pale, distorted smile. His eyes were riveted on Alyosha. They were standing again under a lamp-post.

"No, Ivan. You've told yourself several times that you are the murderer."

"When did I say so? I was in Moscow. . . . When have I said so?" Ivan faltered helplessly.

"You've said so to yourself many times, when you've been alone during these two dreadful months," Alyosha went on softly and distinctly as before. Yet he was speaking now, as it were, not of himself, not of his own will, but obeying some irresistible command. "You have accused yourself and have confessed to yourself that you are the murderer and no one else. But you didn't do it: you are mistaken: you are not the murderer. Do you hear? It was not you! God has sent me to tell you so." (p. 319a-b)

Ivan mutters something about someone who visits him at night, then breaks off all relations with Alyosha, for he "can't endure prophets and epileptics—messengers from God especially."

The narrative turns back to two interviews between Ivan and Smerdyakov. The first is in the hospital, when Smerdyakov is recovering from his fit, which, according to the doctors, was perfectly genuine. Smerdyakov tells Ivan that he did not sham the fits or commit the crime himself, and he accuses Ivan of having gone off to Tchermashnya to avoid what he knew was going to happen. After that interview, Ivan asks Alyosha whether he believed Ivan had the wish to kill his father, or had wanted Dmitri to kill him—("one reptile should devour another")—and was ready to help him to do so? Alyosha admits that he did believe so. Ivan avoids all intercourse with Alyosha after that.

In the second interview with Smerdyakov, this time in his home, Ivan strikes the convalescing man for suggesting that Ivan foresaw that Dmitri would kill Fyodor, thus ensuring that Ivan would get half of the inheritance—both Dmitri and Grushenka having been eliminated as inheritors. When Ivan says that, on the contrary, it was Smerdyakov he had suspected, the latter says it was just that suspicion that indicated what Ivan really wanted. "For if you had a foreboding about me and yet went away, you as good as said to me, 'You can murder my parent, I won't hinder you'" (p. 326d). Indeed, if he had not wanted his father murdered, he should have beaten up Smerdyakov and taken him to the lockup for his menacing suggestion in their conversation before he set off for Moscow. Now it would look very bad for Ivan if he makes their conversation public.

The second interview leaves Ivan in an anguished spirit.

Did he or did he not want his father murdered? he asks himself, and he feels sure that he did. He goes to Katerina, talking like a madman, then announces to her:

"If it's not Dmitri, but Smerdyakov who's the murderer, I share his guilt, for I put him up to it. Whether I did, I don't know yet. But if he is the murderer, and not Dmitri, then, of course, I am the murderer, too." (p. 327d)

Thereupon Katerina takes out a letter from Dmitri, written in a drunken state, on the evening he met Alyosha after Grushenka had insulted Katerina.

FATAL KATYA: To-morrow I will get the money and repay your three thousand and farewell, woman of great wrath, but farewell, too, my love! Let us make an end! To-morrow I shall try and get it from everyone, and if I can't borrow it, I give you my word of honour I shall go to my father and break his skull and take the money from under the pillow, if only Ivan has gone. If I have to go to Siberia for it, I'll give you back your three thousand. And farewell. I bow down to the ground before you, for I've been a scoundrel to you. Forgive me! No, better not forgive me, you'll be happier and so shall I! Better Siberia than your love, for I love another woman and you got to know her too well to-day, so how can you forgive? I will murder the man who's robbed me! I'll leave you all and go to the East so as to see no one again. Not *her* either, for you are not my only tormentress; she is too. Farewell!

P.S.—I write my curse, but I adore you! I hear it in my heart. One string is left, and it vibrates. Better tear my heart in two! I shall kill myself, but first of all that cur. I shall tear three thousand from him and fling it to you. Though I've been a scoundrel to you, I am not a thief! You can expect three thousand. The cur keeps it under his mattress, in pink ribbon. I am not a thief, but I'll murder my thief. Katya, don't look disdainful. Dmitri is not a thief! but a murderer! He has murdered his father and ruined himself to hold his ground, rather than endure your pride. And he doesn't love you.

P.P.S.—I kiss your feet, farewell! P.P.P.S.—Katya, pray to God that someone'll give me the money. Then I shall not be steeped in gore, and if no one does—I shall! Kill me!

Your slave and enemy,
D. KARAMAZOV (p. 328b-c)

Ivan is relieved by this "document" of all feeling of guilt, and considers it a "conclusive proof" that it is Dmitri and not Smerdyakov (acting for Ivan) who committed the murder. Ivan has hated Dmitri because of his jealousy of him as a rival for the affections of Katerina, who drives Ivan mad with her "returns" to favorable feeling for Dmitri. But now he realizes he hates Dmitri simply *"because he was the murderer of his father."* Yet he proposes a plan of escape to Dmitri, which he, Ivan, will finance himself, since he feels guilty about Smerdyakov's suggestion that he will profit by Dmitri's being disinherited as a felon. He realizes that another reason for aiding Dmitri to escape may be that he feels like a murderer in his heart.

The flashback in the narrative is now completed, and we return to the point where Ivan has his revealing conversation with Alyosha. Now he goes to his third and final interview with Smerdyakov, on the eve of the trial. This time Smerdyakov reveals to Ivan that he killed Fyodor, acting, so he thought, as Ivan's "instrument" and "faithful servant." He shows him the three thousand roubles he had taken from the envelope, tells of how he shammed an epileptic fit and lay waiting, expecting Dmitri to murder the old man or at least beat him senseless. But when events turned out as they did, he decided to do the deed himself. He paints a pathetic picture of how he enticed the sensual old man with the lure of Grushenka hiding in the bushes, and how he battered in Fyodor's skull with a paperweight when he leaned out the window to see the object of his desires. As for the open door, Grigory was all wrong—it had been closed all the time, and Fyodor had opened it to Smerdyakov, expecting Grushenka. After the murder, Smerdyakov had taken the money, replaced the paperweight, and hidden the money in the hollow of a tree. He foresaw correctly the suspicious circumstances pointing to Dmitri and the way the prosecutor and investigator would reason and interpret the facts. He also calculated that Ivan, feeling guilty and profiting from his increased inheritance, would reward him for the rest of his life.

Smerdyakov says that Ivan is the real murderer, for Ivan not only had the desire to kill his father and provided the opportunity for the murder, but he also provided the intellectual incitation that Smerdyakov needed for the deed. If "all things are lawful" and there is no God, then there is no human virtue, no difference between right and wrong. Ivan protests that he will make public at the trial all that Smerdyakov has told him, and he takes the stolen bank notes to exhibit in court.

Going home in a blinding snowstorm, Ivan is full of resolution to begin anew, but when he enters his room he feels "something like a touch of ice on his heart, like a recollection or, more exactly, a reminder, of something agonising and revolting that was in that room now, at that moment, and had been there before" (p. 336d). He is in a delirium, on the verge of an attack of brain fever, which he has been holding off for some time. It is at this point that Ivan has an interview with the devil, who has been visiting him frequently of late. (See Book XI, Ch. 9.)

Ivan's devil appears in the form of a Russian gentleman down on his luck, his once fashionable clothes rather shabby now, a sort of "poor relation" who comes around to his better-off friends and relatives for tea and company. This devil does not remember ever having been a fallen angel, but he does love the solid reality of earthly life, even though he has caught rheumatism on his sudden journey through space. Unlike Mephistopheles, he wants to do good, not evil, but he has been given the role of negation, without which there would be no events, no world, no human existence. At the time of the Resurrection, he confesses, he too wanted to shout hosannah with the heavenly choir, but "common sense—oh, a most unhappy trait in my character—kept me in due bounds and I let the moment pass!" (p. 344b). If he ever bawled hosannah, "the indispensable minus would disappear at once," and the universe with it. Throughout this discourse Ivan calls the devil a stupid fool and insists that he does not really exist, but is merely an expression of Ivan's soul—of his worst, stupidest, nastiest side. The devil concludes with a picture of how the new morality that Ivan has been preaching will replace the old "slave morality."

". . . ‘. . . I maintain that nothing need be destroyed, that we only need to destroy the idea of God in man, that's how we have to set to work. It's that, that we must begin with. Oh, blind race of men who have no understanding! As soon as men have all of them denied God—and I believe that period, analogous with geological periods, will come to pass—the old conception of the universe will fall of itself without cannibalism, and, what's more, the old morality, and everything will begin anew. Men will unite to take from life all it can give, but only for joy and happiness in the present world. Man will be lifted up with a spirit of divine Titanic pride and the man-god will appear. From hour to hour extending his conquest of nature infinitely by his will and his science, man will feel such lofty joy from hour to hour in doing it that it will make up for all his old dreams of the joys of heaven. Everyone will know that he is mortal and will accept death proudly and serenely like a god. His pride will teach him that it's useless for him to repine at life's being a moment, and he will love his brother without need of reward. Love will be sufficient only for a moment of life, but the very consciousness of its momentariness will intensify its fire, which now is dissipated in dreams of eternal love beyond the grave' . . ." (p. 345a-b)

A loud knocking at the window ends their interview, as the devil tells Ivan it is his brother Alyosha, "with the most interesting and surprising news." It is Alyosha outside the window, with this news: "An hour ago Smerdyakov hanged himself." Ivan tells Alyosha about his conversation with the devil, and his fear that the devil is the basest part of himself. He ends in delirium, and the concerned Alyosha comments:

"The anguish of a proud determination. An earnest conscience!" God, in Whom he disbelieved, and His truth were gaining mastery over his heart, which still refused to submit . . . "He will either rise up in the light of truth, or . . . he'll perish in hate, revenging on himself and on everyone his having served the cause he does not believe in," . . . (p. 348c-d)

Book XII, "A Judicial Error," presents the trial of Dmitri Karamazov. The sensational case has brought in lawyers and other notables fom other localities, including Moscow and St. Petersburg. The local court has become the center of interest for the Russian newspapers, which present "inside" stories on the defendant and his relation to the two women in the case. Most of the men spectators are against Dmitri and want his conviction, while the women are tenderly and enthusiastically for his acquittal, even if he is guilty. A celebrated criminal lawyer has assumed Dmitri's defense, while the local prosecutor is determined to give the case his all, for it is the great opportunity of his life, and he sincerely believes Dmitri is guilty.

The trial opens with the statement of the charge against Dmitri and the reason why he is being held for trial. Dmitri pleads not guilty to the charges of murder and robbery, although admitting his debauchery and other moral findings. It soon becomes apparent that the preponderant evidence and material witnesses are on the side of the prosecution, and it is the task of the defense to impugn their cogency, credibility, or relevance. The defense attorney proves to be a master in "taking down" the prosecution witnesses. The psychiatric evidence presented by the medical experts is conflicting; even the doctors who agree that Dmitri is mentally unbalanced disagree on which symptoms indicate his abnormality. Dmitri cheers the doctor who pronounces him perfectly normal.

Alyosha presents the most telling evidence for the defense when he recalls that Dmitri struck himself on the breast the night of their conversation after Grushenka had humiliated Katerina, claiming he could regain his honor and remove "half of the disgrace," apparently referring to the rag with the fifteen hundred roubles. (See above, pp. 214-215.) Dmitri confirms that this was what he meant by his gesture. Katerina Ivanovna also gives favorable testimony about Dmitri, presenting the account of how she had humiliated herself before him at the time he lent her the forty-five hundred roubles for her father, without indicating that Dmitri himself had proposed that she make the visit. But the narrator (who was present in court) tells how he "turned cold and trembled," and had a "painful misgiving at heart" at her extraordinary, self-sacrificial testimony. She has laid herself open to all kinds of nasty suspicions and innuendoes. But Dmitri oddly cries out "Katya, why have you ruined me?" and "Now I am condemned!"

The key witness for the defense, however, is Ivan Karamazov, who bears the news of Smerdyakov's confession. He acts strangely, says he has nothing to tell the court, then suddenly pulls out three thousand roubles and announces he got them from Smerdyakov, who murdered Fyodor Karamazov, acting under Ivan's incitation. "Who doesn't desire his father's death?"

he asks the startled court. He accuses the spectators of sham-
ming horror at the parricide. "They all desire the death of their
fathers." When he is asked for proof about his statement about
Smerdyakov, he says he has only one witness, the one with a
tail, who is probably here in the courtroom, along with the
material evidence—"a paltry, pitiful devil." He becomes in-
coherent, knocks down an attendant, and is led from the room
screaming furiously.

This unleases the "sudden catastrophe" which decisively
turns the case against Dmitri. For Katerina Ivanovna, in a fit of
hysterics over Ivan's collapse, begs to introduce new evidence—
the letter which Dmitri wrote to her announcing his intention
to kill his father—what Ivan had once called the "mathematical
proof" that Dmitri was the murderer. Dmitri confirms that he
wrote the letter. Katerina goes on to reveal her resentment of
Dmitri and how she purposely gave him the three thousand
roubles to prove he was a scoundrel and would spend it on
another woman. She believes he has despised her ever since
the day she humbled herself before him to get the loan for her
father, and tells how she tried to conquer him with her love,
her infinite, forgiving love. But now she recognizes him as "the
monster and murderer" who killed his father and drove his
brother Ivan mad.

It is a tremendous moment for Katerina—the narrator likens
it to "the hour of death, for instance, on the way to the
scaffold!" She has her grand moment of revenge for what she
believes to have been Dmitri's scornful humiliation of her. This
is the final expression of her "hysterical, 'lacerated' love only
from pride, from wounded pride," a love that is more like revenge. But in betraying Dmitri, she has betrayed herself, and
at the end she feels empty and ashamed. She falls into another
violent fit of hysterics and is carried from the courtroom, while
the anguished Grushenka cries to Dmitri, "Mitya . . . your serpent has destroyed you!"

The speeches of both the prosecutor and the defense attorney are magnificent examples of forensic logic and rhetoric,
and they include perceptive though slanted sketches of the
main characters, as well as thoughtful considerations on the

state and future of Russia. (For a full discussion of the legal aspects of the trial, see the Fifteenth Reading in the Reading Plan *Law and Jurisprudence.*) Dmitri, in his final plea, reiterates his innocence despite his errors ("I was erring, but I loved what is good"), tells the jurymen not to believe the doctors ("I am perfectly sane, only my heart is heavy"), and begs them to spare him ("do not rob me of my God! I know myself, I shall rebel!"). But his plea as to no avail, for the jury finds him guilty of both murder and robbery. (He is sentenced later to twenty years of penal servitude in Siberia.) He shouts out his innocence again as he is led away.

The Epilogue deals with the plans for Dmitri's escape, the reconciliation of Katerina and Dmitri, and the funeral of Illusha that sounds the note that ends the book. Katerina is helping Alyosha make the arrangements for Dmitri's escape. She still talks bitterly about Dmitri, perhaps because of her sense of guilt at betraying him. Alyosha goes to Dmitri to persuade him that he must escape, since he is innocent, and it is not his vocation to bear the "cross" of needless suffering. Indeed, that would be an easy evasion of his duty in the world.

". . . You wanted to make yourself another man by suffering. I say, only remember that other man always, all your life and wherever you go; and that will be enough for you. Your refusal of that great cross will only serve to make you feel all your life an even greater duty, and that constant feeling will do more to make you a new man, perhaps, than if you went there. For there you would not endure it and would repine, and perhaps at last would say: 'I am quits.' The lawyer was right about that. Such heavy burdens are not for all men. For some they are impossible . . ." (p. 405d)

Dmitri assents and concocts a fantastic plan for him and Grushenka to come back from America, disguised as American citizens, so that they may die on Russian soil.

At this point Katerina enters, in response to Dmitri's request and Alyosha's urging. She and Dmitri, holding hands, declare the unending love that will always be between them, although each now loves another person. She confesses that she never believed that Dmitri was guilty and now wants to punish herself for what she has done to him. When Grushenka enters, Katerina turns white and begs her, "Forgive me!" But Gru-

shenka, recalling the hatred between them, says she will forgive her only if she saves Dmitri. Katerina admits to Alyosha
later that she only begged Grushenka's forgiveness in order
to punish herself and says she admires Grushenka for refusing
to forgive her, but her eyes flash "with fierce resentment."

Alyosha proceeds from this emotional encounter to the
burial of little Ilusha. Alyosha joins the procession of Ilusha's
schoolmates—who had first mistreated him cruelly and then
come to love him—and his family, including the father whom
Dmitri had so cruelly insulted. When the interment is completed, his father crumbles bread on the grave, so the birds
will sing over him and give him company, as he requested. On
the way back, Alyosha delivers a short memorial address on
the meaning of Ilusha's death for them. He says that their
friendship for the dead boy and the good and kind feeling that
was in them when they loved him will become the essential
good memory that will stay with them when they grow up.
When they are tempted to cruel and wicked actions and attitudes, or even when they succumb to them, this memory of a
time when they were good and kind will sustain them and protect them from the evil to which they are exposed. Above all,
they are to remember one another as long as they live and be
with each other in spirit all their lives long. And it is Ilusha,
"the good boy, the dear boy, precious to us for ever!" who has
wrought this community among them. Finally, he begs the
children not to be afraid of life, which is wonderful when one
is good and just, and to look forward to the resurrection beyond death when they shall all meet again.

After this lofty note, Alyosha invites the boys to proceed
hand in hand to the funeral dinner where they will eat pan-
cakes. "And always so, all our lives hand in hand! Hurrah for
Karamazov!" shouts one of the boys. And the rest of the boys
shout, "Hurrah for Karamazov!" On this note of praise and
joy, the turbulent story of the Karamazovs ends.

VI

Do the ideas and actions of this novel fit together?

In this Reading Plan and in *Imaginative Literature I* we have
discussed various allegorical renderings of metaphysical and

theological themes, such as *The Divine Comedy, Paradise Lost, Faust,* and *Moby Dick.* We have seen how the authors of these works expressed ideas through poetic fiction. How does Dostoevsky perform the task of rendering the tension between sin and suffering on the one hand and redemption and joy on the other, between the evil and the good in men's hearts?

If we think back, we recall immediately the direct expression of the ideas in discourses or conversations among the characters. These vary from the full-scale lectures or sermons of Ivan and Father Zossima to the simpler and more impulsive utterances of Dmitri and Grushenka. There are also the inset pieces, such as "The Grand Inquisitor" or Ivan's interview with the devil, which are imaginatively presented discussions of the basic themes. Do you find these direct expressions of ideas acceptable in a novel, or do you feel that they are out of place? Would you rather have the meaning of the story carried through the concrete events and characters, without commentary?

Let us now recall the main line of the story, with its cardinal events and the development of the main characters. Does Dostoevsky convey his themes through the events and characters? Does the murder of Fyodor Karamazov and all that leads up to it and follows from it convey the meaning of Dostoevsky's theme to you? What of the psychological responses and development of the characters? Do they emerge from and reinforce the major ideas of the novel? Are the symbolic actions of Zossima bowing to Dmitri and of Alyosha kissing the earth too pat, or are they quite natural and concrete symbols? What about the recollections of Father Zossima about his wild and vicious young manhood and the "good seed" of his brother's memory? Are they impressive and convincing, or too preachy, too evangelical? What of the quick corruption of Father Zossima's body? Is this a direct, concrete, and fitting symbol?

How does Dostoevsky present psychological states and motivations?

It has been said that Dostoevsky concentrates on the inner life of his characters, so that we know them far better inwardly than outwardly. Do you have any clear image of the appearance of the Karamazovs? Does it matter for this kind of story? How does Dostoevsky present the inner life and mo- tives of his characters—through interior monologue (stream of consciousness), exterior dialogue, description of mental states, psychological analysis, or through actions? Which of these methods does he use in presenting Katerina's motiva- tions in the courtroom scene? Which method does he use in revealing the motivations behind Lise's abuse of Alyosha and of herself? Do you prefer a direct or indirect revelation of character and motive? Does Dostoevsky combine many meth- ods? How would you compare him with Fielding as an analyst of human character?

Who is the narrator of the novel?

In this novel, the narrator appears from time to time, acting like Fielding's omiscient author. Most of the time he is not present, and sometimes it is impossible for him to be present, as when a character is alone or his inner meditations are pre- sented. This evanescent narrator tells us of being present in the courtroom and of his reaction to the testimony. But he is not and cannot be present at other significant scenes. Does this off-again, on-again role of the narrator weaken the credi- bility of the story? Or is it hardly noticeable and without effect on your capacity to take in the story? Do his brief appearances and comments, as for instance, the remark that Alyosha is his favorite character, add verisimilitude or not? Could we just as well do without the narrator? Is his role essential to the telling of the story?

Who is the hero of the novel?

Does this story have an individual hero, or are all the Kara- mazovs the center of the action? If there is an individual hero, who is he? Alyosha? Ivan? Dmitri? Which of the three has the most scenes or "sides," as they say in the theater? Are the three brothers distinct types of human character or complementary aspects of the human person? Would this story and its render- ing of the theme be possible without each and all of the Karamazovs? How are the three brothers linked to Fyodor in character and nature? What do Smerdyakov and the devil mean by identifying Ivan with Fyodor? How is Ivan's nihilism linked to Fyodor's grasping sensuality? And are Dmitri and Fyodor alike, as Ivan says, both lusting animals, "reptiles"? Is Alyosha really one of "them," as he says, sharing in the Karamazov sensuality? What is the link between this sensuality and the love of life that Dmitri says all the Karamazovs have?

What does "joy in the world" mean?

Does "joy in the world" mean the same thing for Father Zossima and Alyosha as it does for Ivan and Dmitri? Does Fyodor, too, have joy in the world, but in perverted form? What about the women characters—Grushenka, Katerina, and Lise? Which of them has joy in the world?

Is joy in the world, as here presented, concordant with traditional, orthodox Christianity? Is there a pantheistic element in this notion, or is it a response to the divine creativity, as in the Psalms and in such religious figures as Francis of Assisi? What is the religious meaning of the counsel to love life regardless of logic and meaning? Is it contrary to a rational theology or theodicy, which attempts to justify God's ways to man?

Many of the passages in this novel are directed against the obsession with material signs and wonders and with rigorous religious observances. Does this indicate the type of religion or Christianity that Dostoevsky espouses in this work? Is it Ivan or Alyosha who speaks for Dostoevsky's views? Does the author intend to express doubt or faith—or both?

What does the subplot about the children contribute to the story?

Why does Dostoevsky introduce the story of Ilusha, his family, and his friends, often returning to it, and ending his book with Ilusha's funeral? Does the subplot reinforce and reiterate the main theme of the novel, adding depth and richness through a different milieu and set of characters? Does it add any new and distinct notes, counterpointing the main theme? What is the main impression upon you of this minor theme about Ilusha, Kolya, Snegiryov, and the boys? Do any of these minor characters correspond to the major characters of the story? Or do you feel that this subplot is an annoying and baffling intrusion on the main line of the story?

The following questions are designed to help you test the thoroughness of your reading. Each question is to be answered by giving a page or pages of the reading assignment. Answers will be found on page 248 of this Reading Plan.

1 Which of the Karamazov brothers have the same mother?

2 Who is Pyotr Alexandrovitch Miüsov, and what role does he play in the story?

3 Who is Lizaveta, and what is her role in the story?

4 What causes antagonism between Grigory and the young Smerdyakov?

5 Who is Samsonov and what part does he play in the story?

6 What event laid the foundation of Pyotr Ilyitch Perhotin's official career?

7 What is Grushenka's full name?

8 Whom does Grushenka take home with her after Dmitri's arrest?

9 What does Dmitri mean by "a Bernard"?

10 Who bought Dmitri a pound of nuts when he was a boy?

ANSWERS
to self-testing questions

First Reading

1. 23a
2. 37c-38c
3. 59c
4. 109c-111a
5. 126c
6. 137d
7. 148b-162d
8. 217d-220c
9. 237b-c
10. 252c-256a

Second Reading

1. 108a
2. 112a-b
3. 113b-116a
4. 127a-129a
5. 130b-132b
6. 157a, 160b
7. 162a-b
8. 168b-169a
9. 206b-207a
10. 217b

Third Reading

1. 6c-8c
2. 17d-19c
3. 21c, 44a
4. 36a-41a, 45d-46d
5. 101a
6. 117d
7. 141b-151d, 191c-193c, 202c-204c
8. 229b-233d, 235b-241c
9. 227a-228c
10. 271c-273c, 287c-289b, 290a-292b

Fourth Reading

1. 8b
2. 51b
3. 77b
4. 101b
5. 121b
6. 153a
7. 194a-195b
8. 224a-b

Fifth Reading

1. 23b-25b
2. 47b-50a
3. 73b-74a
4. 106a
5. 136b
6. 178b
7. 203a-205a
8. 292a-295a
9. 310a-b
10. 356a-357b

Sixth Reading

1. 3c
2. 656d
3. 173d-175a
4. 195a-198b
5. 275a
6. 247a-b
7. 425c
8. 476c-479d
9. 589c-590c
10. 469a-470d

Seventh Reading

1. 4a-d
2. 14c, Bk. II
3. 48c-50c
4. 62d-63a
5. 180a-181b, 193c-197a
6. 235b-238a
7. 180b, 355b
8. 298c-d
9. 312a-c, 355d
10. 358d-359b

ADDITIONAL READINGS

I. Works included in *Great Books of the Western World*

Vol. 7: PLATO, *Phaedrus; Ion; The Republic,* Books II-III, Book X

9: ARISTOTLE, *Politics,* Book VIII; *Rhetoric,* Book III; *Poetics*

18: AUGUSTINE, *On Christian Doctrine,* Books II-IV

25: MONTAIGNE, *The Essays,* I.39, "A Consideration Upon Cicero"; II.10, "Of Books"; II.17, "Of Presumption"; II.36, "Of the Most Excellent Men"

30: BACON, *Advancement of Learning,* Book II, Section IV

32: MILTON, *Samson Agonistes,* "Of that sort of Dramatic Poem which is call'd Tragedy"; *Aeropagitica*

42: KANT, *The Critique of Judgment,* Part I, "Critique of Aesthetic Judgment"

44: BOSWELL, *Life of Samuel Johnson, LL.D.*

54: FREUD, *The Interpretation of Dreams,* VI, "The Dream-Work"; *A General Introduction to Psychoanalysis,* Part II, Chapters 10-11

II. Other Works

A. Criticism and Appreciation

ABRAMS, MEYER H., *The Mirror and the Lamp: Romantic Theory and the Critical Tradition.* New York: W. W. Norton & Co., Inc. 1958

ARNOLD, MATTHEW, *Essays in Criticism,* 2nd series, ed. by S. R. Littlewood. New York: St. Martin's Press, Inc., 1938

ARVIN, NEWTON, *Herman Melville: A Critical Biography.* New York: Compass Books, 1957

AUERBACH, ERICH, *Mimesis: The Representation of Reality in Western Literature.* New York: Doubleday Anchor Books, 1957

BABBITT, IRVING, *Rousseau and Romanticism*. New York: Meridian Books, Inc., 1960

BATE, W. J., *From Classic to Romantic: Premises of Taste in 18th Century England*. New York: Harper Torchbooks, 1961

BERDYAEV, NICOLAS, *Dostoevsky*. New York: Living Age Books, 1960

BERLIN, ISAIAH, *The Hedgehog and the Fox*. New York: New American Library (A Mentor Book), 1957

BOWRA, CECIL MAURICE, *From Virgil to Milton*. New York: St. Martin's Press, Inc., 1946

BRIDGES, ROBERT, *Milton's Prosody*. London: Oxford University Press, 1921

BROOKS, CLEANTH, *The Well-Wrought Urn*. New York: Harvest Books, 1956

BROOKS, CLEANTH and WARREN, ROBERT PENN, *Understanding Fiction*. New York: Appleton-Century-Crofts, Inc., 1959; *Understanding Poetry*. New York: Holt, Rinehart and Winston, Inc., 1960

COLERIDGE, S. T., *Biographia Literaria*. New York: Everyman's Library, 1908

CRANE, RONALD S., ed., *Critics and Criticism: Ancient and Modern*. Chicago: University of Chicago Press, 1952

DREW, ELIZABETH, *Poetry: A Modern Guide to Its Understanding and Enjoyment*. New York: Dell Books, 1959

ECKERMANN, JOHANN PETER, *Conversations with Goethe*. New York: Everyman's Library, 1931

ELIOT, T. S., *Selected Prose*, ed. by John Hayward. Hammondsworth, Middlesex, England: Penguin Books Inc., 1953

ENRIGHT, D. J., *Commentary on Goethe's Faust*. New York: New Directions, 1949

GIDE, ANDRÉ, *Dostoevsky*. New York: New Directions, 1949

GOODMAN, PAUL, *The Structure of Literature*. Chicago: University of Chicago Press, 1954

GORKY, MAXIM, *Reminiscences of Tolstoy, Chekhov, and Andreyev*. New York: Compass Books, 1959

GRIERSON, H. J. C., *Cross-Currents in Seventeenth Century English Literature*. New York: Harper Torchbooks, 1958

HAMBURGER, MICHAEL, *Reason and Energy*. New York: Evergreen Books, 1957

HAZLITT, WILLIAM, *Lectures on the English Comic Writers*. New York: Dolphin Books, 1960; *Lectures on the English Poets*. New York: World's Classics, Oxford University Press, 1925

HELLER, ERICH, *The Disinherited Mind*. New York: Meridian Books, 1959

JOHNSON, SAMUEL, *The Lives of the English Poets*, 2 vols. New York: Dolphin Books, 1961

JONES, EDMUND DAVID, ed., *English Critical Essays (16th, 17th and 18th Centuries)*. New York: World's Classics, Oxford University Press, 1922; *English Critical Essays (19th Century)*. New York: World's Classics, Oxford University Press, 1916

LAWRENCE, D. H., *Studies in Classic American Literature*. New York: Doubleday Anchor Books, 1953

LEWES, GEORGE H., *The Life and Works of Goethe*. New York: Everyman's Library, 1908

LEWIS, C. S., *Preface to Paradise Lost*. New York: Oxford University Press, 1942

LOWES, JOHN LIVINGSTON, *The Road to Xanadu*. New York: Vintage Books, 1959

MADARIAGA, SALVADOR DE, *Don Quixote: An Introductory Essay in Psychology*, rev. ed., New York: Oxford Paperbacks, 1961

MANN, THOMAS, *Essays of Three Decades*. New York: Vintage Books, 1947

POUND, EZRA, *ABC of Reading*. New York: New Directions Paperbooks, 1960

PRAZ, MARIO, *The Romantic Agony*, 2nd ed. London: Oxford University Press, 1951

SANTAYANA, GEORGE, *Interpretations of Poetry and Religion*. New York: Harper Torchbooks, 1957; *Three Philosophical Poets*. New York: Doubleday Anchor Books, 1953

SCOTT, A. F., *Meaning and Style*. New York: St. Martin's Press, Inc., 1938

SIMMONS, ERNEST J., *Leo Tolstoy*, 2 vols. New York: Vintage Books, 1945

STEINER, GEORGE, *Tolstoy or Dostoevsky*. New York: Alfred A. Knopf, Inc., 1959

THORPE, JAMES, ed., *Milton Criticism: Selections from Four Centuries*. New York: Rinehart, 1950

TILLYARD, E. M. W., *Studies in Milton*. New York: The Macmillan Company, 1951

TOLSTOY, LEO, *What Is Art? and Essays on Art*, trans. by Aylmer Maude. New York: World's Classics, Oxford University Press, 1930

UNAMUNO, MIGUEL DE, *The Life of Don Quixote and Sancho*, trans. by Homer P. Earle. New York: Alfred A. Knopf, Inc., 1927

VAN DOREN, MARK, *Don Quixote's Profession*. New York: Columbia University Press, 1958; *Shakespeare*. New York: Doubleday Anchor Books, 1953; *The Noble Voice*. New York: Holt, 1946

WILLEY, BASIL, *The Seventeenth Century Background*. New York: Doubleday Anchor Books, 1953

B. Works on the Novel

ALLEN, WALTER, *The English Novel*. New York: Everyman's Library, 1957; *Writers on Writing*, ed. by Walter Allen. New York: Everyman's Library, 1959

ALLOTT, MIRIAM, ed., *Novelists on the Novel*. New York: Columbia University Press, 1959

BEACH, JOSEPH WARREN, *The Twentieth Century Novel: Studies in Technique*. New York: Appleton-Century-Crofts, Inc., 1932

CHASE, RICHARD, *The American Novel and Its Tradition*. New York: Doubleday Anchor Books, 1957

COWLEY, MALCOLM, ed., *Writers at Work: The Paris Review Interviews*. New York: Compass Books, 1959

DAICHES, DAVID, *The Novel and the Modern World.*, rev. ed. Chicago: University of Chicago Press, 1960

FORSTER, E. M., *Aspects of the Novel*. New York: Harvest Books, 1956

JAMES, HENRY, *The Art of the Novel: Critical Prefaces*, ed. by R. P. Blackmur. New York: Charles Scribner's Sons, 1934;

The Future of the Novel: Essays, ed. by Leon Edel. New York: Vintage Books, 1956

KRUTCH, JOSEPH WOOD, *Five Masters.* Bloomington: Indiana University Press, 1959

LEAVIS, F. R., *The Great Tradition.* New York: Doubleday Anchor Books, 1948

LUBBOCK, PERCY, *The Craft of Fiction.* New York: Compass Books, 1957

MUIR, EDWIN, *The Structure of the Novel.* New York: Harcourt, Brace and Co., Inc., 1929

ORTEGA Y GASSET, JOSÉ, "Notes on the Novel," in *The Dehumanization of Art and Other Writings on Art and Culture.* New York: Doubleday Anchor Books, 1956

TURNELL, MARTIN, *The Novel in France.* New York: Vintage Books, 1958

WATT, IAN, *The Rise of the Novel: Studies in Defoe, Richardson, and Fielding.* Berkeley: University of California Press, 1959

ZABEL, MORTON DAUWEN, *Craft and Character: Texts, Method and Vocation in Modern Fiction.* New York: Viking Press, 1957

C. Reference Works, Literary Histories, and Language Studies

BENÉT, WILLIAM ROSE, ed., *The Reader's Encyclopedia.* New York: Thomas Y. Crowell Co., 1955

BRENAN, GERALD, *The Literature of the Spanish People.* New York: Meridian Books, 1960

BRERETON, GEOFFREY, *A Short History of French Literature.* Baltimore: Penguin Books Inc., 1955

COHEN, J. M., *A History of Western Literature.* Baltimore: Penguin Books Inc., 1956

CUNLIFFE, MARCUS, *The Literature of the United States,* Baltimore: Penguin Books Inc., 1959

DAICHES, DAVID, *A Critical History of English Literature.* New York: Ronald Press Co., 1960

EVANS, IFOR, *A Short History of English Literature.* Baltimore: Penguin Books Inc., 1956

FORD, BORIS, ed., *The Pelican Guide to English Literature.* Volume III. *From Donne to Marvell,* Volume IV. *From Dryden to Johnson;* Volume V. *From Blake to Byron;* Volume VI. *From Dickens to Hardy.* Baltimore: Penguin Books Inc., 1957

HART, JAMES D., *The Oxford Companion to American Literature,* 3rd. ed. New York: Oxford University Press, 1956

JESPERSEN, OTTO, *The Growth and Structure of the English Language.* New York: Doubleday Anchor Books, 1955

LANIER, SIDNEY, *The Science of English Verse and Essays on Music* (Centennial edition of the works and letters of Sidney Lanier, Vol. 2), ed. by Paull F. Baum. Baltimore: Johns Hopkins Press, 1945

MIRSKY, D. S., *A History of Russian Literature.* New York: Vintage Books, 1958

PARRINGTON, VERNON L., *Main Currents in American Thought,* 2 vols. New York: Harvest Books, 1954

READ, HERBERT, *English Prose Style.* Boston: Beacon Press, Inc., 1955

ROBERTSON, JOHN G., *A History of German Literature,* rev. ed. New York: British Books, 1956

SAINTSBURY, GEORGE, *A History of English Prose Rhythms.* London: The Macmillan Company, 1922; *A Short History of English Literature.* New York: St. Martin's Press, Inc., 1898

TORRES-RIOSECO, ARTURO, *The Epic of Latin American Literature.* Berkeley: University of California Press, 1959

WHITFIELD, J. H., *A Short History of Italian Literature.* Baltimore: Penguin Books Inc., 1960